M000295337

Java EE 8 Application Development

Develop Enterprise applications using the latest versions of CDI, JAX-RS, JSON-B, JPA, Security, and more

David R. Heffelfinger

BIRMINGHAM - MUMBAI

Java EE 8 Application Development

First published: December 2017

Production reference: 1111217

Published by Packt Publishing Ltd.
Livery Place
35 Livery Street
Birmingham
B3 2PB, UK.

ISBN 978-1-78829-367-9

www.packtpub.com

Credits

Author
David R. Heffelfinger

Reviewers
Omar El-Prince
Sachin Baveja

Commissioning Editor
Aaron Lazar

Acquisition Editor
Karan Sadawana

Content Development Editors
Siddhi Chavan
Lawrence Veigas

Technical Editor
Mehul Singh

Copy Editor
Safis Editing

Project Coordinator
Prajakta Naik

Proofreader
Safis Editing

Indexer
Tejal Daruwale Soni

Graphics
Tom Scaria

Production Coordinator
Aparna Bhagat

About the Author

David R. Heffelfinger is an independent consultant based in the Washington D.C. area. He is a Java Champion, a member of the NetBeans Dream Team, and is a part of the JavaOne content committee.

He has written several books on Java EE, application servers, NetBeans, and JasperReports. His previous titles include *Java EE 7 Development with NetBeans 8*, *Java EE 7 with GlassFish 4 Application Server*, and *JasperReports 3.5 For Java Developers*, and others.

David has been a speaker at software conferences such as JavaOne and Oracle Code on multiple occasions. He has also been a speaker at NetBeans Day in San Francisco and Montreal, showcasing NetBeans features that greatly enhance the development of Java EE applications. You can follow him on Twitter at `@ensode`.

I would like to thank everyone that help made this book a reality.
I would like to thank the content development editors, Siddhi Chavan and Lawrence Veigas, for their guidance and professionalism during the book's development. I would also like to thank the technical reviewers, Sachin Baveja and Omar El-Prince, for their insightful comments and suggestions.

Additionally, I would like to thank the Java EE expert group for their hard work in putting together such an outstanding set of specifications, and particularly Security API expert group members, Rudy De Busscher, Guillermo González de Agüero, and Arjan Tijms, for their invaluable help and insight on material related to the new Security API.

Finally, I would like to thank my wife and daughters for putting up with the long hours of work that kept me away from the family.

About the Reviewers

Omar El-Prince is an experienced software engineer with a computer engineering graduate degree and master's degree in computer science from Johns Hopkins University. He has experience working in large Java EE projects at CSRA, Booz Allen Hamilton, HP, EDS, and other companies. He enjoys programming and technology blogging that is focused on agile culture, software development, and architecture. He is a Java EE enthusiastic, and he loves learning, mentoring, and helping others.

Sachin Baveja is a technology enthusiast with close to 20 years of experience in the field of IT, the majority of it developing applications in Java/JEE. He is a math graduate from Delhi University and did his MBA at ENPC, Paris with specialization in Management of Technology. He has experience working with some of the top fortune 500 companies, such as IBM, Wells Fargo, Fannie Mae, Customs, Border Protection, and Capital One, to name a few.

www.PacktPub.com

For support files and downloads related to your book, please visit www.PacktPub.com.

Did you know that Packt offers eBook versions of every book published, with PDF and ePub files available? You can upgrade to the eBook version at www.PacktPub.com and as a print book customer, you are entitled to a discount on the eBook copy. Get in touch with us at service@packtpub.com for more details.

At www.PacktPub.com, you can also read a collection of free technical articles, sign up for a range of free newsletters and receive exclusive discounts and offers on Packt books and eBooks.

https://www.packtpub.com/mapt

Get the most in-demand software skills with Mapt. Mapt gives you full access to all Packt books and video courses, as well as industry-leading tools to help you plan your personal development and advance your career.

Why subscribe?

- Fully searchable across every book published by Packt
- Copy and paste, print, and bookmark content
- On demand and accessible via a web browser

Customer Feedback

Thanks for purchasing this Packt book. At Packt, quality is at the heart of our editorial process. To help us improve, please leave us an honest review on this book's Amazon page at https://www.amazon.com/dp/1788293673.

If you'd like to join our team of regular reviewers, you can e-mail us at customerreviews@packtpub.com. We award our regular reviewers with free eBooks and videos in exchange for their valuable feedback. Help us be relentless in improving our products!

Table of Contents

Preface

Java Enterprise Edition 8, the latest version of the Java EE specification, adds several new features to the specification. Several existing Java EE APIs have seen major improvements in this version of the specification, and some brand new APIs have been added to Java EE. This book covers the latest versions of the most popular Java EE specifications, including &`vaServer Faces (JSF), the Java Persistence API (JPA), Enterprise JavaBeans (EJB), Contexts and Dependency Injection (CDI), the Java API for JSON Processing (JSON-P), the new Java API for JSON Binding (JSON-B), the Java API for WebSocket, the Java Messaging Service (JMS) API 2.0, the Java API for XML Web Services (JAX-WS), and the Java API for RESTful Web Services (JAX-RS). It also covers securing Java EE applications via the brand new Java EE 8 Security API.

What this book covers

Chapter 1, *Introduction to Java EE*, provides a brief introduction to Java EE, explaining how it is developed as a community effort. It also clears some common misconceptions about Java EE.

Chapter 2, *JavaServer Faces*, covers the development of web applications using JSF, including features such as HTML5 friendly markup and Faces Flows.

Chapter 3, *Object Relational Mapping with JPA*, discusses how to develop code that interacts with a Relational Database Management System (RDBMS) such as Oracle or MySQL through the Java Persistence API.

Chapter 4, *Enterprise JavaBeans*, explains how to develop applications using both session and message-driven beans. Major EJB features such as transaction management, the EJB timer service, and security are covered.

Chapter 5, *Contexts and Dependency Injection*, discusses CDI-named beans, dependency injection using CDI and CDI qualifiers, as well as CDI-event functionality.

Chapter 6, *JSON Processing with JSON-B and JSON-P*, explains how to generate and parse JavaScript Object Notation (JSON) data using the JSON-P API, and the new JSON-B API.

Chapter 7, *WebSocket*, explains how to develop web-based applications featuring full duplex communication between the browser and the server, as opposed to relying on the traditional HTTP request/response cycle.

Chapter 8, *Java Message Service*, discusses how to develop messaging applications using the completely revamped JMS 2.0 API.

Chapter 9, *Securing Java EE Applications*, covers how to secure Java EE applications via the new Java EE 8 security API.

Chapter 10, *RESTful Web Services with JAX-RS*, discusses how to develop RESTful web services via the Java API for RESTful web services, as well as how to develop RESTful web service clients via the brand new standard JAX-RS client API. The chapter also covers server-sent events, a new JAX-RS feature introduced in Java EE 8.

Chapter 11, *Microservices Development with Java EE*, explains how to develop microservices by leveraging Java EE 8 APIs.

Chapter 12, *Web Services with JAX-WS*, explains how to develop SOAP-based web services via the Java API for XML Web Services.

Chapter 13, *Servlet Development and Deployment*, explains how to develop server-side functionality in Java EE applications via the Servlet API.

Appendix, *Configuring and Deploying to GlassFish*, explains how to configure GlassFish so that we can use it to deploy our applications, as well as various methods we can use to deploy our applications to GlassFish.

What you need for this book

The following software needs to be installed to follow the material in this book:

- Java Development Kit (JDK) 1.8 or newer
- A Java EE 8 compliant application server such as GlassFish 5, Payara 5, or OpenLiberty
- Maven 3 or newer is needed to build the examples
- A Java IDE such as NetBeans, Eclipse, or IntelliJ IDEA (optional, but recommended)

Who this book is for

This book assumes familiarity with the Java language. The target market for this book is existing Java developers wishing to learn Java EE, and existing Java EE developers wishing to update their skills to the latest Java EE specification.

Conventions

In this book, you will find a number of text styles that distinguish between different kinds of information. Here are some examples of these styles and an explanation of their meaning.

Code words in text, database table names, folder names, filenames, file extensions, pathnames, dummy URLs, user input, and Twitter handles are shown as follows: "The @Named class annotation designates this bean as a CDI named bean."

A block of code is set as follows:

```
if (!emailValidator.isValid(email)) {
    FacesMessage facesMessage =
        new FacesMessage(htmlInputText.getLabel()
        + ": email format is not valid");
    throw new ValidatorException(facesMessage);
        }
```

When we wish to draw your attention to a particular part of a code block, the relevant lines or items are set in bold:

```
@FacesValidator(value = "emailValidator")
```

Any command-line input or output is written as follows:

```
/asadmin start-domain domain1
```

New terms and **important words** are shown in bold. Words that you see on the screen, for example, in menus or dialog boxes, appear in the text like this: "Clicking the **Next** button moves you to the next screen."

Warnings or important notes appear like this.

Tips and tricks appear like this.

Reader feedback

Feedback from our readers is always welcome. Let us know what you think about this book—what you liked or disliked. Reader feedback is important for us as it helps us develop titles that you will really get the most out of.

To send us general feedback, simply e-mail `feedback@packtpub.com`, and mention the book's title on the subject of your message.

If there is a topic that you have expertise in and you are interested in either writing or contributing to a book, see our author guide at `www.packtpub.com/authors`.

Customer support

Now that you are the proud owner of a Packt book, we have a number of things to help you to get the most from your purchase.

Downloading the example code

You can download the example code files for this book from your account at `http://www.packtpub.com`. If you purchased this book elsewhere, you can visit `http://www.packtpub.com/support` and register to have the files e-mailed directly to you.

You can download the code files by following these steps:

1. Log in or register to our website using your e-mail address and password.
2. Hover the mouse pointer on the **SUPPORT** tab at the top.
3. Click on **Code Downloads & Errata**.
4. Enter the name of the book in the **Search** box.
5. Select the book for which you're looking to download the code files.
6. Choose from the drop-down menu where you purchased this book from.
7. Click on **Code Download**.

Once the file is downloaded, please make sure that you unzip or extract the folder using the latest version of:

- WinRAR / 7-Zip for Windows
- Zipeg / iZip / UnRarX for Mac
- 7-Zip / PeaZip for Linux

The code bundle for the book is also hosted on GitHub at https://github.com/PacktPublishing/Java-EE-8-Application-Development. We also have other code bundles from our rich catalog of books and videos available at https://github.com/PacktPublishing/. Check them out!

Errata

Although we have taken every care to ensure the accuracy of our content, mistakes do happen. If you find a mistake in one of our books—maybe a mistake in the text or the code—we would be grateful if you could report this to us. By doing so, you can save other readers from frustration and help us improve subsequent versions of this book. If you find any errata, please report them by visiting http://www.packtpub.com/submit-errata, selecting your book, clicking on the **Errata Submission Form** link, and entering the details of your errata. Once your errata are verified, your submission will be accepted and the errata will be uploaded to our website or added to any list of existing errata under the Errata section of that title.

To view the previously submitted errata, go to https://www.packtpub.com/books/content/support and enter the name of the book in the search field. The required information will appear under the **Errata** section.

Piracy

Piracy of copyrighted material on the Internet is an ongoing problem across all media. At Packt, we take the protection of our copyright and licenses very seriously. If you come across any illegal copies of our works in any form on the Internet, please provide us with the location address or website name immediately so that we can pursue a remedy.

Please contact us at copyright@packtpub.com with a link to the suspected pirated material.

We appreciate your help in protecting our authors and our ability to bring you valuable content.

Questions

If you have a problem with any aspect of this book, you can contact us at questions@packtpub.com, and we will do our best to address the problem.

1
Introduction to Java EE

The **Java Platform, Enterprise Edition (Java EE)** consists of a set of **Application Programming Interface (API)** specifications used to develop server-side, enterprise Java applications. In this chapter, we will provide a high-level overview of Java EE.

We will cover the following topics in this chapter:

- Introduction to Java EE
- One standard, multiple implementations
- Java EE, J2EE, and the Spring Framework

Introduction to Java EE

The Java Platform, Enterprise Edition (Java EE) is a collection of API specifications designed to work together when developing server-side, enterprise Java applications. Java EE is a standard; there are multiple implementations of the Java EE specifications. This fact prevents vendor lock-in since code developed against the Java EE specification can be deployed to any Java EE-compliant application server with minimal or no modifications.

Java EE is developed under the **Java Community Process (JCP)**, an organization responsible for the development of Java technology. JCP members include Oracle (the current steward of the Java platform), and the Java community at large.

Java community process

The **Java Community Process (JCP)** allows interested parties to assist in developing standard technical specification for Java technology. Both companies and individuals can become members of the JCP and contribute to any technical specification they may be interested in. Each Java EE API specification is developed as part of a **Java Specification Request (JSR)**. Each JSR is assigned a unique number. **JavaServer Faces (JSF)** 2.3 is developed as JSR 372, for instance.

Since Java EE is developed under the JCP, no one company has complete control over the Java EE specification, since, as mentioned before, the JCP is available to the Java community at large, both software vendors and interested individuals.

Different JCP members have different interests, and contribute to different Java EE specifications; the end result is that Java EE is jointly developed by various members of the Java community.

Java EE APIs

As previously mentioned, Java EE is a collection of API specifications designed to work together when developing server-side enterprise Java applications. Java EE 8 APIs include:

- JavaServer Faces (JSF) 2.3
- Java Persistence API (JPA) 2.2
- Enterprise JavaBeans (EJB) 3.2
- Contexts and Dependency Injection for the Java EE Platform (CDI) 2.0
- Java API for JSON Processing (JSON-P) 1.1
- Java API for JSON Binding (JSON-B) 1.0
- Java API for WebSocket 1.0
- Java Message Service (JMS) 2.0
- Java EE Security API 1.0
- Java API for RESTful Web Services (JAX-RS) 2.1
- Java API for XML Web Services (JAX-WS) 2.2
- Servlet 4.0

- Expression Language (EL) 3.0
- JavaServer Pages (JSP) 2.3
- Java Naming and Directory Interface (JNDI) 1.2
- Java Transaction API (JTA) 1.2
- Java Transaction Service (JTS) 1.0
- JavaMail 1.5
- Java EE Connector Architecture (JCA) 1.7
- Java Architecture for XML Binding (JAXB) 2.2
- Java Management Extensions (JMX) 1.2
- Standard Tag Library for JavaServer Pages (JSTL) 1.2
- Bean Validation 2.0
- Managed Beans 1.0
- Interceptors 1.2
- Concurrency Utilities for Java EE 1.0
- Batch Applications for the Java Platform 1.0

The preceding list is a list of specifications, application server vendors or the open source community need to provide implementations for each Java EE API specification. Application server vendors then bundle a set of Java EE API implementations together as part of their application server offerings. Since each implementation is compliant with the corresponding Java EE JSR, code developed against one implementation can run unmodified against any other implementation, avoiding vendor lock-in.

Due to time and space constraints, we won't cover every single Java EE API specification in this book, instead focusing on the most popular Java EE APIs. The following table summarizes the APIs that we will be covering:

Java EE API	Description
JavaServer Faces (JSF) 2.3	JSF is a component library that greatly simplifies the development of web applications.
Java Persistence API (JPA) 2.2	JPA is the Java EE standard **Object-Relational Mapping (ORM)** API. It makes it easy to interact with relational databases.
Enterprise JavaBeans (EJB) 3.2	EJB's allow us to easily add enterprise features such as transactions and scalability to our Java EE applications.

Contexts and Dependency Injection (CDI) 2.0	CDI allows us to easily define the life cycle of Java objects and provides the ability to easily inject dependencies into Java objects; it also provides a powerful event mechanism.
Java API for **JSON Processing (JSON-P)** 1.1	JSON-P is an API that allows working with JSON strings in Java.
Java API for **JSON Binding (JSON-B)** 1.0	JSON-B provides the ability to easily populate Java objects from JSON streams and back.
Java API for WebSocket 1.0	WebSocket is a standard Java EE implementation of the **Internet Engineering Task Force** (**IETF**) WebSocket protocol, which allows full duplex communication over a single TCP connection.
Java Message Service (JMS) 2.0	JMS is a standard API that allows Java EE developers to interact with **Message Oriented Middleware** (**MOM**).
Java EE Security API 1.0	The Java EE Security API aims to standardize and simplify the task of securing Java EE applications.
Java API for RESTful Web Services (JAX-RS) 2.1	JAX-RS is an API for creating RESTful web services endpoints and clients.
Java API for XML Web Services (JAX-WS) 2.2	JAX-WS is an API that allows the creation of **Simple Object Access Protocol** (**SOAP**) web services.
Servlet 4.0	The servlet API is a low-level API used to implement server-side logic in web applications.

We will also cover how to develop microservices by leveraging standard Java EE APIs. Microservices are a modern, popular architectural style in which applications are split up into small modules deployed independently, interacting with each other via the network, typically by leveraging RESTful web services.

We should also note that, with the possible exception of the chapter on microservices, each chapter on this book is standalone; feel free to read the chapters in any order.

Now that we have covered the different APIs provided by Java EE, it is worth reiterating that Java EE is a single standard with multiple implementations, some commercial, and some open source.

One standard, multiple implementations

At its core, Java EE is a specification—a piece of paper, if you will. Implementations of Java EE specifications need to be developed so that application developers can actually develop server-side, enterprise Java applications against the Java EE standard. Each Java EE API has multiple implementations; the popular Hibernate Object-Relational Mapping tool, for example, is an implementation of Java EE's Java Persistence API (JPA). However, it is by no means the only JPA implementation; other JPA implementations include EclipseLink and OpenJPA. Similarly, there are multiple implementations of every single Java EE API specification.

Java EE applications are typically deployed to an application server; some popular application servers include JBoss, Websphere, Weblogic, and GlassFish. Each application server is considered to be a Java EE implementation. Application server vendors either develop their own implementation of the several Java EE API specifications or choose to include an existing implementation.

Application developers benefit from the Java EE standard by not being tied to a specific Java EE implementation. As long as an application is developed against standard Java EE APIs, it should be very portable across application server vendors.

Java EE, J2EE, and the Spring framework

Java EE was introduced back in 2006; the first version of Java EE was Java EE 5. Java EE replaced J2EE; the last version of J2EE was J2EE 1.4, released back in 2003. Even though J2EE can be considered a dead technology, replaced by Java EE over 11 years ago, the term J2EE refuses to die. Many individuals to this day still refer to Java EE as J2EE; many companies advertise on their websites and job boards that they are looking for "J2EE developers", seemingly unaware that they are referring to a technology that has been dead for several years. The correct term is and has been for a long time, Java EE.

Additionally, the term J2EE has become a "catch-all" term for any server-side Java technology; frequently Spring applications are referred to as J2EE applications. Spring is not, and has never been, J2EE; as a matter of fact, Spring was created by Rod Johnson as an alternative to J2EE back in 2002. Just like with Java EE, Spring applications are frequently erroneously referred to as J2EE applications.

Summary

In this chapter, we provided an introduction to Java EE, supplying a list of several technologies and application programming interfaces (APIs) included with Java EE.

We also covered how Java EE is developed both by software vendors and the Java community at large via the Java community process.

Additionally, we explained how there are multiple implementations of the Java EE standard, a fact that avoids vendor lock-in and allow us to easily migrate our Java EE code from one application server to another.

Finally, we cleared up the confusion between Java EE, J2EE, and Spring, explaining how Java EE and Spring applications are frequently referred to as J2EE applications, even though J2EE has been a dead technology for several years.

2
JavaServer Faces

In this chapter, we will cover **JavaServer Faces** (**JSF**), the standard component framework of the Java EE platform. Java EE 8 includes JSF 2.3, the latest version of JSF. JSF relies a lot on convention over configuration—if we follow JSF conventions then we don't need to write a lot of configuration. In most cases, we don't need to write any configuration at all. This fact, combined with the fact that `web.xml` has been optional since Java EE 6, means that, in many cases, we can write complete web applications without having to write a single line of XML.

We will cover the following topics in this chapter:

- Facelets
- JSF project stages
- Data validation
- Named beans
- Navigation
- Ajax-enabling JSF applications
- JSF HTML5 support
- Faces flows
- JSF artifact injection
- JSF WebSocket support
- JSF component libraries

Introducing JSF

JSF 2.0 introduced a number of enhancements to make JSF application development easier. In the following few sections, we will explore some of these features.

 Readers not familiar with earlier versions of JSF may not understand the following few sections completely. Not to worry, everything will be perfectly clear by the end of this chapter.

Facelets

One notable difference between modern versions of JSF and earlier versions is that Facelets is now the preferred view technology. Earlier versions of JSF used **Java Server Pages** (**JSP**) as their default view technology. Since the JSP technology predates JSF, sometimes using JSP with JSF felt unnatural or created problems. For example, the JSP lifecycle is different from the JSF lifecycle; this mismatch introduced some problems for JSF 1.x application developers.

JSF was designed from the beginning to support multiple view technologies. To take advantage of this capability, Jacob Hookom wrote a view technology specifically for JSF. He named his view technology **Facelets**. Facelets was so successful it became a de-facto standard for JSF. The JSF expert group recognized Facelets' popularity and made it the official view technology for JSF in version 2.0 of the JSF specification.

Optional faces-config.xml

Legacy J2EE applications suffered from what some have considered to be excessive XML configuration.

Java EE 5 took some measures to reduce XML configuration considerably. Java EE 6 reduced the required configuration even further, making the JSF configuration file, `faces-config.xml`, optional in JSF 2.0.

In JSF 2.0 and newer versions, JSF managed beans can be configured via the `@ManagedBean` annotation, obviating the need to configure them in `faces-config.xml`. Java EE 6 introduced the **Contexts and Dependency Injection** (**CDI**) API, which provides an alternate way of implementing functionality typically implemented with JSF managed beans. As of JSF 2.2, CDI named beans are preferred over JSF managed beans; JSF 2.3 went even further, deprecating specific JSF-managed beans in favor of CDI named beans.

Additionally, there is a convention for JSF navigation: if the value of the action attribute of a JSF 2.0 command link or command button matches the name of a facelet (minus the XHTML extension), then by convention, the application will navigate to the facelet matching the action name. This convention allows us to avoid having to configure application navigation in `faces-config.xml`.

For many modern JSF applications, `faces-config.xml` is completely unnecessary as long as we follow established JSF conventions.

Standard resource locations

JSF 2.0 introduced standard resource locations. Resources are artifacts a page or JSF component needs to render properly. Resource examples include CSS stylesheets, JavaScript files, and images.

In JSF 2.0 and newer versions, resources can be placed in a subdirectory under a folder called `resources`, either at the root of the WAR file or under its `META-INF` directory. By convention, JSF components know they can retrieve resources from one of these two locations.

In order to avoid cluttering the `resources` directory, `resources` are typically placed in a subdirectory. This subdirectory is referred to from the `library` attribute of JSF components.

For example, we could place a CSS stylesheet called `styles.css` under `/resources/css/styles.css`.

In our JSF pages, we could retrieve this CSS file using the `<h:outputStylesheet>` tag, as follows:

```
<h:outputStylesheet library="css"  name="styles.css"/>
```

The value of the `library` attribute must match the subdirectory where our `stylesheet` is located.

Similarly, we could have a JavaScript file under `/resources/scripts/somescript.js` and an image under `/resources/images/logo.png`, and we could access these `resources` as follows:

```
<h:graphicImage library="images" name="logo.png"/>
```

And:

```
<h:outputScript library="scripts" name="somescript.js"/>
```

Notice that, in each case, the value of the `library` attribute matches the corresponding subdirectory name under the `resources` directory, and the value of the `name` attribute matches the resource's file name.

Developing our first JSF application

To illustrate basic JSF concepts, we will develop a simple application consisting of two Facelet pages and a single CDI named bean.

Facelets

As we mentioned in this chapter's introduction, the default view technology for JSF 2.0 and newer versions is **Facelets**. Facelets need to be written using standard XML. The most popular way to develop Facelet pages is to use XHTML in conjunction with JSF-specific XML namespaces. The following example shows how a typical Facelet page looks:

```
<?xml version='1.0' encoding='UTF-8' ?>
<!DOCTYPE html PUBLIC "-//W3C//DTD XHTML 1.0 Transitional//EN"
 "http://www.w3.org/TR/xhtml1/DTD/xhtml1-transitional.dtd">
 <html xmlns="http://www.w3.org/1999/xhtml"
        xmlns:h="http://java.sun.com/jsf/html"
        xmlns:f="http://java.sun.com/jsf/core">
     <h:head>
         <title>Enter Customer Data</title>
     </h:head>
     <h:body>
         <h:outputStylesheet library="css" name="styles.css"/>
         <h:form id="customerForm">
             <h:messages></h:messages>
             <h:panelGrid columns="2"
              columnClasses="rightAlign,leftAlign">
                 <h:outputLabel for="firstName" value="First Name:">
                 </h:outputLabel>
                 <h:inputText id="firstName"
                  label="First Name"
                  value="#{customer.firstName}"
                  required="true">
                     <f:validateLength minimum="2" maximum="30">
                     </f:validateLength>
```

```
    </h:inputText>
    <h:outputLabel for="lastName" value="Last Name:">
    </h:outputLabel>
    <h:inputText id="lastName"
     label="Last Name"
     value="#{customer.lastName}"
     required="true">
        <f:validateLength minimum="2" maximum="30">
        </f:validateLength>
        </h:inputText>
    <h:outputLabel for="email" value="Email:">
    </h:outputLabel>
    <h:inputText id="email"
     label="Email"
     value="#{customer.email}">
    <f:validateLength minimum="3" maximum="30">
    </f:validateLength>
        </h:inputText>
        <h:panelGroup></h:panelGroup>
    <h:commandButton action="confirmation" value="Save">
    </h:commandButton>
        </h:panelGrid>
    </h:form>
  </h:body>
</html>
```

The following screenshot illustrates how the previous page renders in the browser:

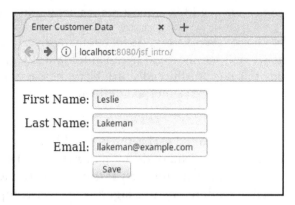

The preceding screenshot, of course, was taken after entering some data in every text field; originally each text field was blank.

Pretty much any Facelet JSF page will include the two namespaces illustrated in the example. The first namespace (xmlns:h="http://xmlns.jcp.org/jsf/html") is for tags that render HTML components; by convention, the prefix h (for HTML) is used when using this tag library.

The second namespace (xmlns:f="http://xmlns.jcp.org/jsf/core") is the core JSF tag library, by convention, the prefix f (for faces) is used when using this tag library.

The first JSF-specific tags we see in the preceding example are the <h:head> and <h:body> tags. These tags are analogous to the standard HTML <head> and <body> tags, and are rendered as such when the page is displayed in the browser.

The <h:outputStylesheet> tag is used to load a CSS stylesheet from a well-known location (JSF standardizes the locations of resources, such as CSS stylesheets and JavaScript files; this will be discussed in detail later in the chapter). The value of the library attribute must correspond to the directory where the CSS file resides (this directory must be under a resources directory). The name attribute must correspond to the name of the CSS stylesheet we want to load.

The next tag we see is the <h:form> tag. This tag generates an HTML form when the page is rendered. As can be seen in the example, there is no need to specify an action or a method attribute for this tag; as a matter of fact, there is no action or method attribute for this tag. The action attribute for the rendered HTML form will be generated automatically, and the method attribute will always be post. The id attribute of <h:form> is optional; however, it is a good idea to always add it, since it makes debugging JSF applications easier.

The next tag we see is the <h:messages> tag. As its name implies, this tag is used to display any messages. As we will see shortly, JSF can automatically generate validation messages, displayed inside this tag. Additionally, arbitrary messages can be added programmatically via the addMessage() method defined in javax.faces.context.FacesContext.

The next JSF tag we see is <h:panelGrid>. This tag is roughly equivalent to an HTML table, but it works a bit differently. Instead of declaring rows (<tr>) and cells (<td>), the <h:panelGrid> tag has a columns attribute; the value of this attribute indicates the number of columns in the table rendered by this tag. As we place components inside this tag, they will be placed in a row until the number of columns defined in the columns attribute is reached, when the next component will be placed in the next row. In the example, the value of the columns attribute is 2, therefore the first two tags will be placed in the first row, the next two will be placed in the second row, and so forth.

Another interesting attribute of `<h:panelGrid>` is the `columnClasses` attribute. This attribute assigns a CSS class to each column in the rendered table. In the example, two CSS classes (separated by a comma) are used as the value for this attribute. This has the effect of assigning the first CSS class to the first column, and the second one to the second column. Had there been three or more columns, the third one would have gotten the first CSS class, the fourth one the second one, and so on, alternating between the first one and the second one. To clarify how this works, the next code snippet illustrates a portion of the source of the HTML markup generated by the preceding page:

```
<table>
    <tbody>
        <tr>
            <td class="rightAlign">
                <label for="customerForm:firstName">
                    First Name:
                </label>
            </td>
            <td class="leftAlign">
                <input id="customerForm:firstName" type="text"
                name="customerForm:firstName" />
            </td>
        </tr>
        <tr>
            <td class="rightAlign">
                <label for="customerForm:lastName">
                Last Name:
                </label>
            </td>
            <td class="leftAlign">
                <input id="customerForm:lastName" type="text"
                name="customerForm:lastName" />
            </td>
        </tr>
        <tr>
            <td class="rightAlign">
                <label for="customerForm:lastName">
                    Email:
                </label>
            </td>
            <td class="leftAlign">
                <input id="customerForm:email" type="text"
                name="customerForm:email" />
            </td>
        </tr>
        <tr>
            <td class="rightAlign"></td>
```

```
            <td class="leftAlign">
                <input type="submit" name="customerForm:j_idt12"
                value="Save" />
            </td>
        </tr>
    </tbody>
</table>
```

Notice how each <td> tag has an alternating CSS tag—"rightAlign" or "leftAlign"; we achieved this by assigning the value "rightAlign,leftAlign" to the columnClasses attribute of <h:panelGrid>. We should note that the CSS classes we are using in our example are defined in the CSS stylesheet we loaded via the <h:outputStylesheet> we discussed earlier. The ID's of the generated markup are a combination of the ID we gave to the <h:form> component, plus the ID of each individual component. Notice that we didn't assign an ID to the <h:commandButton> component near the end of the page, so the JSF runtime assigned one automatically.

At this point in the example, we start adding components inside <h:panelGrid>. These components will be rendered inside the table rendered by <h:panelGrid>. As we mentioned before, the number of columns in the rendered table is defined by the columns attribute of <h:panelGrid>. Therefore, we don't need to worry about columns (or rows), we can just start adding components and they will be placed in the right place.

The next tag we see is the <h:outputLabel> tag. This tag renders as an HTML label element. Labels are associated with other components via the for attribute, whose value must match the ID of the component that the label is for.

Next, we see the <h:inputText> tag. This tag generates a text field in the rendered page. Its label attribute is used for any validation messages; it lets the user know what field the message refers to.

Although it is not mandatory for the value of the label attribute of <h:inputText> to match the label displayed on the page, it is highly recommended to use this value. In case of an error, this will let the user know exactly what field the message is referring to.

Of particular interest is the tag's `value` attribute. What we see as the value for this attribute is a **value binding expression**. What this means is that this value is tied to a property of one of the application's named beans. In the example, this particular text field is tied to a property called `firstName` in a named bean called `customer`. When a user enters a value for this text field and submits the form, the corresponding property in the named bean is updated with this value. The tag's `required` attribute is optional; valid values for it are `true` and `false`. If this attribute is set to `true`, the container will not let the user submit the form until the user enters some data for the text field. If the user attempts to submit the form without entering a required value, the page will be reloaded and an error message will be displayed inside the `<h:messages>` tag:

The preceding screenshot illustrates the default error message shown when the user attempts to save the form in the example without entering a value for the customer's first name. The first part of the message (**First Name**) is taken from the value of the `label` attribute of the corresponding `<h:inputTextField>` tag. The text of the message can be customized, as well as its style (font, color, and more.). We will cover how to do this later in the chapter.

Project stages

Having a <h:messages> tag on every JSF page is a good idea; without it, the user might not see validation messages and will have no idea why the form submission is not going through. By default, JSF validation messages do not generate any output in the application server log. A common mistake new JSF developers make is failing to add a <h:messages> tag to their pages; without it, if validation fails, then the navigation seems to fail for no reason (the same page is rendered if navigation fails and, without a <h:messages> tag, no error messages are displayed in the browser).

To avoid this situation, JSF 2.0 introduced the concept of **project stages**.

The following project stages are defined in JSF 2.0 and newer versions:

- Production
- Development
- UnitTest
- SystemTest

We can define the project stage as an initialization parameter to the Faces servlet in web.xml, or as a custom JNDI resource. The preferred way of setting the project stage is through a custom JNDI resource.

 The process to map global JNDI resources to component resources is application server-specific; when using GlassFish, a change needs to be made to the application's web.xml, plus we need to use a GlassFish-specific deployment descriptor.

Setting up a custom JNDI resource is application server-specific, consult your application server documentation for details. If we are using GlassFish to deploy our application, we can set up a custom JNDI by logging in to the web console, navigating to **JNDI | Custom Resources**, then clicking the **New...** button:

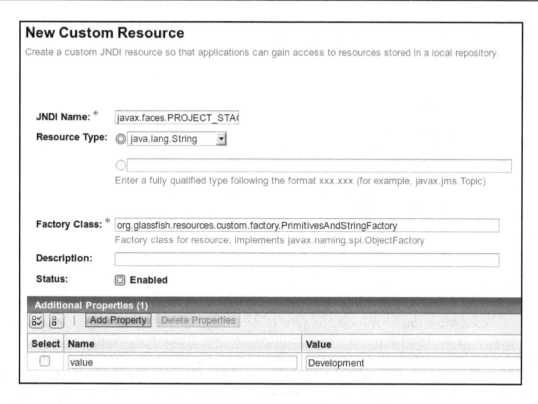

In the resulting page, we need to enter the following information:

JNDI Name	`javax.faces.PROJECT_STAGE`
Resource Type	`java.lang.String`

After entering these two values, the **Factory Class** field will be automatically populated with the value :
`org.glassfish.resources.custom.factory.PrimitivesAndStringFactory`.

After entering the values, we need to add a new property with a name of **value** and a value corresponding to the project stage we want to use (**Development**, in the preceding screenshot).

Setting the project stage allows us to perform some logic only if we are running in a specific stage. For instance, in one of our named beans, we could have code that looks like this:

```
Application application = facesContext.getApplication();

if (application.getProjectStage().equals(
    ProjectStage.Production)) {
  //do production stuff
} else if (application.getProjectStage().equals(
    ProjectStage.Development)) {
  //do development stuff
} else if (application.getProjectStage().equals(
    ProjectStage.UnitTest)) {
  //do unit test stuff
} else if (application.getProjectStage().equals(
    ProjectStage.SystemTest)) {
  //do system test stuff
}
```

As we can see, project stages allow us to modify our code's behavior for different environments. More importantly, setting the project stage allows the JSF engine to behave a bit differently based on the project stage setting. Relevant to our discussion, setting the project stage to Development results in additional logging statements in the application server log. Therefore, if we forget to add a <h:messages> tag to our page, our project stage is Development, and validation fails; a **Validation Error** will be displayed on the page even if we omit the <h:messages> component:

In the default Production stage, this error message is not displayed in the page, leaving us confused as to why our page navigation doesn't seem to be working.

Validation

Notice that each `<h:inputField>` tag has a nested `<f:validateLength>` tag. As its name implies, this tag validates that the entered value for the text field is between a minimum and maximum length. Minimum and maximum values are defined by the tag's `minimum` and `maximum` attributes. `<f:validateLength>` is one of the standard validators included with JSF. Just like with the `required` attribute of `<h:inputText>`, JSF will automatically display a default error message when a user attempts to submit a form with a value that does not validate:

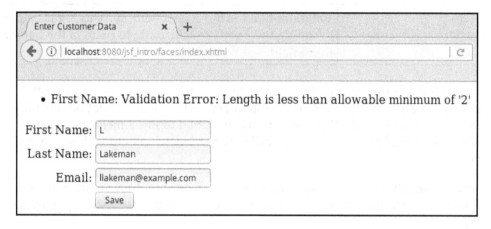

Again, the default message and style can be overridden; we will cover how to do this later in the chapter.

In addition to `<f:validateLength>`, JSF includes other standard validators, which are listed in the following table:

Validation tag	Description
`<f:validateBean>`	Bean validation allows us to validate named `bean` values by using annotations in our named beans without having to add validators to our JSF tags. This tag allows us to fine-tune bean validation if necessary.
`<f:validateDoubleRange>`	Validates that the input is a valid `Double` value between the two values specified by the tag's `minimum` and `maximum` attributes, inclusive.

`<f:validateLength>`	Validates that the input's length is between the values specified by the tag's `minimum` and `maximum` values, inclusive.
`<f:validateLongRange>`	Validates that the input is a valid `Double` value between the values specified by the tag's `minimum` and `maximum` attributes, inclusive.
`<f:validateRegex>`	Validates that the input matches a regular expression pattern specified in the tag's `pattern` attribute.
`<f:validateRequired>`	Validates that the input is not empty. This tag is equivalent to setting the `required` attribute to `true` in the parent input field.

Notice that in the description for `<f:validateBean>`, we briefly mentioned bean validation. The bean validation JSR aims to standardize JavaBean validation. JavaBeans are used across several other APIs that, up until recently, had to implement their own validation logic. JSF 2.0 adopted the bean validation standard to help validate named bean properties.

If we want to take advantage of bean validation, all we need to do is annotate the desired field with the appropriate bean validation annotation, without having to explicitly use a JSF validator.

For a complete list of bean validation annotations, refer to the `javax.validation.constraints` package in the Java EE 8 API at `https://javaee.github.io/javaee-spec/javadocs/`.

Grouping components

`<h:panelGroup>` is the next new tag in the example. Typically, `<h:panelGroup>` is used to group several components together so that they occupy a single cell in an `<h:panelGrid>`. This can be accomplished by adding components inside `<h:panelGroup>` and adding `<h:panelGroup>` to `<h:panelGrid>`. As can be seen in the example, this particular instance of `<h:panelGroup>` has no child components. In this particular case, the purpose of `<h:panelGroup>` is to have an empty cell and have the next component, `<h:commandButton>`, align with all other input fields in the form.

Form submission

`<h:commandButton>` renders an HTML submit button in the browser. Just like with standard HTML, its purpose is to submit the form. Its `value` attribute simply sets the button's label. This tag's `action` attribute is used for navigation; the next page to show is based on the value of this attribute. The `action` attribute can have a `String` constant or a **method binding expression**, meaning that it can point to a `method` in a named bean that returns a string.

If the base name of a page in our application matches the value of the `action` attribute of a `<h:commandButton>` tag, then we navigate to this page when clicking the button. This JSF feature frees us from having to define navigation rules, like we used to have to do in older versions of JSF. In our example, our confirmation page is called `confirmation.xhtml`; therefore by convention, this page will be shown when the button is clicked, since the value of its `action` attribute (confirmation) matches the base name of the page.

> Even though the label for the button reads **Save**, in our simple example, clicking on the button won't actually save any data.

Named beans

There are two types of Java Beans that can interact with JSF pages: JSF managed beans and CDI named beans. JSF managed beans have been around since the first version of the JSF specification and can be used only in a JSF context. CDI named beans were introduced in Java EE 6 and can interoperate with other Java EE APIs, such as Enterprise JavaBeans. For this reason, CDI named beans are preferred over JSF managed beans.

To make a Java class a CDI named bean, all we need to do is make sure the class has a public, no argument constructor (one is created implicitly if there are no other constructors declared, which is the case in our example) and add the `@Named` annotation at the class level. Here is the managed bean for our example:

```
package net.ensode.glassfishbook.jsf;
import javax.enterprise.context.RequestScoped;
import javax.inject.Named;

@Named
@RequestScoped
public class Customer {
```

```
    private String firstName;
    private String lastName;
    private String email;

    public String getEmail() {
        return email;
    }

    public void setEmail(String email) {
        this.email = email;
    }

    public String getFirstName() {
        return firstName;
    }

    public void setFirstName(String firstName) {
        this.firstName = firstName;
    }

    public String getLastName() {
        return lastName;
    }

    public void setLastName(String lastName) {
        this.lastName = lastName;
    }
}
```

The @Named class annotation designates this bean as a CDI named bean. This annotation has an optional value attribute we can use to give our bean a logical name for use in our JSF pages. However, by convention, the value of this attribute is the same as the class name (Customer, in our case), with its first character switched to lower case. In our example, we let this default behavior take place, therefore we access our bean's properties via the customer logical name. Notice the value attribute of any of the input fields in our example page to see this logical name in action.

Notice that, other than the @Named and @RequestScoped annotations, there is nothing special about this bean. It is a standard JavaBean with private properties and corresponding getter and setter methods. The @RequestScoped annotation specifies that the bean should live through a single request. The different named bean, scopes, available for our JSF applications, are covered in the next section.

Named bean scopes

Managed beans always have a scope. A managed bean scope defines the lifespan of the application. The managed bean scope is defined by a class level annotation. The following table lists all valid managed bean scopes:

Named bean scope annotation	Description
@ApplicationScoped	The same instance of application scoped named beans is available to all of our application's clients. If one client modifies the value of an application scoped managed bean, the change is reflected across clients.
@SessionScoped	An instance of each session scoped named bean is assigned to each of our application's clients. A session-scoped named bean can be used to hold client-specific data across requests.
@RequestScoped	Request scoped named beans only live through a single HTTP request.
@Dependent	Dependent scoped named beans are assigned the same scope as the bean they are injected to.
@ConversationScoped	The conversation scope can span multiple requests, but is typically shorter than the session scope.

Navigation

As can be seen in our input page, when clicking on the **Save** button in the customer_data_entry.xhtml page, our application will navigate to a page called confirmation.xhtml. This happens because we are taking advantage of JSF's convention over configuration feature; if the value of the action attribute of a command button or link matches the base name of another page, then this navigation takes us to this page.

Same page reloading when clicking on a button or link that should navigate to another page? When JSF does not recognize the value of the action attribute of a command button or command link, it will by default navigate to the same page that was displayed in the browser when the user clicked on a button or link that is meant to navigate to another page.

If navigation does not seem to be working properly, chances are there is a typo in the value of this attribute. Remember that, by convention, JSF will look for a page whose base name matches the value of the action attribute of a command button or link.

The source for confirmation.xhtml looks like this:

```xml
<?xml version='1.0' encoding='UTF-8' ?>
<!DOCTYPE html PUBLIC "-//W3C//DTD XHTML 1.0 Transitional//EN"
"http://www.w3.org/TR/xhtml1/DTD/xhtml1-transitional.dtd">
<html xmlns="http://www.w3.org/1999/xhtml"
      xmlns:h="http://java.sun.com/jsf/html">
  <h:head>
    <title>Customer Data Entered</title>
  </h:head>
  <h:body>
    <h:panelGrid columns="2" columnClasses="rightAlign,leftAlign">
      <h:outputText value="First Name:"></h:outputText>
      <h:outputText value="#{customer.firstName}"></h:outputText>
      <h:outputText value="Last Name:"></h:outputText>
      <h:outputText value="#{customer.lastName}"></h:outputText>
      <h:outputText value="Email:"></h:outputText>
      <h:outputText value="#{customer.email}"></h:outputText>
    </h:panelGrid>
  </h:body>
</html>
```

The <h:outputText> is the only tag on this page we haven't covered before. This tag simply displays the value of its value attribute to the rendered page, its value attribute can be a simple string or a value binding expression. Since the value binding expressions in our <h:outputText> tags are the same expressions used in the previous page for the <h:inputText> tags, their values will correspond to the data the user entered:

In traditional (that is, non-JSF) Java web applications, we define URL patterns to be processed by specific servlets. Specifically for JSF, the suffixes .jsf or .faces are commonly used; another commonly used URL mapping for JSF is the /faces prefix. Under certain conditions, modern application servers automatically add all three mappings to the faces servlet, if these conditions are met, we don't have to specify any URL mappings at all.

If any of these conditions are met, then the FacesServlet will be automatically mapped:

- There is a faces-config.xml file in the WEB-INF directory of our web application
- There is a faces-config.xml file in the META-INF directory of one of the dependencies of our web application
- There is a filename ending in .faces-config.xml in the META-INF directory of one of the dependencies of our web application
- We declare a context parameter named javax.faces.CONFIG_FILES in our web.xml or a web-fragment.xml in one of the dependencies
- We pass a non-empty set of classes when invoking the onStartup() method of ServletContextInitializer

When none of the preceding conditions are met, we need to explicitly map the Faces servlet in our web.xml deployment descriptor, as illustrated here:

```xml
<?xml version="1.0" encoding="UTF-8"?>
<web-app xmlns="http://xmlns.jcp.org/xml/ns/javaee"
         xmlns:xsi="http://www.w3.org/2001/XMLSchema-instance"
         xsi:schemaLocation="http://xmlns.jcp.org/xml/ns/javaee
http://xmlns.jcp.org/xml/ns/javaee/web-app_3_1.xsd"
         version="3.1">
    <servlet>
        <servlet-name>Faces Servlet</servlet-name>
        <servlet-class>javax.faces.webapp.FacesServlet</servlet-
        class>
        <load-on-startup>1</load-on-startup>
    </servlet>
    <servlet-mapping>
        <servlet-name>Faces Servlet</servlet-name>
        <url-pattern>/faces/*</url-pattern>
    </servlet-mapping>
</web-app>
```

The URL we used for the pages in our application was the name of our Facelets pages, prefixed by /faces.

Custom data validation

In addition to providing standard validators for our use, JSF allows us to create `custom validator`s. This can be done in one of two ways—by creating a `custom validator` class or by adding `validation` methods to our named beans.

Creating custom validators

In addition to the standard validators, JSF allows us to create custom validators by creating a Java class implementing the `javax.faces.validator.Validator` interface.

The following class implements an email validator, which we will use to validate the email text input field in our customer data entry screen:

```
package net.ensode.glassfishbook.jsfcustomval;

import javax.faces.application.FacesMessage;
import javax.faces.component.UIComponent;
import javax.faces.component.html.HtmlInputText;
import javax.faces.context.FacesContext;
import javax.faces.validator.FacesValidator;
import javax.faces.validator.Validator;
import javax.faces.validator.ValidatorException;
import org.apache.commons.lang3.StringUtils;

@FacesValidator(value = "emailValidator")
public class EmailValidator implements Validator {

  @Override
  public void validate(FacesContext facesContext,
    UIComponent uiComponent,
    Object value) throws ValidatorException {
    org.apache.commons.validator.routines.EmailValidator
emailValidator =
org.apache.commons.validator.routines.EmailValidator.getInstance();
    HtmlInputText htmlInputText = (HtmlInputText) uiComponent;

    String email = (String) value;

    if (!StringUtils.isEmpty(email)) {
      if (!emailValidator.isValid(email)) {
        FacesMessage facesMessage = new FacesMessage(htmlInputText.
          getLabel()
          + ": email format is not valid");
```

```
        throw new ValidatorException(facesMessage);
      }
    }
  }
}
```

The @FacesValidator annotation registers our class as a JSF custom validator class. The value of its value attribute is the logical name that JSF pages can use to refer to it.

As can be seen in the example, the only method we need to implement when implementing the Validator interface is a method called validate(). This method takes three parameters—an instance of javax.faces.context.FacesContext, an instance of javax.faces.component.UIComponent, and an object. Typically, application developers only need to be concerned with the last two. The second parameter is the component whose data we are validating, the third parameter is the actual value. In the example, we cast uiComponent to javax.faces.component.html.HtmlInputText; this way, we get access to its getLabel() method, which we can use as part of the error message.

If the entered value is not an invalid email address format, a new instance of javax.faces.application.FacesMessage is created, passing the error message to be displayed in the browser as its constructor parameter. We then throw a new javax.faces.validator.ValidatorException. The error message is then displayed in the browser; it gets there behind the scenes via the JSF API.

Apache Commons Validator: Our custom JSF validator uses Apache Commons Validator to do the actual validation. This library includes many common validations such as dates, credit card numbers, ISBN numbers, and emails. When implementing a custom validator, it's worth investigating whether this library already has a validator that we can use.

In order to use our validator on our page, we need to use the <f:validator> JSF tag. The following Facelets page is a modified version of the customer data entry screen. This version uses the <f:validator> tag to validate email:

```xml
<?xml version='1.0' encoding='UTF-8' ?>
<!DOCTYPE html PUBLIC "-//W3C//DTD XHTML 1.0 Transitional//EN"
  "http://www.w3.org/TR/xhtml1/DTD/xhtml1-transitional.dtd">
<html xmlns="http://www.w3.org/1999/xhtml"
      xmlns:h="http://java.sun.com/jsf/html"
      xmlns:f="http://java.sun.com/jsf/core">
  <h:head>
    <title>Enter Customer Data</title>
  </h:head>
  <h:body>
```

```
      <h:outputStylesheet library="css" name="styles.css"/>
      <h:form>
        <h:messages></h:messages>
        <h:panelGrid columns="2"
         columnClasses="rightAlign,leftAlign">
          <h:outputText value="First Name:">
          </h:outputText>
          <h:inputText label="First Name"
           value="#{customer.firstName}"
           required="true">
            <f:validateLength minimum="2" maximum="30">
            </f:validateLength>
          </h:inputText>
          <h:outputText value="Last Name:"></h:outputText>
          <h:inputText label="Last Name"
           value="#{customer.lastName}"
           required="true">
            <f:validateLength minimum="2" maximum="30">
            </f:validateLength>
          </h:inputText>
          <h:outputText value="Email:">
          </h:outputText>
          <h:inputText label="Email" value="#{customer.email}">
            <f:validator validatorId="emailValidator" />
          </h:inputText>
          <h:panelGroup></h:panelGroup>
          <h:commandButton action="confirmation" value="Save">
          </h:commandButton>
        </h:panelGrid>
      </h:form>
    </h:body>
</html>
```

After writing our custom validator and modifying our page to take advantage of it, we can see our `validator` in action:

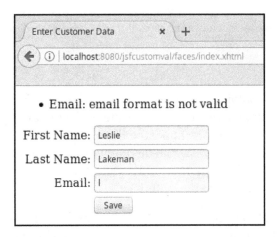

Validator methods

Another way we can implement custom validation is by adding `validation` methods to one or more of the application's named beans. The following `Java` class illustrates the use of `validator` methods for JSF validation:

```
package net.ensode.glassfishbook.jsfcustomval;

import javax.enterprise.context.RequestScoped;
import javax.faces.application.FacesMessage;
import javax.faces.component.UIComponent;
import javax.faces.component.html.HtmlInputText;
import javax.faces.context.FacesContext;
import javax.faces.validator.ValidatorException;
import javax.inject.Named;

import org.apache.commons.lang3.StringUtils;

@Named
@RequestScoped
public class AlphaValidator {

    public void validateAlpha(FacesContext facesContext,
        UIComponent uiComponent,
        Object value) throws ValidatorException {
        if (!StringUtils.isAlphaSpace((String) value)) {
```

```
        HtmlInputText htmlInputText = (HtmlInputText) uiComponent;
        FacesMessage facesMessage = new FacesMessage(htmlInputText.
            getLabel()
            + ": only alphabetic characters are allowed.");
        throw new ValidatorException(facesMessage);
      }
    }
  }
```

In this example, the class contains only the `validator` method, but that does not always have to be the case. We can give our `validator` method any name we want; however its return value must be `void`, and it must take the three parameters illustrated in the example, in that order. In other words, except for the method name, the signature of a `validator` method must be identical to the signature of the `validate()` method defined in the `javax.faces.validator.Validator` interface.

As we can see, the body of the preceding `validator` method is nearly identical to the body of our `custom validator` class, `validate()` method. We check the value entered by the user to make sure it contains only alphabetic characters and/or spaces; if it does not, then we throw a `ValidatorException` passing an instance of `FacesMessage` containing an appropriate error message `String: StringUtils`.

In the example, we used `org.apache.commons.lang3.StringUtils` to perform the actual validation logic. In addition to the method used in the example, this class contains several methods for verifying that a `String` is numeric or alphanumeric. This class, part of the `Apache Commons Lang` library, is very useful when writing `custom validators`.

Since every `validator` method must be in a named bean, we need to make sure the class containing our `validator` method is annotated with the `@Named` annotation, as illustrated in our example.

The last thing we need to do to use our `validator` method is to bind it to our component via the tag's `validator` attribute:

```xml
<?xml version='1.0' encoding='UTF-8' ?>
<!DOCTYPE html PUBLIC "-//W3C//DTD XHTML 1.0 Transitional//EN"
    "http://www.w3.org/TR/xhtml1/DTD/xhtml1-transitional.dtd">
<html xmlns="http://www.w3.org/1999/xhtml"
      xmlns:h="http://java.sun.com/jsf/html"
      xmlns:f="http://java.sun.com/jsf/core">
  <h:head>
    <title>Enter Customer Data</title>
  </h:head>
```

```
<h:body>
  <h:outputStylesheet library="css" name="styles.css"/>
  <h:form>
    <h:messages></h:messages>
    <h:panelGrid columns="2"
                 columnClasses="rightAlign,leftAlign">
      <h:outputText value="First Name:">
      </h:outputText>
      <h:inputText label="First Name"
       value="#{customer.firstName}"
       required="true"
       validator="#{alphaValidator.validateAlpha}">
        <f:validateLength minimum="2" maximum="30">
        </f:validateLength>
      </h:inputText>
      <h:outputText value="Last Name:"></h:outputText>
      <h:inputText label="Last Name"
       value="#{customer.lastName}"
       required="true"
       validator="#{alphaValidator.validateAlpha}">
        <f:validateLength minimum="2" maximum="30">
        </f:validateLength>
      </h:inputText>
      <h:outputText value="Email:">
      </h:outputText>
      <h:inputText label="Email" value="#{customer.email}">
        <f:validateLength minimum="3" maximum="30">
        </f:validateLength>
        <f:validator validatorId="emailValidator" />
      </h:inputText>
      <h:panelGroup></h:panelGroup>
      <h:commandButton action="confirmation" value="Save">
      </h:commandButton>
    </h:panelGrid>
  </h:form>
</h:body>
</html>
```

Since neither the first name nor the last name fields should accept anything other than alphabetic characters or spaces, we added our custom validator method to both of these fields.

Notice that the value of the `validator` attribute of the `<h:inputText>` tag is a JSF expression language; it uses the default named bean name for the bean containing our `validation` method. `alphaValidator` is the name of our bean, and `validateAlpha` is the name of our `validator` method.

After modifying our page to use our `custom validator`, we can now see it in action:

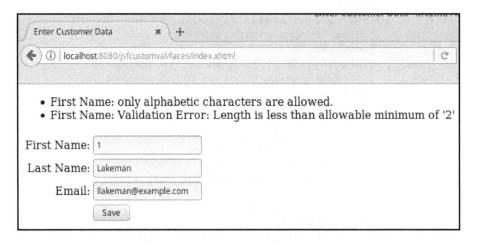

Notice how, for the **First Name** field, both our custom validator message and the standard length validator were executed.

Implementing `validator` methods have the advantage of not having the overhead of creating a whole class just for a single `validator` method (our example does just that, but in many cases, `validator` methods are added to an existing named bean containing other methods); however, the disadvantage is that each component can only be validated by a single `validator` method. When using `validator` classes, several `<f:validator>` tags can be nested inside the tag to be validated, therefore multiple validations, both custom and standard, can be done on the field.

Customizing JSF's default messages

Like we mentioned earlier, it is possible to customize the style (font, color, text, and so on) of JSF's default validation messages. Additionally, it is possible to modify the text of default JSF validation messages. In the following sections, we will explain how to modify error message formatting and text.

Customizing message styles

Customizing message styles can be done via **Cascading Style Sheets** (**CSS**). This can be accomplished by using the <h:message>, style, or styleClass attributes. The style attribute is used when we want to declare the CSS style inline. The styleClass attribute is used when we want to use a predefined style in a CSS style sheet or inside a <style> tag in our page.

The following markup illustrates using the styleClass attribute to alter the style of error messages; it is a modified version of the input page we saw in the previous section:

```
<?xml version='1.0' encoding='UTF-8' ?>
<!DOCTYPE html PUBLIC "-//W3C//DTD XHTML 1.0 Transitional//EN"
  "http://www.w3.org/TR/xhtml1/DTD/xhtml1-transitional.dtd">
<html xmlns="http://www.w3.org/1999/xhtml"
      xmlns:h="http://xmlns.jcp.org/jsf/html"
      xmlns:f="http://xmlns.jcp.org/jsf/core">
  <h:head>
    <title>Enter Customer Data</title>
  </h:head>
  <h:body>
    <h:outputStylesheet library="css" name="styles.css" />
    <h:form>
      <h:messages styleClass="errorMsg"></h:messages>
      <h:panelGrid columns="2"
                   columnClasses="rightAlign,leftAlign">
      <h:outputText value="First Name:">
      </h:outputText>
      <h:inputText label="First Name"
       value="#{customer.firstName}"
       required="true" validator="#
       {alphaValidator.validateAlpha}">
        <f:validateLength minimum="2" maximum="30">
        </f:validateLength>
      </h:inputText>
      <h:outputText value="Last Name:"></h:outputText>
      <h:inputText label="Last Name"
       value="#{customer.lastName}"
       required="true"
       validator="#{alphaValidator.validateAlpha}">
        <f:validateLength minimum="2" maximum="30">
        </f:validateLength>
      </h:inputText>
      <h:outputText value="Email:">
      </h:outputText>
      <h:inputText label="Email" value="#{customer.email}">
```

```
            <f:validator validatorId="emailValidator" />
        </h:inputText>
        <h:panelGroup></h:panelGroup>
        <h:commandButton action="confirmation" value="Save">
        </h:commandButton>
      </h:panelGrid>
    </h:form>
  </h:body>
</html>
```

The only difference between this page and the previous one is the use of the styleClass attribute of the <h:messages> tag. As we mentioned earlier, the value of the styleClass attribute must match the name of a CSS style defined in a cascading stylesheet that our page has access to.

In our case, we defined a CSS style for messages as follows:

```
.errorMsg {
  color: red;
}
```

Then we used this style as the value of the styleClass attribute of our <h:messages> tag.

The following screenshot illustrates how the validation error messages look after implementing this change:

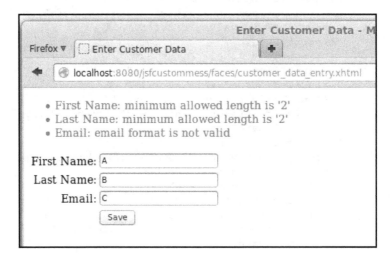

In this particular case, we just set the color of the error message text to red, but we are only limited only by CSS capabilities in setting the style of the error messages.

Pretty much any standard JSF component has both a `style` and a `styleClass` attribute that can be used to alter its style. The former is used for predefined CSS styles, the latter is used for inline CSS.

Customizing message text

Sometimes it is desirable to override the text of JSF's default validation errors. Default validation errors are defined in a resource bundle called `Messages.properties`. This file can typically be found inside one of the JSF JAR Files included with your application server. For example, GlassFish includes it inside a JAR file called `javax.faces.jar` file under `[glassfish installation directory]/glassfish/modules`. The file contains several messages; we are only interested in validation errors at this point. The default validation error messages are defined as follows:

```
javax.faces.validator.DoubleRangeValidator.MAXIMUM={1}: Validation Error:
Value is greater than allowable maximum of "{0}"
javax.faces.validator.DoubleRangeValidator.MINIMUM={1}: Validation Error:
Value is less than allowable minimum of ''{0}''
javax.faces.validator.DoubleRangeValidator.NOT_IN_RANGE={2}: Validation
Error: Specified attribute is not between the expected values of {0} and
{1}.
javax.faces.validator.DoubleRangeValidator.TYPE={0}: Validation Error:
Value is not of the correct type
javax.faces.validator.LengthValidator.MAXIMUM={1}: Validation Error: Length
is greater than allowable maximum of ''{0}''
javax.faces.validator.LengthValidator.MINIMUM={1}: Validation Error: Length
is less than allowable minimum of ''{0}''
javax.faces.validator.LongRangeValidator.MAXIMUM={1}: Validation Error:
Value is greater than allowable maximum of ''{0}''
javax.faces.validator.LongRangeValidator.MINIMUM={1}: Validation Error:
Value is less than allowable minimum of ''{0}''
javax.faces.validator.LongRangeValidator.NOT_IN_RANGE={2}: Validation
Error: Specified attribute is not between the expected values of {0} and
{1}.
javax.faces.validator.LongRangeValidator.TYPE={0}: Validation Error: Value
is not of the correct type.
javax.faces.validator.NOT_IN_RANGE=Validation Error: Specified attribute is
not between the expected values of {0} and {1}.
javax.faces.validator.RegexValidator.PATTERN_NOT_SET=Regex pattern must be
set.
javax.faces.validator.RegexValidator.PATTERN_NOT_SET_detail=Regex pattern
```

```
must be set to non-empty value.
javax.faces.validator.RegexValidator.NOT_MATCHED=Regex Pattern not matched
javax.faces.validator.RegexValidator.NOT_MATCHED_detail=Regex pattern of
''{0}'' not matched
javax.faces.validator.RegexValidator.MATCH_EXCEPTION=Error in regular
expression.
javax.faces.validator.RegexValidator.MATCH_EXCEPTION_detail=Error in
regular expression, ''{0}''
javax.faces.validator.BeanValidator.MESSAGE={0}
```

In order to override the default error messages, we need to create our own resource bundle, using the same keys used in the default one, but altering the values to suit our needs. Here is a very simple customized resource bundle for our application. For example, to overwrite the message for minimum length validation, we would add the following property to our custom resource bundle:

```
javax.faces.validator.LengthValidator.MINIMUM={1}: minimum allowed
length is ''{0}''
```

In this resource bundle, we override the error message for when the value entered for a field validated by the `<f:validateLength>` tag is less than the allowed minimum. In order to let our application know that we have a custom resource bundle for message properties, we need to modify the application's `faces-config.xml` file:

```
<?xml version='1.0' encoding='UTF-8'?>
<faces-config version="2.0"
       xmlns="http://java.sun.com/xml/ns/javaee"
       xmlns:xsi="http://www.w3.org/2001/XMLSchema-instance"
       xsi:schemaLocation="http://java.sun.com/xml/ns/javaee
       http://java.sun.com/xml/ns/javaee/web-facesconfig_2_0.xsd">
    <application>
     <message-bundle>net.ensode.Messages</message-bundle>
    </application>
</faces-config>
```

As we can see, the only thing we need to do to the application's `faces-config.xml` file is to add a `<message-bundle>` element indicating the name and location of the resource bundle containing our custom messages.

Custom error message text definitions are one of the few cases where we still need to define a `faces-config.xml` file for modern JSF applications. However, notice how simple our `faces-config.xml` file is, a far cry from a typical `faces-config.xml` for JSF 1.x, which typically contains named bean definitions, navigation rules, and JSF validator definitions.

After adding our custom message resource bundle and modifying the application's `faces-config.xml` file, we can see our custom validation message in action:

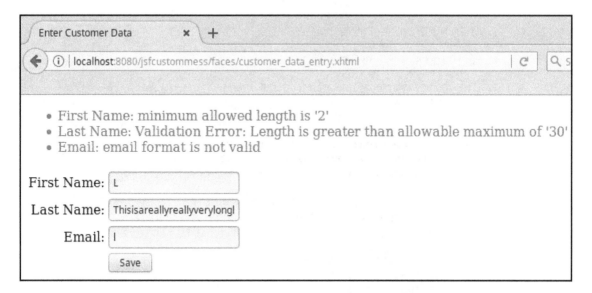

As can be seen in the screenshot, if we haven't overridden a validation message, the default will still be displayed. In our resource bundle we only overrode the minimum length validation error message, therefore our custom error message is shown in the **First Name** text field. Since we didn't override the error message in the other standard JSF validators, the default error message is shown for each one of them. The email validator is the custom validator we developed previously in this chapter; since it is a custom validator, its error message is not affected.

Ajax-enabling JSF applications

JSF allows us to easily implement **Ajax (Asynchronous JavaScript and XML)** functionality into our web applications by simply employing the `<f:ajax>` tag and CDI named beans, without needing to implement any JavaScript code or having to parse JSON strings to implement Ajax with JSF.

The following illustrates a typical usage of the `<f:ajax>` tag:

```
<?xml version='1.0' encoding='UTF-8' ?>
<!DOCTYPE html PUBLIC "-//W3C//DTD XHTML 1.0 Transitional//EN"
"http://www.w3.org/TR/xhtml1/DTD/xhtml1-transitional.dtd">
<html xmlns="http://www.w3.org/1999/xhtml"
```

```
          xmlns:h="http://java.sun.com/jsf/html"
          xmlns:f="http://java.sun.com/jsf/core">
   <h:head>
     <title>JSF Ajax Demo</title>
   </h:head>
   <h:body>
     <h2>JSF Ajax Demo</h2>
     <h:form>
       <h:messages/>
       <h:panelGrid columns="2">

         <h:outputText value="Echo input:"/>
         <h:inputText id="textInput" value="#{controller.text}">
          <f:ajax render="textVal" event="keyup"/>
         </h:inputText>

         <h:outputText value="Echo output:"/>
         <h:outputText id="textVal" value="#{controller.text}"/>
       </h:panelGrid>
       <hr/>
       <h:panelGrid columns="2">
         <h:panelGroup/>
         <h:panelGroup/>
         <h:outputText value="First Operand:"/>
         <h:inputText id="first" value="#{controller.firstOperand}"
         size="3"/>
         <h:outputText value="Second Operand:"/>
         <h:inputText id="second"
          value="#{controller.secondOperand}"
          size="3"/>
         <h:outputText value="Total:"/>
         <h:outputText id="sum" value="#{controller.total}"/>
         <h:commandButton
          actionListener="#{controller.calculateTotal}"
                         value="Calculate Sum">
         <f:ajax execute="first second" render="sum"/>
        </h:commandButton>
        </h:panelGrid>
     </h:form>
   </h:body>
</html>
```

After deploying our application, the preceding page renders as illustrated in the following screenshot:

The preceding page illustrates two uses of the `<f:ajax>` tag. At the top of the page, we use this tag by implementing a typical Ajax Echo example, in which we have a `<h:outputText>` component updating itself with the value of an input text component. Whenever any character is entered into the input field, the value of the `<h:outputText>` component is automatically updated.

To implement the functionality described in the previous paragraph, we put an `<f:ajax>` tag inside an `<h:inputText>` tag. The value of the `render` attribute of the `<f:ajax>` tag must correspond to the ID of a component we want to update after the Ajax request finishes. In our particular example, we want to update the `<h:outputText>` component with an ID of `textVal`, therefore this is the value we use for the render attribute of our `<f:ajax>` tag.

 In some cases we may need to render more than one JSF component after an Ajax event finishes. In order to accommodate this, we can add several IDs as the value of the `render` attribute, we simply need to separate them by spaces.

The other `<f:ajax>` attribute we used in this instance is the `event` attribute. This attribute indicates the JavaScript event that triggers the Ajax event. In this particular case we need to trigger the event any time a key is released while a user is typing into the input field; therefore the appropriate event is to use is `keyup`.

The following table lists all supported JavaScript events:

Event	Description
`blur`	The component loses focus.
`change`	The component loses focus and its value has been modified.
`click`	The component is clicked on.
`dblclick`	The component is double-clicked on.
`focus`	The component gains focus.
`keydown`	A key is pressed while the component has focus.
`keypress`	A key is pressed or held down while the component has focus.
`keyup`	A key is released while the component has focus.
`mousedown`	Mouse button is pressed while the component has focus.
`mousemove`	Mouse pointer is moved over the component.
`mouseout`	Mouse pointer leaves the component.
`mouseover`	Mouse pointer is placed over the component.
`mouseup`	Mouse button is released while the component has focus.
`select`	The component's text is selected.
`valueChange`	Equivalent to change; the component loses focus and its value has been modified.

We use `<f:ajax>` once again further down in the page, to Ajax-enable a command button component. In this instance, we want to recalculate a value based on the value of two input components. In order to have the values on the server updated with the latest user input, we used the `execute` attribute of `<f:ajax>`; this attribute takes a space-separated list of component IDs for use as input. We then use the `render` attribute just like before to specify which components need to be re-rendered after the Ajax request finishes.

Notice we are using the `actionListener` attribute of `<h:commandButton>`. This attribute is typically used whenever we don't need to navigate to another page after clicking the button. The value for this attribute is an `action listener` method we wrote in one of our named beans. `Action listener` methods must return `void`, and take an instance of `javax.faces.event.ActionEvent` as its sole parameter.

The named bean for our application looks like this:

```java
package net.ensode.glassfishbook.jsfajax;
import javax.faces.event.ActionEvent;
import javax.faces.view.ViewScoped;
import javax.inject.Named;
@Named
@ViewScoped
public class Controller {
  private String text;
  private int firstOperand;
  private int secondOperand;
  private int total;
  public Controller() {
  }
  public void calculateTotal(ActionEvent actionEvent) {
    total = firstOperand + secondOperand;
  }
  public String getText() {
    return text;
  }
  public void setText(String text) {
    this.text = text;
  }
  public int getFirstOperand() {
    return firstOperand;
  }
  public void setFirstOperand(int firstOperand) {
    this.firstOperand = firstOperand;
  }
  public int getSecondOperand() {
    return secondOperand;
  }
  public void setSecondOperand(int secondOperand) {
    this.secondOperand = secondOperand;
  }
  public int getTotal() {
    return total;
  }
  public void setTotal(int total) {
    this.total = total;
  }
}
```

Notice that we didn't have to do anything special in our named bean to enable Ajax in our application. It is all controlled by the `<f:ajax>` tag on the page.

As we can see from this example, Ajax-enabling JSF applications is very simple; we simply need to use a single tag to Ajax-enable our page, without having to write a single line of JavaScript, JSON, or XML.

JSF HTML5 support

HTML5 is the latest version of the HTML specification and includes several improvements over the previous version of HTML. Modern versions of JSF include several features to make JSF pages work nicely with HTML5.

HTML5-friendly markup

Through the use of pass-through elements, we can develop our pages using HTML5 and also treat them as JSF components. To do this, we need to specify at least one element attributes using `http://xmlns.jcp.org/jsf namespace`. The following example demonstrates this approach in action:

```
<!DOCTYPE html>
<html xmlns="http://www.w3.org/1999/xhtml"
      xmlns:jsf="http://xmlns.jcp.org/jsf">
    <head jsf:id="head">
        <title>JSF Page with HTML5 Markup</title>
        <link jsf:library="css" jsf:name="styles.css"
rel="stylesheet"
          type="text/css" href="resources/css/styles.css"/>
    </head>
    <body jsf:id="body">
        <form jsf:prependId="false">
            <table style="border-spacing: 0; border-collapse:
              collapse">
                <tr>
                    <td class="rightAlign">
                      <label jsf:for="firstName">First
                      Name</label>
                    </td>
                    <td class="leftAlign">
                      <input type="text" jsf:id="firstName"
                      jsf:value="#{customer.firstName}"/>
                    </td>
```

```
        </tr>
        <tr>
            <td class="rightAlign">
                <label jsf:for="lastName">
                Last Name</label>
            </td>
            <td class="leftAlign">
                <input type="text" jsf:id="lastName"
                jsf:value="#{customer.lastName}"/>
                </td>
        </tr>
        <tr>
            <td class="rightAlign">
                <label jsf:for="email">Email
                Address</label>
            </td>
            <td class="leftAlign">
                <input type="email" jsf:id="email"

                    jsf:value="#{customer.email}"/></td>
        </tr>
        <tr>
            <td></td>
          <td>
            <input type="submit"
            jsf:action="confirmation"
            value="Submit"/>
          </td>
        </tr>
    </table>
  </form>
 </body>
</html>
```

The first thing we should notice about the preceding example is the XML namespace prefixed by jsf near the top of the page. This namespace allows us to add JSF-specific attributes to HTML5 pages. When the JSF runtime encounters attributes prefixed by jsf in any of the tags on the page, it automatically converts the HTML5 tag to the equivalent JSF component. JSF-specific attributes are the same as in regular JSF pages, except they are prefixed with jsf therefore, at this point, they should be self-explanatory and will not be discussed in detail.

The preceding example will render and behave just like the first example in this chapter.

The technique described in this section is useful if we have experienced HTML web designers in our team who prefer to have full control over the look of the page. The pages are developed using standard HTML5 with JSF-specific attributes so that the JSF runtime can manage user input.

If our team consists primarily of Java developers with limited CSS/HTML knowledge, then it is preferable to develop the web pages for our web application using JSF components. HTML5 introduced several new attributes that didn't exist in previous versions of HTML. For this reason, JSF 2.2 introduced the ability to add arbitrary attributes to JSF components; this JSF/HTML5 integration technique is discussed in the next section.

Pass-through attributes

JSF allows the definition of any arbitrary attributes (not processed by the JSF engine); these attributes are simply rendered as-is on the generated HTML displayed in the browser. The following example is a new version of an earlier example in this chapter, modified to take advantage of the HTML5 pass-through attributes:

```
<?xml version='1.0' encoding='UTF-8' ?>
<!DOCTYPE html PUBLIC "-//W3C//DTD XHTML 1.0 Transitional//EN"
"http://www.w3.org/TR/xhtml1/DTD/xhtml1-transitional.dtd">
<html xmlns="http://www.w3.org/1999/xhtml"
      xmlns:h="http://java.sun.com/jsf/html"
      xmlns:f="http://java.sun.com/jsf/core"
      xmlns:p="http://xmlns.jcp.org/jsf/passthrough">
  <h:head>
      <title>Enter Customer Data</title>
  </h:head>
  <h:body>
      <h:outputStylesheet library="css" name="styles.css"/>
      <h:form id="customerForm">
          <h:messages/>
          <h:panelGrid columns="2"
           columnClasses="rightAlign,leftAlign">
              <h:outputLabel for="firstName" value="First Name:">
              </h:outputLabel>
              <h:inputText id="firstName"
               label="First Name"
               value="#{customer.firstName}"
               required="true"
               p:placeholder="First Name">
                  <f:validateLength minimum="2" maximum="30">
                  </f:validateLength>
              </h:inputText>
```

```
<h:outputLabel for="lastName" value="Last Name:">
</h:outputLabel>
<h:inputText id="lastName"
 label="Last Name"
 value="#{customer.lastName}"
 required="true"
 p:placeholder="Last Name">
    <f:validateLength minimum="2" maximum="30">
    </f:validateLength>
</h:inputText>
<h:outputLabel for="email" value="Email:">
</h:outputLabel>
<h:inputText id="email"
 label="Email"
 value="#{customer.email}"
 p:placeholder="Email Address">
    <f:validateLength minimum="3" maximum="30">
    </f:validateLength>
</h:inputText>
<h:panelGroup></h:panelGroup>
<h:commandButton action="confirmation"
 value="Save">
</h:commandButton>
            </h:panelGrid>
        </h:form>
    </h:body>
</html>
```

The first thing we should notice about this example is the addition of the xmlns:p="http://xmlns.jcp.org/jsf/passthrough namespace, which allows us to add any arbitrary attributes to our JSF components.

In our example, we added the HTML5 placeholder attribute to all input text fields in our page; as we can see, we need it to be prefixed by the defined prefix for the namespace at the top of the application (p, in our case). The placeholder HTML attribute simply adds some placeholder text to input fields that are automatically deleted once the user starts typing on the input field (this technique was commonly implemented *by hand* using JavaScript before HTML5).

The following screenshot shows our updated page in action:

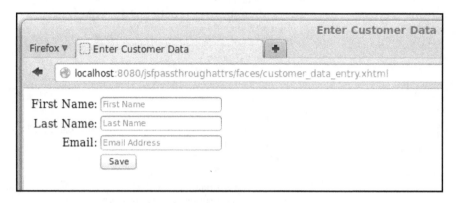

JSF 2.2 Faces flows

JSF 2.2 introduced Faces flows, which defines a scope that can span several pages. Flow scoped beans are created when the user enters a flow (a set of web pages), and are destroyed when the user leaves the flow.

Faces flows adopts the convention over configuration principle of JSF. The following conventions are typically used when developing applications employing faces flows:

- All pages in the flow must be placed in a directory whose name defines the name of the flow
- An XML configuration file named after the directory name, and suffixed with **-flow**, must exist inside the directory that contains the pages in the flow (the file may be empty, but it must exist)
- The first page in the flow must be named after the directory name that contains the flow
- The last page in the flow must not be located inside the directory containing the flow and must be named after the directory name and suffixed with **-return**

The following screenshot illustrates these conventions:

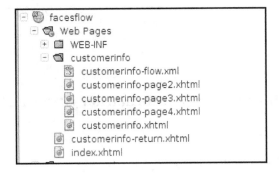

In the preceding example, we define a flow named customerinfo; by convention, these files are inside a directory named customerinfo, and the first page on the flow is named customerinfo.xhtml (there are no restrictions on the names of other pages in the flow). When we exit the flow, we navigate to a page named flowname-return.xml; in our case, since our flow is named customerinfo, the name of the page in question is customerinfo-return.xhtml, which follows the naming convention and takes us out of the flow.

The markup for the pages doesn't illustrate anything we haven't seen before; therefore we will not show it. All example code is available as part of this book's code download bundle.

All of the previous pages store data in a named bean called Customer, which has a flow of scope:

```
@Named
@FlowScoped("customerinfo")
public class Customer implements Serializable {
    //class body omitted
}
```

The @FlowScoped annotation has a value attribute that must match the name of the flow that the bean is meant to work with (customerinfo, in this example).

This example creates a wizard-style set of pages in which data for a user is entered across several pages in the flow.

In the first page, we enter name information:

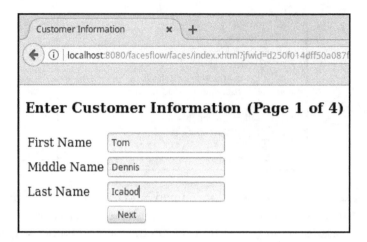

In the second page, we enter address information:

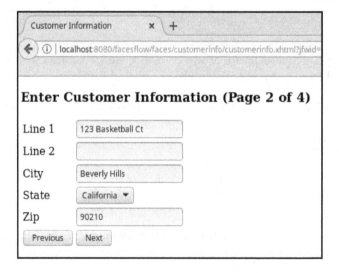

In the next page, we enter phone number information:

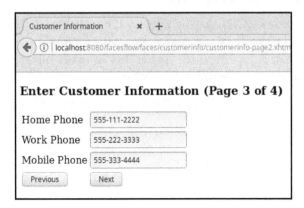

Finally, we display a **Confirmation** page:

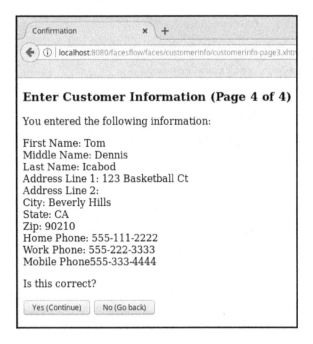

If the user verifies that the information is correct, we navigate outside the flow to customerinfo-return.xhtml; otherwise, we go back to the first page in the flow to allow the user to make any necessary corrections.

Injecting JSF artifacts

The JSF specification predates CDI. As such, many JSF artifacts, such as `FacesContext` and `ExternalContext`, had to be obtained via `static entry` methods; this resulted in hard-to-read boilerplate code. JSF 2.3 introduces the ability to inject JSF artifacts via CDI's `@Inject` annotation, as seen in the following example:

```
package net.ensode.javaee8book.jsfarbitrarymess;

import java.io.Serializable;
import javax.faces.application.FacesMessage;
import javax.faces.context.FacesContext;
import javax.faces.view.ViewScoped;
import javax.inject.Inject;
import javax.inject.Named;

@Named
@ViewScoped
public class ArbitraryMessageController implements Serializable {

    @Inject
    FacesContext facesContext;

    public void saveData() {
        FacesMessage facesMessage = new
         FacesMessage(FacesMessage.SEVERITY_INFO,
         "Data saved successfully", "All Data successfully
           saved.");
        facesContext.addMessage(null, facesMessage);
    }

}
```

In this example, we need an instance of `FacesContext` so that we can send an arbitrary message to an `<h:messages>` component; as of JSF 2.3, we can simply annotate our instance of `FacesContext` with CDI's `@Inject` annotation.

 Chapter 5, *Contexts and Dependency Injection*, covers CDI in detail.

In order for us to be able to successfully inject a JSF artifact into our CDI named beans, we need to add a CDI `beans.xml` deployment descriptor to the `WEB-INF` directory of our WAR file, making sure to set the `bean-discovery-mode` attribute of its `<beans>` tag to all:

```xml
<?xml version="1.0" encoding="UTF-8"?>
<beans xmlns="http://xmlns.jcp.org/xml/ns/javaee"
       xmlns:xsi="http://www.w3.org/2001/XMLSchema-instance"
       xsi:schemaLocation="http://xmlns.jcp.org/xml/ns/javaee
http://xmlns.jcp.org/xml/ns/javaee/beans_1_1.xsd"
       bean-discovery-mode="all">
</beans>
```

Additionally, we need to have a class in our WAR file annotated with the `@FacesConfig` annotation (we use this annotation to specify we are using JSF 2.3):

```java
package net.ensode.javaee8book.jsfarbitrarymess.config;

import javax.faces.annotation.FacesConfig;

@FacesConfig(version = FacesConfig.Version.JSF_2_3)
public class ConfigurationBean {

}
```

As can be seen in the preceding example, the class containing the `@FacesConfig` annotation doesn't have to have any code. We specify that we are using JSF 2.3 by passing `FacesConfig.Version.JSF_2_3` as the value of the annotation's version attribute.

In addition to illustrating how to inject the JSF artifact, this example illustrates a JSF feature we haven't seen before—the ability to send arbitrary messages to an `<h:messages>` component via the `addMessage()` method of `FacesContext`. Next, we show the markup corresponding to the preceding CDI named bean:

```xml
<?xml version='1.0' encoding='UTF-8' ?>
<!DOCTYPE html PUBLIC "-//W3C//DTD XHTML 1.0 Transitional//EN"
"http://www.w3.org/TR/xhtml1/DTD/xhtml1-transitional.dtd">
<html xmlns="http://www.w3.org/1999/xhtml"
      xmlns:h="http://xmlns.jcp.org/jsf/html"
      xmlns:f="http://xmlns.jcp.org/jsf/core">
    <h:head>
        <title>JSF Arbitrary Messages Demo</title>
    </h:head>
    <h:body>
        <h:outputStylesheet library="css" name="styles.css"/>
        <h:messages id="messages" />
        <h:form>
```

```
            <h:panelGrid columns="2"
             columnClasses="rightAlign,leftAlign">
                <!-- Irrelevant markup omitted for brevity -->
              <h:commandButton
              actionListener="#
              {arbitraryMessageController.saveData()}"
               value="Save">
              <f:ajax render="messages"/>
              </h:commandButton>
            </h:panelGrid>
          </h:form>
        </h:body>
     </html>
```

When the user clicks on the button generated by the `<h:commandButton>` component, the `saveData()` method of our CDI named bean is invoked, which in turn creates an instance of `FacesMessage` and passes it to the `addMessage()` method of `FacesContext`, resulting in the message being shown in the browser.

> In case it isn't obvious, this simple example doesn't actually save any data; all we are illustrating here is how to pass arbitrary messages to the JSF `<h:messages>` component.

The following screenshot assumes the user has already pressed the **Save** button. The message at the top is the result of our invocation to the `addMessage()` method of `FacesContext`:

JSF WebSocket support

In typical web applications, servers always respond to requests from a browser; there is no way for a server to send data to the client browser without responding to a request. **WebSocket** technology provides full duplex communication between a browser and a server, allowing servers to independently send data to a client, without having to respond to a request. WebSocket technology allows a myriad of new applications to be developed for the web, including updating stock tickers, multiplayer online games, and chat applications.

 Although some of these types of web applications were developed before the advent of WebSockets, they relied on hacks to work around the limitations of the HTTP protocol. With WebSockets, these hacks are no longer necessary.

Traditionally, writing applications taking advantage of the WebSocket protocol required a lot of JavaScript code. JSF 2.3 introduces WebSocket support and abstracts out most of the JavaScript plumbing, allowing us to focus on developing the business logic of our applications.

The following example illustrates a simple chat application developed using JSF 2.3 WebSocket support.

First, let's take a look at an application-scoped CDI named bean responsible for sending messages to all browser clients:

```
package net.ensode.javaee8book.jsfwebsocket;

import java.io.Serializable;
import javax.enterprise.context.ApplicationScoped;
import javax.faces.push.Push;
import javax.faces.push.PushContext;
import javax.inject.Inject;
import javax.inject.Named;

@Named
@ApplicationScoped
public class JsfWebSocketMessageSender implements Serializable {

    @Inject
    @Push
    private PushContext pushContext;

    public void send(String message) {
        System.out.println("Sending message: " + message);
```

```
              pushContext.send(message);
        }
    }
```

As shown in the preceding example, in order to send data via WebSockets to the clients we need to inject an instance of an implementation of the `javax.faces.push.PushContext` interface, and annotate it with the `@Push` annotation. To actually send the message to the client, we need to invoke the `send()` method of the injected `PushContext` implementation; in our example, this is done in the `send()` method of our CDI named bean.

In our example, there is a session scoped CDI named bean that takes input from the user and passes it to the `send()` method of the preceding application scoped CDI named bean. Our session scoped CDI bean looks as follows:

```
package net.ensode.javaee8book.jsfwebsocket;
import java.io.Serializable;
import javax.enterprise.context.SessionScoped;
import javax.inject.Inject;
import javax.inject.Named;

@Named
@SessionScoped
public class JsfWebSocketController implements Serializable {

    @Inject
    private JsfWebSocketMessageSender jsfWebSocketMessageSender;

    private String userName;
    private String message;

    public void sendMessage() {
      jsfWebSocketMessageSender.send(String.format("%s: %s",
        userName,
        message));
    }

    //setters getters and less relevant methods omitted for
brevity.
}
```

The sendMessage() method of the preceding class calls the send() method of the application scoped CDI bean we discussed earlier, passing the name of the user and the message to be broadcast to all browsers. The aforementioned sendMessage() method is invoked via Ajax when a user clicks a button on the corresponding page, as shown in the following markup:

```
<h:body>
    <f:websocket channel="pushContext"
     onmessage="socketListener" />

    <h:form prependId="false">
        <h:panelGrid columns="2">
            <h:outputLabel for="chatWindow" value="Chat
             Window:"/>
            <textarea id="chatWindow" rows="10"/>
            <h:outputLabel for="chatInput" value="Type
             something here:"/>
            <h:inputText id="chatInput"
             value="#{jsfWebSocketController.message}"/>
            <h:panelGroup/>
            <h:commandButton
             actionListener="#
             {jsfWebSocketController.sendMessage()}"
              value="Send message">
                <f:ajax execute="chatInput"
                 render="chatWindow"/>
            </h:commandButton>
        </h:panelGrid>
    </h:form>

    <script type="text/javascript">
     function socketListener(message, channel, event) {
      var textArea = document.getElementById('chatWindow');
      var textAreaValue = textArea.value;
      if (textAreaValue.trim() !== '') {
       textAreaValue += "\n";
             }
            textAreaValue += message;
            textArea.value = textAreaValue;
            textArea.scrollTop = textArea.scrollHeight;
        }
    </script>
</h:body>
```

The `<f:websocket>` tag in the preceding markup is needed to enable WebSocket support in our page. The value of its `channel` attribute links the page to the corresponding `PushContext` instance on the server (in our example, it is defined in the application scoped `JsfWebSocketMessageSender` CDI named bean). By convention, the value of the `channel` attribute must match the variable name on the corresponding CDI named bean (`pushContext`, in our example).

We're only showing the most relevant sections of the example; the complete example can be downloaded from this book's GitHub repository at `https://github.com/dheffelfinger/Java-EE-8-Application-Development-Code-Samples`.

After building and deploying our application we can see it in action:

Additional JSF component libraries

In addition to the standard JSF component libraries, there are a number of third-party JSF tag libraries available. The following table lists some of the most popular:

Tag library	Distributor	License	URL
ICEfaces	ICEsoft	MPL 1.1	http://www.icefaces.org
RichFaces	Red Hat/JBoss	LGPL	http://www.jboss.org/richfaces
Primefaces	Prime Technology	Apache 2.0	http://www.primefaces.org

Summary

In this chapter, we covered how to develop web-based applications using JavaServer Faces, the standard component framework for the Java EE platform. We looked at how to write a simple application by creating pages using Facelets as the view technology and CDI named beans. We also covered how to validate user input by using JSF's standard validators, by creating our own custom validators or by writing `validator` methods. Additionally, we covered how to customize standard JSF error messages, both the message text and the message style (font, color, and such). Also, we covered how to develop Ajax-enabled JSF pages, as well as how to integrate JSF and HTML5.

3
Object Relational Mapping with the Java Persistence API

Any non-trivial Java EE application will persist data to a relational database. In this chapter, we will cover how to connect to a database and perform CRUD (Create, Read, Update, Delete) operations.

The **Java Persistence API (JPA)** is the standard Java EE **Object Relational Mapping (ORM)** tool. We will discuss this API in detail in this chapter.

Some of the topics covered in this chapter include:

- Retrieving data from a database through JPA
- Inserting data into a database through JPA
- Updating data in a database through JPA
- Deleting data in a database through JPA
- Building queries programmatically through the JPA Criteria API
- Automating data validation through JPA 2.0's Bean Validation support

The Customer database

Examples in this chapter will use a database called `CUSTOMERDB`. This database contains tables to track customer and order information for a fictitious store. The database uses JavaDB for its RDBMS, since it comes bundled with GlassFish, but it can be easily adapted to any other RDBMS.

A script is included with this book's code download to create this database and pre-populate some of its tables. Instructions on how to execute the script, and add a connection pool and data source to access it are included in the download as well.

The schema for the CUSTOMERDB database is depicted in the following diagram:

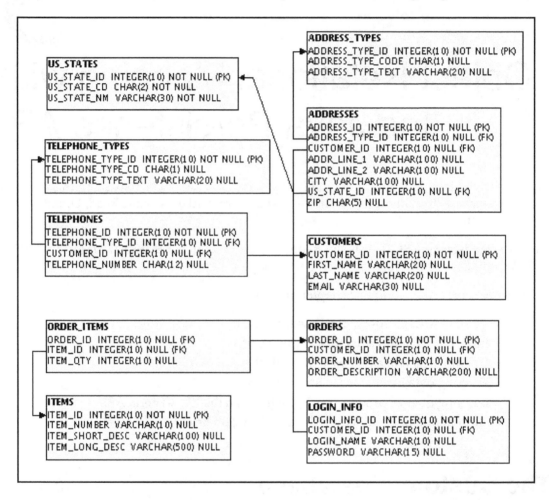

As can be seen in the diagram, the database contains tables to store customer information such as name, address, and email address. It also contains tables to store order and item information.

The `ADDRESS_TYPES` table will store values such as "Home", "Mailing", and "Shipping", to distinguish the type of address in the `ADDRESSES` table; similarly, the `TELEPHONE_TYPES` table stores the "Cell", "Home", and "Work" values. These two tables are prepopulated when creating the database, as well as the `US_STATES` table.

 For simplicity, our database only deals with U.S. addresses.

The Java Persistence API

The **Java Persistence API (JPA)** was introduced to Java EE in version 5 of the specification. Like its name implies, it is used to persist data to a relational database management system. JPA is a replacement for the Entity Beans that were used in J2EE. Java EE Entities are regular Java classes; the Java EE container knows these classes are Entities because they are decorated with the `@Entity` annotation. Let's look at an Entity mapping to the `CUSTOMER` table in the `CUSTOMERDB` database:

```
package net.ensode.javaee8book.jpaintro.entity;

import java.io.Serializable;

import javax.persistence.Column;
import javax.persistence.Entity;
import javax.persistence.Id;
import javax.persistence.Table;

@Entity
@Table(name = "CUSTOMERS")
public class Customer implements Serializable
{
  @Id
  @Column(name = "CUSTOMER_ID")
  private Long customerId;

  @Column(name = "FIRST_NAME")
  private String firstName;

  @Column(name = "LAST_NAME")
  private String lastName;

  private String email;
```

```
public Long getCustomerId()
{
  return customerId;
}
public void setCustomerId(Long customerId)
{
  this.customerId = customerId;
}
public String getEmail()
{
  return email;
}
public void setEmail(String email)
{
  this.email = email;
}
public String getFirstName()
{
  return firstName;
}
public void setFirstName(String firstName)
{
  this.firstName = firstName;
}
public String getLastName()
{
  return lastName;
}
public void setLastName(String lastName)
{
  this.lastName = lastName;
}
}
```

In the preceding code, the `@Entity` annotation lets any other Java EE-compliant application server know that this class is a JPA entity.

The `@Table(name = "CUSTOMERS")` annotation lets the application server know what table to map the entity to. The value of the `name` element contains the name of the database table that the entity maps to. This annotation is optional; if the name of the class maps the name of the database table, then it isn't necessary to specify what table the entity maps to.

The `@Id` annotation indicates that the `customerId` field maps to the primary key.

The @Column annotation maps each field to a column in the table. If the name of the field matches the name of the database column, then this annotation is not needed. This is the reason why the email field is not annotated.

The EntityManager class (this is actually an interface; each Java EE compliant application server provides its own implementation) is used to persist entities to a database. The following example illustrates its usage:

```java
package net.ensode.javaee8book.jpaintro.namedbean;

import javax.annotation.Resource;
import javax.enterprise.context.RequestScoped;
import javax.inject.Named;
import javax.persistence.EntityManager;
import javax.persistence.PersistenceContext;
import javax.transaction.HeuristicMixedException;
import javax.transaction.HeuristicRollbackException;
import javax.transaction.NotSupportedException;
import javax.transaction.RollbackException;
import javax.transaction.SystemException;
import javax.transaction.UserTransaction;
import net.ensode.javaee8book.jpaintro.entity.Customer;

@Named
@RequestScoped
public class JpaDemoBean {

    @PersistenceContext
    private EntityManager entityManager;

    @Resource
    private UserTransaction userTransaction;

    public String updateDatabase() {

        String retVal = "confirmation";

        Customer customer = new Customer();
        Customer customer2 = new Customer();
        Customer customer3;

        customer.setCustomerId(3L);
        customer.setFirstName("James");
        customer.setLastName("McKenzie");
        customer.setEmail("jamesm@notreal.com");

        customer2.setCustomerId(4L);
```

```
                        customer2.setFirstName("Charles");
                        customer2.setLastName("Jonson");
                        customer2.setEmail("cjohnson@phony.org");

                        try {
                            userTransaction.begin();
                            entityManager.persist(customer);
                            entityManager.persist(customer2);
                            customer3 = entityManager.find(Customer.class, 4L);
                            customer3.setLastName("Johnson");
                            entityManager.persist(customer3);
                            entityManager.remove(customer);

                            userTransaction.commit();
                        } catch (HeuristicMixedException |
                                HeuristicRollbackException |
                                IllegalStateException |
                                NotSupportedException |
                                RollbackException |
                                SecurityException |
                                SystemException e) {
                            retVal = "error";
                            e.printStackTrace();
                        }

                        return retVal;
                    }
                }
```

The preceding CDI named bean obtains an instance of a class implementing the
`javax.persistence.EntityManager` interface via dependency injection. This is done by
decorating the `EntityManager` variable with the `@PersistenceContext` annotation.

An instance of a class implementing the `javax.transaction.UserTransaction`
interface is then injected via the `@Resource` annotation. This object is necessary, since,
without it invoking calls to persist Entities to the database, the code would throw a
`javax.persistence.TransactionRequiredException`.

`EntityManager` performs many database-related tasks, such as finding entities in the
database, updating them, or deleting them.

Since JPA Entities are **plain old Java objects** (**POJOs**), they can be instantiated via the new
operator.

The call to the `setCustomerId()` method takes advantage of autoboxing, a feature added to the Java language in JDK 1.5. Notice that the method takes an instance of `java.lang.Long` as its parameter, but we are using `long` primitives. The code compiles and executes properly thanks to this feature.

Calls to the `persist()` method on `EntityManager` must be in a transaction, therefore it is necessary to start one by calling the `begin()` method on `UserTransaction`.

We then insert two new rows to the CUSTOMERS table by calling the `persist()` method on `entityManager` for the two instances of the `Customer` class we populated earlier in the code.

After persisting the data contained in the `customer` and `customer2` objects, we search the database for a row in the CUSTOMERS table with a primary key of four. We do this by invoking the `find()` method on `entityManager`. This method takes the class of the Entity we are searching for as its first parameter, and the primary key of the row corresponding to the object we want to obtain. This method is roughly equivalent to the `findByPrimaryKey()` method on an entity bean's home interface.

The primary key we set for the `customer2` object was 4, therefore what we have now is a copy of this object. The last name for this customer was misspelled when we originally inserted his data into the database. We can now correct Mr. Johnson's last name by invoking the `setLastName()` method on `customer3`, then we can update the information in the database by invoking `entityManager.persist()`.

We then delete the information for the `customer` object by invoking `entityManager.remove()` and passing the `customer` object as a parameter.

Finally, we commit the changes to the database by invoking the `commit()` method on `userTransaction`.

In order for the preceding code to work as expected, an XML configuration file named `persistence.xml` must be deployed in the WAR file containing the previously-named bean. This file must be placed in the `WEB-INF/classes/META-INF/` directory inside the WAR file. The contents of this file for the preceding code are shown here:

```
<?xml version="1.0" encoding="UTF-8"?>
<persistence version="2.2"
xmlns="http://xmlns.jcp.org/xml/ns/persistence"
xmlns:xsi="http://www.w3.org/2001/XMLSchema-instance"
xsi:schemaLocation="http://xmlns.jcp.org/xml/ns/persistence
http://xmlns.jcp.org/xml/ns/persistence/persistence_2_2.xsd">
```

```
<persistence-unit name="customerPersistenceUnit">
  <jta-data-source>jdbc/__CustomerDBPool</jta-data-source>
</persistence-unit>
</persistence>
```

`persistence.xml` must contain at least one `<persistence-unit>` element. Each `<persistence-unit>` element must provide a value for its `name` attribute and must contain a `<jta-data-source>` child element whose value is the JNDI name of the data source to be used for the persistence unit.

The reason more than one `<persistence-unit>` element is allowed is because an application may access more than one database. A `<persistence-unit>` element is required for each database the application will access. If the application defines more than one `<persistence-unit>` element, then the `@PersistenceContext` annotation used to inject `EntityManager` must provide a value for its `unitName` element; the value for this element must match the name attribute of the corresponding `<persistence-unit>` element in `persistence.xml`.

Cannot persist detached object Exception: Frequently, an application will retrieve a JPA entity via the `EntityManager.find()` method, then pass this entity to a business or user interface layer, where it will potentially be modified, and later the database data corresponding to the entity will be updated. In cases such as this, invoking `EntityManager.persist()` will result in an exception. In order to update JPA entities this way, we need to invoke `EntityManager.merge()`. This method takes an instance of the JPA entity as its single argument and updates the corresponding row in the database with the data stored in it.

Entity relationships

In the previous section, we saw how to retrieve, insert, update, and delete single entities from the database. Entities are rarely isolated; in the vast majority of cases they are related to other entities.

Entities can have one-to-one, one-to-many, many-to-one, and many-to-many relationships.

In the `CustomerDB` database, for example, there is a one-to-one relationship between the `LOGIN_INFO` and the `CUSTOMERS` tables. This means that each customer has exactly one corresponding row in the login info table. There is also a one-to-many relationship between the `CUSTOMERS` table and the `ORDERS` table. This is because a customer can place many orders, but each order belongs only to a single customer. Additionally, there is a many-to-many relationships between the `ORDERS` table and the `ITEMS` table. This is because an order can contain many items and an item can be on many orders.

In the next few sections, we will discuss how to establish relationships between JPA entities.

One-to-one relationships

One-to-one relationships occur when an instance of an entity can have zero or one corresponding instance of another entity.

One-to-one entity relationships can be bidirectional (each entity is aware of the relationship) or unidirectional (only one of the entities is aware of the relationship). In the `CUSTOMERDB` database, the one-to-one mapping between the `LOGIN_INFO` and the `CUSTOMERS` tables is unidirectional, since the `LOGIN_INFO` table has a foreign key to the `CUSTOMERS` table, but not the other way around. As we will soon see, this fact does not stop us from creating a bidirectional one-to-one relationship between the `Customer` entity and the `LoginInfo` entity.

The source code for the `LoginInfo` entity, which maps to the `LOGIN_INFO` table, can be seen here:

```
package net.ensode.javaee8book.entityrelationship.entity;

import javax.persistence.Column;
import javax.persistence.Entity;
import javax.persistence.Id;
import javax.persistence.JoinColumn;
import javax.persistence.Table;

@Entity
@Table(name = "LOGIN_INFO")
public class LoginInfo
{
  @Id
  @Column(name = "LOGIN_INFO_ID")
  private Long loginInfoId;

  @Column(name = "LOGIN_NAME")
```

```java
private String loginName;

private String password;

@OneToOne
@JoinColumn(name="CUSTOMER_ID")
private Customer customer;
public Long getLoginInfoId()
{
   return loginInfoId;
}

public void setLoginInfoId(Long loginInfoId)
{
   this.loginInfoId = loginInfoId;
}

public String getPassword()
{
   return password;
}

public void setPassword(String password)
{
   this.password = password;
}

public String getLoginName()
{
   return loginName;
}

public void setLoginName(String userName)
{
   this.loginName = userName;
}

public Customer getCustomer()
{
   return customer;
}

public void setCustomer(Customer customer)
{
   this.customer = customer;
}

}
```

The code for this entity is very similar to the code for the Customer entity. It defines fields that map to database columns. Each field whose name does not match the database column name is decorated with the @Column annotation; in addition to that, the primary key is decorated with the @Id annotation.

Where the preceding code gets interesting is the declaration of the customer field. As can be seen in the code, the customer field is decorated with the @OneToOne annotation; this lets the application server know that there is a one-to-one relationship between this entity and the Customer entity. The customer field is also decorated with the @JoinColumn annotation. This annotation lets the container know which column in the LOGIN_INFO table is the foreign key corresponding to the primary key on the CUSTOMER table. Since LOGIN_INFO, the table that the LoginInfo entity maps to, has a foreign key to the CUSTOMER table, the LoginInfo entity owns the relationship. If the relationship were unidirectional, we wouldn't have to make any changes to the Customer entity. However, since we would like to have a bidirectional relationship between these two entities, we need to add a LoginInfo field to the Customer entity, along with the corresponding getter and setter methods.

Like we mentioned before, in order to make the one-to-one relationship between the Customer and LoginInfo entities bidirectional, we need to make a few simple changes to the Customer entity:

```
package net.ensode.javaee8book.entityrelationship.entity;

import java.io.Serializable;
import java.util.Set;

import javax.persistence.CascadeType;
import javax.persistence.Column;
import javax.persistence.Entity;
import javax.persistence.Id;
import javax.persistence.OneToMany;
import javax.persistence.OneToOne;
import javax.persistence.Table;

@Entity
@Table(name = "CUSTOMERS")
public class Customer implements Serializable
{
  @Id
  @Column(name = "CUSTOMER_ID")
  private Long customerId;

  @Column(name = "FIRST_NAME")
```

```
        private String firstName;

        @Column(name = "LAST_NAME")
        private String lastName;

        private String email;

        @OneToOne(mappedBy = "customer")
        private LoginInfo loginInfo;
        public LoginInfo getLoginInfo()
        {
          return loginInfo;
        }
        public void setLoginInfo(LoginInfo loginInfo)
        {
          this.loginInfo = loginInfo;
        }
        //Additional setters and getters omitted for brevity
    }
```

The only change we need to make to the Customer entity to make the one-to-one
relationship bidirectional is to add a LoginInfo field to it, along with the corresponding
setter and getter methods. The loginInfo field is decorated with the @OneToOne
annotation. Since the Customer entity does not own the relationship (the table it maps to
does not have a foreign key to the corresponding table), the mappedBy element of the
@OneToOne annotation needs to be added. This element specifies which field in the
corresponding entity has the other end of the relationship. In this particular case, the
customer field in the LoginInfo entity corresponds to the other end of this one-to-one
relationship.

The following Java class illustrates the use of the preceding entity:

```
        package net.ensode.javaee8book.entityrelationship.namedbean;

        import javax.annotation.Resource;
        import javax.enterprise.context.RequestScoped;
        import javax.inject.Named;
        import javax.persistence.EntityManager;
        import javax.persistence.PersistenceContext;
        import javax.transaction.HeuristicMixedException;
        import javax.transaction.HeuristicRollbackException;
        import javax.transaction.NotSupportedException;
        import javax.transaction.RollbackException;
        import javax.transaction.SystemException;
        import javax.transaction.UserTransaction;
        import net.ensode.javaee8book.entityrelationship.entity.Customer;
```

```
import net.ensode.javaee8book.entityrelationship.entity.LoginInfo;

@Named
@RequestScoped
public class OneToOneRelationshipDemoBean {

    @PersistenceContext
    private EntityManager entityManager;

    @Resource
    private UserTransaction userTransaction;

    public String updateDatabase() {
        String retVal = "confirmation";
        Customer customer;
        LoginInfo loginInfo = new LoginInfo();

        loginInfo.setLoginInfoId(1L);
        loginInfo.setLoginName("charlesj");
        loginInfo.setPassword("iwonttellyou");

        try {
            userTransaction.begin();

            customer = entityManager.find(Customer.class, 4L);
            loginInfo.setCustomer(customer);

            entityManager.persist(loginInfo);

            userTransaction.commit();

        } catch (NotSupportedException |
                SystemException |
                SecurityException |
                IllegalStateException |
                RollbackException |
                HeuristicMixedException |
                HeuristicRollbackException e) {
            retVal = "error";
            e.printStackTrace();
        }

        return retVal;
    }
}
```

In this example, we first create an instance of the `LoginInfo` entity and populate it with some data. We then obtain an instance of the `Customer` entity from the database by invoking the `find()` method of `EntityManager` (data for this entity was inserted into the `CUSTOMERS` table in one of the previous examples). We then invoke the `setCustomer()` method on the `LoginInfo` entity, passing the customer object as a parameter. Finally, we invoke the `EntityManager.persist()` method to save the data in the database.

What happens behind the scenes is that the `CUSTOMER_ID` column of the `LOGIN_INFO` table gets populated with the primary key of the corresponding row in the `CUSTOMERS` table. This can be easily verified by querying the `CUSTOMERDB` database.

 Notice how the call to `EntityManager.find()` to obtain the customer entity is inside the same transaction from where we call `EntityManager.persist()`. This must be the case; otherwise, the database will not be updated successfully.

One-to-many relationships

JPA one-to-many entity relationships can be bidirectional (one entity contains a many-to-one relationship and the corresponding entity contains an inverse one-to-many relationship).

With SQL, one-to-many relationships are defined by foreign keys in one of the tables. The `many` part of the relationship is the one containing a foreign key to the `one` part of the relationship. One-to-many relationships defined in an RDBMS are typically unidirectional, since making them bidirectional usually results in denormalized data.

Just like when defining a unidirectional one-to-many relationship in an RDBMS, in JPA the many part of the relationship is the one that has a reference to the `one` part of the relationship, therefore the annotation used to decorate the appropriate `setter` method is `@ManyToOne`.

In the `CUSTOMERDB` database, there is a unidirectional one-to-many relationship between customers and orders. We define this relationship in the `Order` entity:

```
package net.ensode.javaee8book.entityrelationship.entity;

import javax.persistence.Column;
import javax.persistence.Entity;
import javax.persistence.Id;
import javax.persistence.JoinColumn;
import javax.persistence.ManyToOne;
```

```
import javax.persistence.Table;

@Entity
@Table(name = "ORDERS")
public class Order
{
  @Id
  @Column(name = "ORDER_ID")
  private Long orderId;

  @Column(name = "ORDER_NUMBER")
  private String orderNumber;

  @Column(name = "ORDER_DESCRIPTION")
  private String orderDescription;

  @ManyToOne  @JoinColumn(name = "CUSTOMER_ID")
  private Customer customer;

  public Customer getCustomer()
  {
    return customer;
  }

  public void setCustomer(Customer customer)
  {
    this.customer = customer;
  }

  public String getOrderDescription()
  {
    return orderDescription;
  }

  public void setOrderDescription(String orderDescription)
  {
    this.orderDescription = orderDescription;
  }

  public Long getOrderId()
  {
    return orderId;
  }

  public void setOrderId(Long orderId)
  {
    this.orderId = orderId;
  }
```

```
  public String getOrderNumber()
  {
    return orderNumber;
  }

  public void setOrderNumber(String orderNumber)
  {
    this.orderNumber = orderNumber;
  }
}
```

If we were to define a unidirectional many-to-one relationship between the Orders entity and the Customer entity, we wouldn't need to make any changes to the Customer entity. To define a bidirectional one-to-many relationship between the two entities, a new field decorated with the @OneToMany annotation needs to be added to the Customer entity:

```
package net.ensode.javaee8book.entityrelationship.entity;

import java.io.Serializable;
import java.util.Set;

import javax.persistence.Column;
import javax.persistence.Entity;
import javax.persistence.Id;
import javax.persistence.OneToMany;
import javax.persistence.Table;

@Entity
@Table(name = "CUSTOMERS")
public class Customer implements Serializable
{
  @Id
  @Column(name = "CUSTOMER_ID")
  private Long customerId;

  @Column(name = "FIRST_NAME")
  private String firstName;

  @Column(name = "LAST_NAME")
  private String lastName;

  private String email;

  @OneToOne(mappedBy = "customer")
  private LoginInfo loginInfo;

  @OneToMany(mappedBy="customer")
```

```java
private Set<Order> orders;

public Long getCustomerId()
{
  return customerId;
}

public void setCustomerId(Long customerId)
{
  this.customerId = customerId;
}

public String getEmail()
{
  return email;
}

public void setEmail(String email)
{
  this.email = email;
}

public String getFirstName()
{
  return firstName;
}

public void setFirstName(String firstName)
{
  this.firstName = firstName;
}

public String getLastName()
{
  return lastName;
}

public void setLastName(String lastName)
{
  this.lastName = lastName;
}

public LoginInfo getLoginInfo()
{
  return loginInfo;
}

public void setLoginInfo(LoginInfo loginInfo)
```

```
{
  this.loginInfo = loginInfo;
}

public Set<Order> getOrders()
{
  return orders;
}
public void setOrders(Set<Order> orders)
{
  this.orders = orders;
}
}
```

The only difference between this version of the Customer entity and the previous one is the addition of the orders field and related getter and setter methods. Of special interest is the @OneToMany annotation decorating this field. The mappedBy attribute must match the name of the corresponding field in the entity corresponding to the many part of the relationship. In simple terms, the value of the mappedBy attribute must match the name of the field decorated with the @ManyToOne annotation in the bean at the other side of the relationship.

The following example code illustrates how to persist one-to-many relationships to the database:

```
package net.ensode.javaee8book.entityrelationship.namedbean;

import javax.annotation.Resource;
import javax.enterprise.context.RequestScoped;
import javax.inject.Named;
import javax.persistence.EntityManager;
import javax.persistence.PersistenceContext;
import javax.transaction.HeuristicMixedException;
import javax.transaction.HeuristicRollbackException;
import javax.transaction.NotSupportedException;
import javax.transaction.RollbackException;
import javax.transaction.SystemException;
import javax.transaction.UserTransaction;
import net.ensode.javaee8book.entityrelationship.entity.Customer;
import net.ensode.javaee8book.entityrelationship.entity.Order;

@Named
@RequestScoped
public class OneToManyRelationshipDemoBean {

    @PersistenceContext
```

```java
private EntityManager entityManager;

@Resource
private UserTransaction userTransaction;

public String updateDatabase() {
    String retVal = "confirmation";

    Customer customer;
    Order order1;
    Order order2;

    order1 = new Order();
    order1.setOrderId(1L);
    order1.setOrderNumber("SFX12345");
    order1.setOrderDescription("Dummy order.");

    order2 = new Order();
    order2.setOrderId(2L);
    order2.setOrderNumber("SFX23456");
    order2.setOrderDescription("Another dummy order.");

    try {
        userTransaction.begin();

        customer = entityManager.find(Customer.class, 4L);

        order1.setCustomer(customer);
        order2.setCustomer(customer);

        entityManager.persist(order1);
        entityManager.persist(order2);

        userTransaction.commit();

    } catch (NotSupportedException |
            SystemException |
            SecurityException |
            IllegalStateException |
            RollbackException |
            HeuristicMixedException |
            HeuristicRollbackException e) {
        retVal = "error";
        e.printStackTrace();
    }

    return retVal;
}
```

```
}
```

The preceding code is pretty similar to the previous example. It instantiates two instances of the Order entity, populates them with some data, then in a transaction an instance of the Customer entity is located and used as the parameter of the setCustomer() method of both instances of the Order entity. We then persist both Order entities by invoking EntityManager.persist() for each one of them.

Just like when dealing with one-to-one relationships, what happens behind the scenes is that the CUSTOMER_ID column of the ORDERS table in the CUSTOMERDB database is populated with the primary key corresponding to the related row in the CUSTOMERS table.

Since the relationship is bidirectional, we can obtain all orders related to a customer by invoking the getOrders() method on the Customer entity.

Many-to-many relationships

In the CUSTOMERDB database, there is a many-to-many relationship between the ORDERS table and the ITEMS table. We can map this relationship by adding a new Collection<Item> field to the Order entity and decorating it with the @ManyToMany annotation:

```java
package net.ensode.javaee8book.entityrelationship.entity;

import java.util.Collection;

import javax.persistence.Column;
import javax.persistence.Entity;
import javax.persistence.Id;
import javax.persistence.JoinColumn;
import javax.persistence.JoinTable;
import javax.persistence.ManyToMany;
import javax.persistence.ManyToOne;
import javax.persistence.Table;

@Entity
@Table(name = "ORDERS")
public class Order
{
  @Id
  @Column(name = "ORDER_ID")
  private Long orderId;

  @Column(name = "ORDER_NUMBER")
```

```
private String orderNumber;

@Column(name = "ORDER_DESCRIPTION")
private String orderDescription;

@ManyToOne
@JoinColumn(name = "CUSTOMER_ID")
private Customer customer;

@ManyToMany
@JoinTable(name = "ORDER_ITEMS",
 joinColumns = @JoinColumn(name = "ORDER_ID",
  referencedColumnName = "ORDER_ID"),
   inverseJoinColumns = @JoinColumn(name = "ITEM_ID",
    referencedColumnName = "ITEM_ID"))
private Collection<Item> items;

public Customer getCustomer()
{
  return customer;
}

public void setCustomer(Customer customer)
{
  this.customer = customer;
}

public String getOrderDescription()
{
  return orderDescription;
}

public void setOrderDescription(String orderDescription)
{
  this.orderDescription = orderDescription;
}

public Long getOrderId()
{
  return orderId;
}

public void setOrderId(Long orderId)
{
  this.orderId = orderId;
}

public String getOrderNumber()
```

```
    {
       return orderNumber;
    }

    public void setOrderNumber(String orderNumber)
    {
       this.orderNumber = orderNumber;
    }

    public Collection<Item> getItems()
    {
       return items;
    }
    public void setItems(Collection<Item> items)
    {
       this.items = items;
    }
}
```

As we can see in the preceding code, in addition to being decorated with the `@ManyToMany`
annotation, the `items` field is also decorated with the `@JoinTable` annotation. Like its
name suggests, this annotation lets the application server know what table is used as a join
table to create the many-to-many relationship between the two entities. This annotation has
three relevant elements: the name element, which defines the name of the join table, and the
`joinColumns` and `inverseJoinColumns` elements, which define the columns that serve as
foreign keys in the join table pointing to the entities' primary keys. Values for the
`joinColumns` and `inverseJoinColumns` elements are yet another annotation: the
`@JoinColumn` annotation. This annotation has two relevant elements: the name element,
which defines the name of the column in the join table, and the `referencedColumnName`
element, which defines the name of the column in the entity table.

The `Item` entity is a simple entity mapping to the `ITEMS` table in the `CUSTOMERDB` database:

```
package net.ensode.javaee8book.entityrelationship.entity;

import java.util.Collection;

import javax.persistence.Column;
import javax.persistence.Entity;
import javax.persistence.Id;
import javax.persistence.ManyToMany;
import javax.persistence.Table;

@Entity
@Table(name = "ITEMS")
public class Item
```

```
{
  @Id
  @Column(name = "ITEM_ID")
  private Long itemId;

  @Column(name = "ITEM_NUMBER")
  private String itemNumber;

  @Column(name = "ITEM_SHORT_DESC")
  private String itemShortDesc;

  @Column(name = "ITEM_LONG_DESC")
  private String itemLongDesc;

  @ManyToMany(mappedBy="items")
  private Collection<Order> orders;
  public Collection<Order> getOrders()
  {
    return orders;
  }
  public void setOrders(Collection<Order> orders)
  {
    this.orders = orders;
  }
  //additional setters and getters removed for brevity
}
```

Just like one-to-one and one-to-many relationships, many-to-many relationships can be unidirectional or bidirectional. Since we would like the many-to-many relationship between the Order and Item entities to be bidirectional, we added a Collection<Order> field and decorated it with the @ManyToMany annotation. Since the corresponding field in the Order entity already has the join table defined, it is not necessary to do it again here. The entity containing the @JoinTable annotation is said to own the relationship; in a many-to-many relationship, either entity can own the relationship. In our example, the Order entity owns it, since its Collection<Item> field is decorated with the @JoinTable annotation.

Just like with one-to-one and one-to-many relationships, the @ManyToMany annotation in the non-owning side of a bidirectional many-to-many relationship must contain a mappedBy element indicating which field in the owning entity defines the relationship.

Now that we have seen the changes necessary to establish a bidirectional many-to-many relationship between the Order and Item entities, we can see the relationship in action in the following example:

```
package net.ensode.javaee8book.entityrelationship.namedbean;

import java.util.ArrayList;
import java.util.Collection;
import javax.annotation.Resource;
import javax.enterprise.context.RequestScoped;
import javax.inject.Named;
import javax.persistence.EntityManager;
import javax.persistence.PersistenceContext;
import javax.transaction.HeuristicMixedException;
import javax.transaction.HeuristicRollbackException;
import javax.transaction.NotSupportedException;
import javax.transaction.RollbackException;
import javax.transaction.SystemException;
import javax.transaction.UserTransaction;
import net.ensode.javaee8book.entityrelationship.entity.Item;
import net.ensode.javaee8book.entityrelationship.entity.Order;

@Named
@RequestScoped
public class ManyToManyRelationshipDemoBean {

    @PersistenceContext
    private EntityManager entityManager;

    @Resource
    private UserTransaction userTransaction;

    public String updateDatabase() {
        String retVal = "confirmation";

        Order order;
        Collection<Item> items = new ArrayList<Item>();
        Item item1 = new Item();
        Item item2 = new Item();

        item1.setItemId(1L);
        item1.setItemNumber("BCD1234");
        item1.setItemShortDesc("Notebook Computer");
        item1.setItemLongDesc("64 bit Quad core CPU, 4GB memory");

        item2.setItemId(2L);
        item2.setItemNumber("CDF2345");
```

```
item2.setItemShortDesc("Cordless Mouse");
item2.setItemLongDesc("Three button, infrared, "
        + "vertical and horizontal scrollwheels");

items.add(item1);
items.add(item2);

try {
    userTransaction.begin();

    entityManager.persist(item1);
    entityManager.persist(item2);
    order = entityManager.find(Order.class, 1L);
    order.setItems(items);
    entityManager.persist(order);

    userTransaction.commit();

} catch (NotSupportedException |
        SystemException |
        SecurityException |
        IllegalStateException |
        RollbackException |
        HeuristicMixedException |
        HeuristicRollbackException e) {
    retVal = "error";
    e.printStackTrace();
}

    return retVal;
    }
}
```

The preceding code creates two instances of the Item entity and populates them with some data. It then adds these two instances to a collection. A transaction is then started and the two Item instances are persisted to the database. Then an instance of the Order entity is retrieved from the database. The setItems() method of the Order entity instance is then invoked, passing the collection containing the two Item instances as a parameter. The Customer instance is then persisted into the database. At this point, two rows are created behind the scenes to the ORDER_ITEMS table, which is the join table between the ORDERS and ITEMS tables.

Composite primary keys

Most tables in the CUSTOMERDB database have a column with the sole purpose of serving as a primary key (this type of primary key is sometimes referred to as a surrogate primary key or as an artificial primary key). However, some databases are not designed this way; instead a column in the database that is known to be unique across rows is used as the primary key. If there is no column whose value is not guaranteed to be unique across rows, then a combination of two or more columns is used as the table's primary key. It is possible to map this kind of primary key to JPA entities by using a primary key class.

There is one table in the CUSTOMERDB database that does not have a surrogate primary key: the ORDER_ITEMS table. This table serves as a join table between the ORDERS and the ITEMS tables, in addition to having foreign keys for these two tables, this table has an additional column called ITEM_QTY ;this column stores the quantity of each item in an order. Since this table does not have a surrogate primary key, the JPA entity mapping to it must have a custom primary key class. In this table, the combination of the ORDER_ID and the ITEM_ID columns must be unique, therefore this is a good combination for a composite primary key:

```java
package net.ensode.javaee8book.compositeprimarykeys.entity;

import java.io.Serializable;

public class OrderItemPK implements Serializable
{
  public Long orderId;
  public Long itemId;

  public OrderItemPK()
  {

  }

  public OrderItemPK(Long orderId, Long itemId)
  {
    this.orderId = orderId;
    this.itemId = itemId;
  }

  @Override
  public boolean equals(Object obj)
  {
    boolean returnVal = false;

    if (obj == null)
```

```
    {
      returnVal = false;
    }
    else if (!obj.getClass().equals(this.getClass()))
    {
      returnVal = false;
    }
    else
    {
      OrderItemPK other = (OrderItemPK) obj;

      if (this == other)
      {
        returnVal = true;
      }
      else if (orderId != null && other.orderId != null
          && this.orderId.equals(other.orderId))
      {
        if (itemId != null && other.itemId != null
            && itemId.equals(other.itemId))
        {
          returnVal = true;
        }
      }
      else
      {
        returnVal = false;
      }
    }

    return returnVal;
  }

  @Override
  public int hashCode()
  {
    if (orderId == null || itemId == null)
    {
      return 0;
    }
    else
    {
      return orderId.hashCode() ^ itemId.hashCode();
    }
  }
}
```

A custom `primary key` class must satisfy the following requirements:

- The class must be public
- It must implement `java.io.Serializable`
- It must have a public constructor that takes no arguments
- Its fields must be `public` or `protected`
- Its field names and types must match those of the entity
- It must override the default `hashCode()` and `equals()` methods defined in the `java.lang.Object` class

The preceding `OrderPK` class meets all of these requirements. It also has a convenience constructor that takes two `Long` objects to initialize its `orderId` and `itemId` fields. This constructor was added for convenience; this is not a prerequisite for the class to be used as a primary key class.

When an entity uses a custom `primary key` class, it must be decorated with the `@IdClass` annotation. Since the `OrderItem` class uses `OrderItemPK` as its custom `primary key` class, it must be decorated with the aforementioned annotation:

```java
package net.ensode.javaee8book.compositeprimarykeys.entity;

import javax.persistence.Column;
import javax.persistence.Entity;
import javax.persistence.Id;
import javax.persistence.IdClass;
import javax.persistence.Table;

@Entity
@Table(name = "ORDER_ITEMS")
@IdClass(value = OrderItemPK.class)
public class OrderItem
{
  @Id
  @Column(name = "ORDER_ID")
  private Long orderId;

  @Id
  @Column(name = "ITEM_ID")
  private Long itemId;

  @Column(name = "ITEM_QTY")
  private Long itemQty;

  public Long getItemId()
```

```
  {
    return itemId;
  }

  public void setItemId(Long itemId)
  {
    this.itemId = itemId;
  }

  public Long getItemQty()
  {
    return itemQty;
  }

  public void setItemQty(Long itemQty)
  {
    this.itemQty = itemQty;
  }

  public Long getOrderId()
  {
    return orderId;
  }

  public void setOrderId(Long orderId)
  {
    this.orderId = orderId;
  }
}
```

There are two differences between the preceding entity and the previous entities we have seen. The first difference is that this entity is decorated with the @IdClass annotation, indicating the primary key class corresponding to it. The second difference is that the preceding entity has more than one field decorated with the @Id annotation. Since this entity has a composite primary key, each field that is part of the primary key must be decorated with this annotation.

Obtaining a reference of an entity with a composite primary key is not much different from obtaining a reference to an entity with a primary key consisting of a single field. The following example demonstrates how to do this:

```
package net.ensode.javaee8book.compositeprimarykeys.namedbean;

import javax.enterprise.context.RequestScoped;
import javax.inject.Named;
import javax.persistence.EntityManager;
```

```
import javax.persistence.PersistenceContext;
import
net.ensode.javaee8book.compositeprimarykeys.entity.OrderItem;
import
net.ensode.javaee8book.compositeprimarykeys.entity.OrderItemPK;

@Named
@RequestScoped
public class CompositePrimaryKeyDemoBean {

    @PersistenceContext
    private EntityManager entityManager;

    private OrderItem orderItem;

    public String findOrderItem() {
        String retVal = "confirmation";

        try {
            orderItem = entityManager.find(OrderItem.class,
            new OrderItemPK(1L, 2L));
        } catch (Exception e) {
            retVal = "error";
            e.printStackTrace();
        }

        return retVal;
    }

    public OrderItem getOrderItem() {
        return orderItem;
    }

    public void setOrderItem(OrderItem orderItem) {
        this.orderItem = orderItem;
    }

}
```

As can be seen in this example, the only difference between locating an entity with a composite primary key and an entity with a primary key consisting of a single field is that an instance of the custom `primary key` class must be passed as the second argument of the `EntityManager.find()` method. Fields for this instance must be populated with the appropriate values for each field that is part of the primary key.

Java Persistence Query Language

All of our examples that obtain entities from the database so far have conveniently assumed that the primary key for the entity is known ahead of time. We all know that frequently this is not the case. Whenever we need to search for an entity by a field other than the entity's primary key, we must use the **Java Persistence Query Language** (**JPQL**).

JPQL is a SQL-like language used for retrieving, updating, and deleting entities in a database. The following example illustrates how to use JPQL to retrieve a subset of states from the US_STATES table in the CUSTOMERDB database:

```
package net.ensode.javaee8book.jpql.namedbean;

import java.util.List;
import javax.enterprise.context.RequestScoped;
import javax.inject.Named;
import javax.persistence.EntityManager;
import javax.persistence.PersistenceContext;
import javax.persistence.Query;
import net.ensode.javaee8book.jpql.entity.UsState;

@Named
@RequestScoped
public class SelectQueryDemoBean {

    @PersistenceContext
    private EntityManager entityManager;

    private Stream<UsState> matchingStatesStream;
    private List<UsState> matchingStatesList;

    public String findStates() {
        String retVal = "confirmation";

        try {
            Query query = entityManager
            .createQuery(
             "SELECT s FROM UsState s WHERE s.usStateNm "
             + "LIKE :name");
            query.setParameter("name", "New%");
            matchingStatesStream = query.getResultStream();
            if (matchingStatesStream != null) {
             matchingStatesList =
              matchingStatesStream.collect(Collectors.toList());
            }
        } catch (Exception e) {
```

```
                        retVal = "error";
                        e.printStackTrace();
                }
                return retVal;
        }

        public List<UsState> getMatchingStatesList() {
                return matchingStatesList;
        }

        public void setMatchingStatesList(List<UsState>
matchingStatesList) {
                this.matchingStatesList = matchingStatesList;
        }


    }
```

The preceding code invokes the `EntityManager.createQuery()` method, passing a `String` containing a JPQL query as a parameter. This method returns an instance of `javax.persistence.Query`. The query retrieves all `UsState` entities whose name starts with the word `New`.

As can be seen in the preceding code, JPQL is similar to SQL; however, there are some differences that may confuse readers with some knowledge of SQL. The equivalent SQL code for the query in the code would be:

```
SELECT * from US_STATES s where s.US_STATE_NM like 'New%'
```

The first difference between JPQL and SQL is that in JPQL we always reference entity names, wherein SQL table names are referenced. The `s` after the entity name in the JPQL query is an alias for the entity. Table aliases are optional in SQL, but entity aliases are required in JPQL. Keeping these differences in mind, the JPQL query should now be a lot less confusing.

The `:name` in the query is a **named parameter;** named parameters are meant to be substituted with actual values. This is done by invoking the `setParameter()` method in the instance of `javax.persistence.Query` returned by the call to `EntityManager.createQuery()`. A JPQL query can have multiple named parameters.

To actually run the query and retrieve the entities from the database, the `getResultList()` method must be invoked in the instance of `javax.persistence.Query` obtained from `EntityManager.createQuery()`. This method returns an instance of a class implementing the `java.util.List` interface; this list contains the entities matching the query criteria. If no entities match the criteria, then an empty list is returned.

If we are certain that the query will return exactly one entity, then the `getSingleResult()` method may be alternatively called on `Query`; this method returns an `Object` that must be cast to the appropriate entity.

The preceding example uses the `LIKE` operator to find entities whose names start with the word "New". This is accomplished by substituting the query's named parameter with the value "New%". The percent sign at the end of the parameter value means that any number of characters after the word "New" will match the expression. The percent sign can be used anywhere in the parameter value, for example, a value of "%Dakota" would match any entities whose name end in "Dakota", a value of "A%a" would match any states whose name starts with a capital "A" and end with a lowercase "a". There can be more than one % sign in a parameter value. The underscore sign, (_), can be used to match a single character; all the rules for the % sign apply to the underscore as well.

In addition to the `LIKE` operator, there are other operators that can be used to retrieve entities from the database:

- The = operator will retrieve entities whose field at the left of the operator exactly match as the value to the right of the operator
- The > operator will retrieve entities whose field at the left of the operator is greater than the value to the right of the operator
- The < operator will retrieve entities whose field at the left of the operator is less than the value to the right of the operator
- The >= operator will retrieve entities whose field at the left of the operator is greater than or equal to the value to the right of the operator
- The <= operator will retrieve entities whose field at the left of the operator is less than or equal to the value to the right of the operator

All of the preceding operators work the same way as the equivalent operators in SQL. Just like in SQL, these operators can be combined with the `AND` and `OR` operators. Conditions combined with the `AND` operator match if both conditions are true; conditions combined with the `OR` operator match if at least one of the conditions is true.

If we intend to use a query many times, it can be stored in a **named query**. Named queries can be defined by decorating the relevant entity class with the `@NamedQuery` annotation. This annotation has two elements: a `name` element used to set the name of the query, and a `query` element defining the query itself. To execute a named query, the `createNamedQuery()` method must be invoked in an instance of `EntityManager`. This method takes a `String` containing the query name as its sole parameter, and returns an instance of `javax.persistence.Query`.

In addition to retrieving entities, JPQL can be used to modify or delete entities. However, entity modification and deletion can be done programmatically via the `EntityManager` interface; doing so results in code that tends to be more readable than when using JPQL. Because of this, we will not cover entity modification and deletion via JPQL. Readers interested in writing JPQL queries to modify and delete entities, as well as readers wishing to know more about JPQL, are encouraged to review the Java Persistence 2.2 specification. This specification can be downloaded at `http://jcp.org/en/jsr/detail?id=338`.

The Criteria API

One of the main additions to JPA in the 2.0 specification was the introduction of the **Criteria API**. The Criteria API is meant as a complement to JPQL.

Although JPQL is very flexible, it has some problems that make working with it more difficult than necessary. For starters, JPQL queries are stored as strings, and the compiler has no way of validating the JPQL syntax. Additionally, JPQL is not type-safe: we could write a JPQL query in which our where clause could have a string value for a numeric property and our code would compile and deploy just fine.

To get around the JPQL limitations described in the previous paragraph, the Criteria API was introduced to JPA in version 2.0 of the specification. The Criteria API allows us to write JPA queries programmatically, without having to rely on JPQL.

The following code example illustrates how to use the Criteria API in our Java EE applications:

```
package net.ensode.javaee8book.criteriaapi.namedbean;

import java.util.List;
import javax.enterprise.context.RequestScoped;
import javax.inject.Named;
import javax.persistence.EntityManager;
import javax.persistence.PersistenceContext;
import javax.persistence.TypedQuery;
```

```
import javax.persistence.criteria.CriteriaBuilder;
import javax.persistence.criteria.CriteriaQuery;
import javax.persistence.criteria.Path;
import javax.persistence.criteria.Predicate;
import javax.persistence.criteria.Root;
import javax.persistence.metamodel.EntityType;
import javax.persistence.metamodel.Metamodel;
import javax.persistence.metamodel.SingularAttribute;
import net.ensode.javaee8book.criteriaapi.entity.UsState;

@Named
@RequestScoped
public class CriteriaApiDemoBean {

    @PersistenceContext
    private EntityManager entityManager;

    private List<UsState> matchingStatesList;
    private List<UsState> matchingStatesList;

    public String findStates() {
        String retVal = "confirmation";
        try {
            CriteriaBuilder criteriaBuilder = entityManager.
             getCriteriaBuilder();
            CriteriaQuery<UsState> criteriaQuery = criteriaBuilder.
             createQuery(UsState.class);
            Root<UsState> root = criteriaQuery.from(UsState.class);
            Metamodel metamodel = entityManager.getMetamodel();
            EntityType<UsState> usStateEntityType =
             metamodel.entity(
               UsState.class);
            SingularAttribute<UsState, String> usStateAttribute=
             usStateEntityType.getDeclaredSingularAttribute(
              "usStateNm",
               String.class);
            Path<String> path = root.get(usStateAttribute);
            Predicate predicate = criteriaBuilder.like(path,
            "New%");
            criteriaQuery = criteriaQuery.where(predicate);
            TypedQuery typedQuery = entityManager.createQuery(
             criteriaQuery);
            matchingStatesStream = typedQuery.getResultStream();
            if (matchingStatesStream != null) {
             matchingStatesList =
             matchingStatesStream.collect(Collectors.toList());
            }
```

```
                    } catch (Exception e) {
                        retVal = "error";
                        e.printStackTrace();
                    }

                    return retVal;
                }

                public List<UsState> getMatchingStatesList() {
                    return matchingStatesList;
                }

                public void setMatchingStatesList(List<UsState>
                 matchingStatesList) {
                    this.matchingStatesList = matchingStatesList;
                }


            }
```

The preceding example is equivalent to the JPQL example we saw earlier in this chapter. This example, however, takes advantage of the Criteria API instead of relying on JPQL.

When writing code using the Criteria API, the first thing we need to do is obtain an instance of a class implementing the `javax.persistence.criteria.CriteriaBuilder` interface; as we can see in the preceding example, we need to obtain this instance by invoking the `getCriteriaBuilder()` method on our `EntityManager`.

From our `CriteriaBuilder` implementation, we need to obtain an instance of a class implementing the `javax.persistence.criteria.CriteriaQuery` interface. We do this by invoking the `createQuery()` method in our `CriteriaBuilder` implementation. Notice that `CriteriaQuery` is generically typed. The generic type argument dictates the type of result that our `CriteriaQuery` implementation will return upon execution. By taking advantage of generics in this way, the Criteria API allows us to write type-safe code.

Once we have obtained a `CriteriaQuery` implementation, from it we can obtain an instance of a class implementing the `javax.persistence.criteria.Root` interface. The root implementation dictates which JPA Entity we will be querying from. It is analogous to the FROM query in JPQL (and SQL).

The next two lines in our example take advantage of another new addition to the JPA specification: the **Metamodel API**. In order to take advantage of the Metamodel API, we need to obtain an implementation of the `javax.persistence.metamodel.Metamodel` interface by invoking the `getMetamodel()` method on our `EntityManager`.

From our `Metamodel` implementation, we can obtain a generically typed instance of the `javax.persistence.metamodel.EntityType` interface. The generic type argument indicates the JPA entity our `EntityType` implementation corresponds to. `EntityType` allows us to browse the `persistent` attributes of our JPA entities at runtime. This is exactly what we do in the next line in our example. In our case, we get an instance of `SingularAttribute`, which maps to a simple, singular attribute in our JPA entity. `EntityType` has methods to obtain attributes that map to collections, sets, lists, and maps. Obtaining these attribute types is very similar to obtaining a `SingularAttribute`, therefore we won't be covering those directly. Please refer to the Java EE 8 API documentation at `https://javaee.github.io/javaee-spec/javadocs/` for more information.

As we can see in our example, `SingularAttribute` contains two generic type arguments. The first argument dictates the JPA entity we are working with, and the second one indicates the type of the attribute. We obtain our `SingularAttribute` by invoking the `getDeclaredSingularAttribute()` method on our `EntityType` implementation and passing the attribute name (as declared in our JPA entity) as a string.

Once we have obtained our `SingularAttribute` implementation, we need to obtain an import `javax.persistence.criteria.Path` implementation by invoking the `get()` method in our `Root` instance, and passing our `SingularAttribute` as a parameter.

In our example, we will get a list of all the *new* states in the United States; that is, all states whose names start with `New`. This, of course, is a job for a "like" condition. We can do this with the criteria API by invoking the `like()` method on our `CriteriaBuilder` implementation. The `like()` method takes our `Path` implementation as its first parameter, and the value to search for as its second parameter.

`CriteriaBuilder` has a number of methods that are analogous to SQL and JPQL clauses, such as `equals()`, `greaterThan()`, `lessThan()`, `and()`, and `or()` (for the complete list, refer to the Java EE 8 documentation at `https://javaee.github.io/javaee-spec/javadocs/`). These methods can be combined to create complex queries via the Criteria API.

The `like()` method in `CriteriaBuilder` returns an implementation of the `javax.persistence.criteria.Predicate` interface, which we need to pass to the `where()` method in our `CriteriaQuery` implementation. This method returns a new instance of `CriteriaBuilder`, which we assign to our `criteriaBuilder` variable.

At this point we are ready to build our query. When working with the Criteria API, we deal with the `javax.persistence.TypedQuery` interface, which can be thought of as a type-safe version of the `Query` interface we use with JPQL. We obtain an instance of `TypedQuery` by invoking the `createQuery()` method in `EntityManager`, and passing our `CriteriaQuery` implementation as a parameter.

To obtain our query results as a list, we simply invoke `getResultList()` on our `TypedQuery` implementation. It is worth reiterating that the Criteria API is type-safe, therefore attempting to assign the results of `getResultList()` to a list of the wrong type would result in a compilation error.

Updating data with the Criteria API

When the JPA Criteria API was initially added to JPA 2.0, it only supported selecting data from the database. Modifying existing data was not supported.

JPA 2.1, introduced in Java EE 7, added support for updating database data via the `CriteriaUpdate` interface; the following example illustrates how to use it:

```java
package net.ensode.javaee8book.criteriaupdate.namedbean;

//imports omitted for brevity

@Named
@RequestScoped
public class CriteriaUpdateDemoBean {

    @PersistenceContext
    private EntityManager entityManager;

    @Resource
    private UserTransaction userTransaction;

    private int updatedRows;

    public String updateData() {
        String retVal = "confirmation";

        try {

            userTransaction.begin();
            insertTempData();

            CriteriaBuilder criteriaBuilder =
```

```
        entityManager.getCriteriaBuilder();
        CriteriaUpdate<Address> criteriaUpdate =
         criteriaBuilder.createCriteriaUpdate(Address.class);
        Root<Address> root =
         criteriaUpdate.from(Address.class);
        criteriaUpdate.set("city", "New York");
        criteriaUpdate.where(criteriaBuilder.equal(
         root.get("city"), "New Yorc"));
        Query query =
         entityManager.createQuery(criteriaUpdate);
        updatedRows = query.executeUpdate();
        userTransaction.commit();
    } catch (Exception e) {
        retVal = "error";
        e.printStackTrace();
    }
    return retVal;
}

public int getUpdatedRows() {
    return updatedRows;
}

public void setUpdatedRows(int updatedRows) {
    this.updatedRows = updatedRows;
}

private void insertTempData() throws NotSupportedException,
        SystemException, RollbackException,
HeuristicMixedException,
        HeuristicRollbackException {
    //body omitted since it is not relevant to the discussion at
hand
    //full source code available as part of this book's code
download
}
```

What this example is actually doing is finding all of the database rows with "New Yorc" (a typo) as a city, and replacing the value with the correct spelling of "New York".

Just like in the previous example, we obtain an instance of a class implementing the CriteriaBuilder interface by invoking the getCriteriaBuilder() method on our EntityManager instance.

We then obtain an instance of a class implementing `CriteriaUpdate` by invoking `createCriteriaUpdate()` on our `CriteriaBuilder` instance.

The next step is to obtain an instance of a class implementing `Root` by invoking the `from()` method on our `CriteriaUpdate` instance.

We then invoke the `set()` method on `CriteriaUpdate` to specify the new values our rows will have after they have been updated; the first parameter of the `set()` method must be a `String` matching the property name in the `Entity` class, and the second parameter must be the new value.

At this point, we build the where clause by invoking the `where()` method on `CriteriaUpdate`, and passing the `Predicate` returned by the `equal()` method invoked in `CriteriaBuilder`.

Then we get a `Query` implementation by invoking `createQuery()` on `EntityManager`, and passing our `CriteriaUpdate` instance as a parameter.

Finally, we execute our query as usual by invoking `executeUpdate()` on our `Query` implementation.

Deleting data with the Criteria API

In addition to adding support for data updates via the Criteria API, JPA 2.1 added the ability to bulk-delete database rows with the new `CriteriaDelete` interface. The following code snippet illustrates its usage:

```
package net.ensode.javaee8book.criteriadelete.namedbean;

//imports omitted

@Named
@RequestScoped
public class CriteriaDeleteDemoBean {

    @PersistenceContext
    private EntityManager entityManager;

    @Resource
    private UserTransaction userTransaction;

    private int deletedRows;

    public String deleteData() {
```

```
            String retVal = "confirmation";

            try {

                userTransaction.begin();

                CriteriaBuilder criteriaBuilder =
                entityManager.getCriteriaBuilder();
                CriteriaDelete<Address> criteriaDelete
                = criteriaBuilder.createCriteriaDelete(Address.class);
                Root<Address> root =
                criteriaDelete.from(Address.class);
                criteriaDelete.where(criteriaBuilder.or
                (criteriaBuilder.equal(root.get("city"), "New York"),
                 criteriaBuilder.equal(root.get("city"), "New York")));

                Query query =
                entityManager.createQuery(criteriaDelete);

                deletedRows = query.executeUpdate();
                userTransaction.commit();
            } catch (Exception e) {
                retVal = "error";
                e.printStackTrace();
            }
            return retVal;
        }

    public int getDeletedRows() {
        return deletedRows;
    }

    public void setDeletedRows(int updatedRows) {
        this.deletedRows = updatedRows;
    }
}
```

To use `CriteriaDelete`, we first obtain an instance of `CriteriaBuilder` as usual, then invoke the `createCriteriaDelete()` method on our `CriteriaBuilder` instance to obtain an implementation of `CriteriaDelete`.

Once we have an instance of `CriteriaDelete`, we build the where clause in the normal way with the Criteria API.

Once we have built our where clause, we obtain an implementation of the `Query` interface and invoke `executeUpdate()` on it as usual.

Bean Validation support

Another feature introduced in JPA 2.0 is support for JSR 303 **Bean Validation**. Bean Validation support allows us to annotate our JPA entities with Bean Validation annotations. These annotations allow us to easily validate user input and perform data sanitation.

Taking advantage of Bean Validation is very simple; all we need to do is annotate our JPA Entity fields or getter methods with any of the validation annotations defined in the `javax.validation.constraints` package. Once our fields are annotated as appropriate, the `EntityManager` will prevent non-validating data from being persisted.

The following code example is a modified version of the `Customer` JPA entity we saw earlier in this chapter. It has been modified to take advantage of Bean Validation in some of its fields:

```
net.ensode.javaee8book.beanvalidation.entity;

import java.io.Serializable;

import javax.persistence.Column;
import javax.persistence.Entity;
import javax.persistence.Id;
import javax.persistence.Table;
import javax.validation.constraints.NotNull;
import javax.validation.constraints.Size;

@Entity
@Table(name = "CUSTOMERS")
public class Customer implements Serializable
{
  @Id
  @Column(name = "CUSTOMER_ID")
  private Long customerId;

  @Column(name = "FIRST_NAME")
  @NotNull  @Size(min=2, max=20)
  private String firstName;

  @Column(name = "LAST_NAME")
  @NotNull  @Size(min=2, max=20)
  private String lastName;

  private String email;

  public Long getCustomerId()
  {
```

```
      return customerId;
   }

   public void setCustomerId(Long customerId)
   {
      this.customerId = customerId;
   }

   public String getEmail()
   {
      return email;
   }

   public void setEmail(String email)
   {
      this.email = email;
   }

   public String getFirstName()
   {
      return firstName;
   }

   public void setFirstName(String firstName)
   {
      this.firstName = firstName;
   }

   public String getLastName()
   {
      return lastName;
   }

   public void setLastName(String lastName)
   {
      this.lastName = lastName;
   }
}
```

In this example, we used the `@NotNull` annotation to prevent the `firstName` and `lastName` of our entity from being persisted with `null` values. We also used the `@Size` annotation to restrict the minimum and maximum length of these fields.

That is all we need to do to take advantage of Bean Validation in JPA. If our code attempts to persist or update an instance of our entity that does not pass the declared validation, an exception of type `javax.validation.ConstraintViolationException` will be thrown, and the entity will not be persisted.

As we can see, Bean Validation pretty much automates data validation, freeing us from having to manually write validation code.

In addition to the two annotations discussed in the previous example, the `javax.validation.constraints` package contains several additional annotations we can use to automate validation on our JPA entities. Please refer to the Java EE 8 API documentation at `https://javaee.github.io/javaee-spec/javadocs/` for the complete list.

Final notes

In the examples for this chapter, we showed database access performed directly from CDI named beans serving as controllers. We did this to get the point across without getting mired in the details; however, in general, this is not a good practice. Database access code should be encapsulated in **Data Access Objects (DAOs)**.

For more information on the DAO design pattern, see `http://www.oracle.com/technetwork/java/dao-138818.html`.

Named beans typically assume the role of controllers and/or model when using the **Model-View-Controller (MVC)** design pattern, a practice so common that it has become the de facto standard for Java EE applications.

For more information about the MVC design pattern, see `http://www.oracle.com/technetwork/java/mvc-140477.html`.

Additionally, we chose not to show any user interface code in our examples since it is irrelevant to the topic at hand. However, code downloads for this chapter include JSF pages that invoke named beans in this chapter, and display a confirmation page once the named bean invocation finishes.

Summary

This chapter covered how to access data in a database via the Java Persistence API (JPA).

We covered how to mark a Java class as a JPA entity by decorating it with the `@Entity` annotation. Additionally, we covered how to map an entity to a database table via the `@Table` annotation. We also covered how to map entity fields to database columns via the `@Column` annotation, as well as declaring an entity's primary key via the `@Id` annotation.

Using the `javax.persistence.EntityManager` interface to find, persist, and update JPA entities was also covered.

Defining both unidirectional and bidirectional one-to-one, one-to-many, and many-to-many relationships between JPA entities was covered as well.

Additionally, we explored how to use JPA composite primary keys by developing custom primary key classes.

Also, we covered how to retrieve entities from a database by using the Java Persistence Query Language (JPQL).

We discussed additional JPA features such as the Criteria API, which allows us to build JPA queries programmatically; the Metamodel API, which allows us to take advantage of Java's type safety when working with JPA; and Bean Validation, which allows us to easily validate input by simply annotating our JPA entity fields.

4

Enterprise JavaBeans

Enterprise JavaBeans are server-side components that encapsulate the business logic of an application. **Enterprise JavaBeans (EJB)** simplify application development by automatically taking care of transaction management and security. There are two types of Enterprise JavaBean: session beans, which perform business logic, and message-driven beans, which act as a message listener.

Readers familiar with previous versions of J2EE will notice that entity beans were not mentioned in the preceding paragraph. In Java EE 5, entity beans were deprecated in favor of the **Java Persistence API (JPA)**. Entity beans are still supported for backwards compatibility; however, the preferred way of doing **Object Relational Mapping (ORM)** is through the JPA.

The following topics will be covered in this chapter:

- Session beans
- A simple session bean
- A more realistic example
- Using a session bean to implement the DAO design pattern
    - Singleton session beans
- Message-driven beans
- Transactions in enterprise JavaBeans
- Container-managed transactions
- Bean-managed transactions
- Enterprise JavaBeans life cycles
- Stateful session bean life cycle

- Stateless session bean life cycle
- Message-driven bean life cycle
- EJB timer service
- EJB Security

Session beans

Like we previously mentioned, session beans typically encapsulate business logic. In Java EE, only one or two artifacts need to be created in order to create a session bean: the bean itself, and an optional business interface. These artifacts need to be decorated with the proper annotations to let the EJB container know they are session beans.

 J2EE required application developers to create several artifacts in order to create a session bean. These artifacts include the bean itself, a local or remote interface (or both), a local home or a remote home interface (or both), and an XML deployment descriptor. As we shall see in this chapter, EJB development was greatly simplified in Java EE.

A simple session bean

The following example illustrates a very simple session bean.:

```
package net.ensode.javaeebook;

import javax.ejb.Stateless;

@Stateless
public class SimpleSessionBean implements SimpleSession
{
  private String message =
      "If you don't see this, it didn't work!";
  public String getMessage()
  {
    return message;
  }
}
```

The `@Stateless` annotation lets the EJB container know that this class is a stateless session bean. There are three types of session bean: stateless, stateful, and singleton. Before we explain the difference between these types of session bean, we need to clarify how an instance of an EJB is provided to an EJB client application.

When a stateless session bean is deployed, the EJB container creates a series of instances of each session bean. This is what is typically referred to as the EJB pool. When an EJB client application obtains an instance of an EJB, one of the instances in the pool is provided to this client application.

The difference between stateful and stateless session beans is that stateful session beans maintain a conversational state with the client, whereas stateless session beans do not. In simple terms, this means that, when an EJB client application obtains an instance of a stateful session bean, we are guaranteed that the value of any instance variables in the bean will be consistent across method calls. Therefore, it is safe to modify any instance variables on a stateful session bean, since they will retain their value for the next method call. The EJB container saves the conversational state by passivating stateful session beans and retrieves the state when the bean is activated. Conversational state is the reason why the life cycle of stateful session beans is a bit more complex than the life cycle of stateless session beans or message-driven beans (the EJB life cycle is discussed later in this chapter).

The EJB container may provide any instance of an EJB in the pool when an EJB client application requests an instance of a stateless session bean. Since we are not guaranteed the same instance for every method call, values set to any instance variables in a stateless session bean may be "lost" (they are not really lost, the modification is in another instance of the EJB in the pool).

Other than being decorated with the `@Stateless` annotation, there is nothing special about this class. Notice that it implements an interface called **SimpleSession**. This interface is the bean's business interface. The `SimpleSession` interface is shown here:

```
package net.ensode.javaeebook;

import javax.ejb.Remote;

@Remote
public interface SimpleSession
{
   public String getMessage();
}
```

The only peculiar thing about this interface is that it is decorated with the `@Remote` annotation. This annotation indicates that this is a remote business interface. What this means is that the interface may be in a different JVM than the client application invoking it. Remote business interfaces may even be invoked across the network.

Business interfaces may also be decorated with the @Local interface. This annotation indicates that the business interface is a local business interface. Local business interface implementations must be in the same JVM as the client application invoking its methods.

Since remote business interfaces can be invoked either from the same JVM or from a different JVM as the client application, at first glance we might be tempted to make all of our business interfaces remote. Before doing so, we must be aware of the fact that the flexibility provided by remote business interfaces comes with a performance penalty, since method invocations are made on the assumption that they will be made across the network. As a matter of fact, most typical Java EE applications consist of web applications acting as client applications for EJBs. In this case, the client application and the EJB are running on the same JVM, therefore local interfaces are used a lot more frequently than remote business interfaces.

Once we have compiled the session bean and its corresponding business interface, we need to place them in a JAR file and deploy them. How to deploy an EJB JAR file depends on what application server we are using. However, most modern application servers have an autodeploy directory; we can simply copy our EJB JAR file to this directory in most cases. Consult your application server documentation to find the exact location of its autodeploy directory.

Implementing EJB client code

Now that we have seen the session bean and its corresponding business interface, let's take a look at a client sample application:

```java
package net.ensode.javaeebook;

import javax.ejb.EJB;

public class SessionBeanClient
{
  @EJB
  private static SimpleSession simpleSession;

  private void invokeSessionBeanMethods()
  {
    System.out.println(simpleSession.getMessage());

    System.out.println("\nSimpleSession is of type: "
        + simpleSession.getClass().getName());
  }
```

```
public static void main(String[] args)
{
  new SessionBeanClient().invokeSessionBeanMethods();
}

}
```

The preceding code simply declares an instance variable of type `net.ensode.SimpleSession`, which is the business interface for our session bean. The instance variable is decorated with the `@EJB` annotation; this annotation lets the EJB container know that this variable is a business interface for a session bean. The EJB container then injects an implementation of the business interface for the client code to use.

Since our client is a standalone application (as opposed to a Java EE artifact such as a WAR file or another EJB JAR file), it isn't actually deployed to the application server. In order for it to be able to access code deployed to the server, it must have access to the application server's client libraries. The procedure on how to accomplish this varies from application server to application server. When using GlassFish, our client code must be placed in a JAR file and executed through the `appclient` utility. This utility can be found at `[glassfish installation directory]/glassfish/bin/`. Assuming this directory is in the PATH environment variable, and assuming we placed our client code in a JAR file called `simplesessionbeanclient.jar`, we would execute the preceding client code by typing the following command in the command line:

`appclient -client simplesessionbeanclient-jar-with-dependencies.jar`

Executing the preceding command results in the following console output:

If you don't see this, it didn't work!
SimpleSession is of type: net.ensode.javaeebook._SimpleSession_Wrapper

This is the output of the `SessionBeanClient` class.

We are using Maven to build our code. For this example, we used the Maven Assembly plugin (`http://maven.apache.org/plugins/maven-assembly-plugin/`) to build a client JAR file that includes all dependencies. This frees us from having to specify all the dependent JAR files in the `-classpath` command line option of `appclient`. To build this JAR file, simply invoke `mvn assembly:assembly` from the command line.

The first line of output is simply the return value of the `getMessage()` method we implemented in the session bean. The second line of output displays the fully qualified class name of the class implementing the business interface. Notice that the class name is not the fully qualified name of the session bean we wrote; instead, what is actually provided is an implementation of the business interface created behind the scenes by the EJB container.

A more realistic example

In the previous section, we saw a very simple "Hello world" type of example. In this section, we will use a more realistic example. Session beans are frequently used as Data Access Objects (**DAOs**). Sometimes they are used as a wrapper for JDBC calls, other times they are used to wrap calls to obtain or modify JPA entities. In this section, we will take the latter approach.

The following example illustrates how to implement the DAO design pattern in a session bean. Before looking at the bean implementation, let's look at its corresponding business interface:

```
package net.ensode.javaeebook;

import javax.ejb.Remote;

@Remote
public interface CustomerDao
{
  public void saveCustomer(Customer customer);

  public Customer getCustomer(Long customerId);

  public void deleteCustomer(Customer customer);
}
```

As we can see, this is a remote interface implementing three methods; the `saveCustomer()` method saves customer data to the database, the `getCustomer()` method obtains data for a customer from the database, and the `deleteCustomer()` method deletes customer data from the database. All of these methods take an instance of the `Customer` entity we developed in Chapter 3, *Object Relational Mapping with JPA* as a parameter.

Let's now take a look at the session bean implementing the preceding business interface. As we are about to see, there are some differences between the way JPA code is implemented in a session bean and in a plain old `Java` object:

```
package net.ensode.javaeebook;

import javax.ejb.Stateful;
import javax.persistence.EntityManager;
import javax.persistence.PersistenceContext;

@Stateful
public class CustomerDaoBean implements CustomerDao {

    @PersistenceContext
    private EntityManager entityManager;

    public void saveCustomer(Customer customer) {
        if (customer.getCustomerId() == null) {
            saveNewCustomer(customer);
        } else {
            updateCustomer(customer);
        }
    }

    private void saveNewCustomer(Customer customer) {
        entityManager.persist(customer);
    }

    private void updateCustomer(Customer customer) {
        entityManager.merge(customer);
    }

    public Customer getCustomer(Long customerId) {
        Customer customer;

        customer = entityManager.find(Customer.class, customerId);

        return customer;
    }

    public void deleteCustomer(Customer customer) {
        entityManager.remove(customer);
    }
}
```

The main difference between the preceding session bean and previous JPA examples is that in previous examples, JPA calls were wrapped between calls to `UserTransaction.begin()` and `UserTransaction.commit()`. The reason we had to do this is because JPA calls are required to be wrapped in a transaction; if they are not in a transaction, most JPA calls will throw a `TransactionRequiredException`. The reason we don't have to explicitly wrap JPA calls in a transaction like in previous examples is because session bean methods are implicitly transactional, there is nothing we need to do to make them that way. This default behavior is what is known as container-managed transactions. Container-managed transactions are discussed in detail later in this chapter.

As mentioned in `Chapter 3`, *Object Relational Mapping with Java Persistence API*, when a JPA entity is retrieved in one transaction and updated in a different transaction, the `EntityManager.merge()` method needs to be invoked to update the data in the database. Invoking `EntityManager.persist()` in this case will result in a "Cannot persist detached object" exception.

Invoking session beans from web applications

Frequently, Java EE applications consist of web applications acting as clients for EJBs. Before Java EE 6, the most common way of deploying a Java EE application that consists of both a web application and one or more session beans was to package both the WAR file for the web application and the EJB JAR files into an **EAR (Enterprise ARchive)** file.

Java EE 6 simplified the packaging and deployment of applications consisting of both EJBs and web components.

In this section, we will develop a JSF application with a CDI named bean acting as a client to the DAO session bean we just discussed in the previous section.

In order to make this application act as an EJB client, we will develop a `CustomerController` named bean so that it delegates the logic to save a new customer to the database to the `CustomerDaoBean` session bean we developed in the previous section:

```
package net.ensode.javaeebook.jsfjpa;

//imports omitted for brevity

@Named
@RequestScoped
public class CustomerController implements Serializable {

    @EJB
```

```java
    private CustomerDaoBean customerDaoBean;

    private Customer customer;

    private String firstName;
    private String lastName;
    private String email;

    public CustomerController() {
        customer = new Customer();
    }

    public String saveCustomer() {
        String returnValue = "customer_saved";

        try {
            populateCustomer();
            customerDaoBean.saveCustomer(customer);
        } catch (Exception e) {
            e.printStackTrace();
            returnValue = "error_saving_customer";
        }

        return returnValue;
    }

    private void populateCustomer() {
        if (customer == null) {
            customer = new Customer();
        }
        customer.setFirstName(getFirstName());
        customer.setLastName(getLastName());
        customer.setEmail(getEmail());
    }

    //setters and getters omitted for brevity

}
```

As we can see, all we had to do was to declare an instance of the CustomerDaoBean session bean, and decorate it with the @EJB annotation so that an instance of the corresponding EJB is injected, then invoke the EJB's saveCustomer() method.

Notice that we injected an instance of the session bean directly into our client code. The reason we can do this is because of a feature introduced in Java EE 6. When using Java EE 6 or newer, we can do away with local interfaces and use session bean instances directly in our client code.

Now that we have modified our web application to be a client for our session bean, we need to package it in a **WAR** (**web archive**) file and deploy it in order to use it.

Singleton session beans

A new type of session bean that was introduced in Java EE 6 is the singleton session bean. A single instance of each singleton session bean exists in the application server.

Singleton session beans are useful to cache database data. Caching frequently-used data in a singleton session bean increases performance since it greatly minimizes trips to the database. The common pattern is to have a method in our bean decorated with the @PostConstruct annotation; in this method we retrieve the data we want to cache. Then we provide a setter method for the bean's clients to call. The following example illustrates this technique:

```
package net.ensode.javaeebook.singletonsession;

import java.util.List;
import javax.annotation.PostConstruct;
import javax.ejb.Singleton;
import javax.persistence.EntityManager;
import javax.persistence.PersistenceContext;
import javax.persistence.Query;
import net.ensode.javaeebook.entity.UsStates;

@Singleton
public class SingletonSessionBean implements
    SingletonSessionBeanRemote {

  @PersistenceContext
  private EntityManager entityManager;
  private List<UsStates> stateList;

  @PostConstruct
  public void init() {
    Query query = entityManager.createQuery(
        "Select us from UsStates us");
    stateList = query.getResultList();
  }
```

```
@Override
public List<UsStates> getStateList() {
  return stateList;
}
}
```

Since our bean is a singleton, all of its clients would access the same instance, avoiding having duplicate data in memory. Additionally, since it is a singleton, it is safe to have an instance variable, since all clients access the same instance of the bean.

Asynchronous method calls

Sometimes it is useful to have some processing done asynchronously, that is, invoking a method call and returning control immediately to the client, without having the client wait for the method to finish.

In earlier versions of Java EE, the only way to invoke EJB methods asynchronously was to use message-driven beans (discussed in the next section). Although message-driven beans are fairly easy to write, they do require some configuration, such as setting up JMS message queues or topics, before they can be used.

EJB 3.1 introduced the @Asynchronous annotation, which can be used to mark a method in a session bean as asynchronous. When an EJB client invokes an asynchronous method, control immediately goes back to the client, without waiting for the method to finish.

Asynchronous methods can only return void or an implementation of the java.util.concurrent.Future interface. The following example illustrates both scenarios:

```
package net.ensode.javaeebook.asynchronousmethods;
import java.util.concurrent.Future;
import java.util.logging.Level;
import java.util.logging.Logger;
import javax.ejb.AsyncResult; .
import javax.ejb.Asynchronous;
import javax.ejb.Stateless;

@Stateless
public class AsynchronousSessionBean implements
    AsynchronousSessionBeanRemote {

  private static Logger logger = Logger.getLogger(
      AsynchronousSessionBean.class.getName());
```

```
@Asynchronous
@Override
public void slowMethod() {
  long startTime = System.currentTimeMillis();
  logger.info("entering " + this.getClass().getCanonicalName()
      + ".slowMethod()");
  try {
    Thread.sleep(10000); //simulate processing for 10 seconds
  } catch (InterruptedException ex) {
    Logger.getLogger(AsynchronousSessionBean.class.getName()).
        log(Level.SEVERE, null, ex);
  }
  logger.info("leaving " + this.getClass().getCanonicalName()
      + ".slowMethod()");
  long endTime = System.currentTimeMillis();
  logger.info("execution took " + (endTime - startTime)
      + " milliseconds");
}

@Asynchronous
@Override
public Future<Long> slowMethodWithReturnValue() {
  try {
    Thread.sleep(15000); //simulate processing for 15 seconds
  } catch (InterruptedException ex) {
    Logger.getLogger(AsynchronousSessionBean.class.getName()).
        log(Level.SEVERE, null, ex);
  }

  return new AsyncResult<Long>(42L);
}
}
```

When our asynchronous method returns void, the only thing we need to do is decorate the method with the @Asynchronous annotation, then call it as usual from the client code.

If we need a return value, this value needs to be wrapped in an implementation of the java.util.concurrent.Future interface. The Java EE API provides a convenience implementation in the form of the javax.ejb.AsyncResult class. Both the Future interface and the AsyncResult class use generics; we need to specify our return type as the type parameter of these artifacts.

The `Future` interface has several methods we can use to cancel execution of an asynchronous method, check to see if the method is done, get the return value of the method, or check to see if the method is canceled. The following table lists these methods:

Method	Description
`cancel(boolean mayInterruptIfRunning)`	Cancels method execution. If the `boolean` parameter is true, then this method will attempt to cancel the method execution even if it is already running.
`get()`	Will return the "unwrapped" return value of the method; the return value will be of the `type` parameter of the `Future` interface implementation returned by the method.
`get(long timeout, TimeUnit unit)`	Will attempt the "unwrapped" return value of the method; the return value will be of the `type` parameter of the `Future` interface implementation returned by the method. This method will block the amount of time specified by the first parameter. The unit of time to wait is determined by the second parameter; the `TimeUnit` enum has constants for NANOSECONDS, MILLISECONDS, SECONDS, MINUTES, and so on. Refer to its Javadoc documentation for the complete list.
`isCancelled()`	Returns true if the method has been canceled, false otherwise.
`isDone()`	Returns true if the method has finished executing, false otherwise.

As we can see, the `@Asynchronous` annotation makes it very easy to make asynchronous calls without having the overhead of having to set up message queues or topics. It is certainly a welcome addition to the EJB specification.

Message-driven beans

The purpose of a message-driven bean is to consume messages from a Java Message Service (JMS) queue or a JMS topic, depending on the messaging domain used (refer to Chapter 8, *Java Message Service*). A message-driven bean must be decorated with the @MessageDriven annotation; the mappedName attribute of this annotation must contain the **Java Naming and Directory Interface** (JNDI) name of the JMS message queue or JMS message topic that the bean will be consuming messages from. The following example illustrates a simple message-driven bean:

```java
package net.ensode.javaeebook;

import javax.ejb.MessageDriven;
import javax.jms.JMSException;
import javax.jms.Message;
import javax.jms.MessageListener;
import javax.jms.TextMessage;

@MessageDriven(mappedName = "jms/JavaEE8BookQueue")
public class ExampleMessageDrivenBean implements MessageListener
{
  public void onMessage(Message message)
  {
    TextMessage textMessage = (TextMessage) message;
    try
    {
      System.out.print("Received the following message: ");
      System.out.println(textMessage.getText());
      System.out.println();
    }
    catch (JMSException e)
    {
      e.printStackTrace();
    }
  }
}
```

Message-driven beans must be decorated with the @MessageDriven annotation. They listen for messages on the queue or topic defined in the mappedName attribute of the @MessageDriven interface (jms/JavaEEBookQueue in this example).

It is recommended, but not required, for message-driven beans to implement the javax.jms.MessageListener interface; however message-driven beans must have a method called onMessage() whose signature is identical to the preceding example.

Client applications never invoke a message-driven bean's methods directly; instead they put messages in the message queue or topic, then the bean consumes those messages and acts appropriately. The preceding example simply prints the message to standard output; since message-driven beans execute inside an EJB container, standard output gets redirected to a log. If using GlassFish, the server log file can be found at `[GlassFish installation directory]/glassfish/domains/domain1/logs/server.log`.

Transactions in enterprise JavaBeans

Like we mentioned earlier in this chapter, by default all EJB methods are automatically wrapped in a transaction. This default behavior is known as container-managed transactions, since transactions are managed by the EJB container. Application developers may also choose to manage transactions themselves, which can be accomplished by using bean-managed transactions. Both of these approaches are discussed in the following sections.

Container-managed transactions

Because EJB methods are transactional by default, we run into an interesting dilemma when an EJB method is invoked from client code that is already in a transaction. How should the EJB container behave? Should it suspend the client transaction, execute its method in a new transaction, and then resume the client transaction? Should it not create a new transaction and execute its method as part of the client transaction? Should it throw an exception?

By default, if an EJB method is invoked by client code that is already in a transaction, the EJB container will simply execute the session bean method as part of the client transaction. If this is not the behavior we need, we can change it by decorating the method with the `@TransactionAttribute` annotation. This annotation has a `value` attribute that determines how the EJB container will behave when the session bean method is invoked within an existing transaction and when it is invoked outside any transactions. The value of the `value` attribute is typically a constant defined in the `javax.ejb.TransactionAttributeType` enum.

The following table lists the possible values for the `@TransactionAttribute` annotation:

Values	Description
`TransactionAttributeType.MANDATORY`	Forces the method to be invoked as part of a client transaction. If the method is called outside any transactions, it will throw a `TransactionRequiredException`.
`TransactionAttributeType.NEVER`	The method is never executed in a transaction. If the method is invoked as part of a client transaction, it will throw a `RemoteException`. No transaction is created if the method is not invoked inside a client transaction.
`TransactionAttributeType.NOT_SUPPORTED`	If the method is invoked as part of a client transaction, the client transaction is suspended and the method is executed outside any transaction; after the method completes, the client transaction is resumed. No transaction is created if the method is not invoked inside a client transaction.
`TransactionAttributeType.REQUIRED`	If the method is invoked as part of a client transaction, the method is executed as part of this transaction. If the method is invoked outside any transaction, a new transaction is created for the method. This is the default behavior.
`TransactionAttributeType.REQUIRES_NEW`	If the method is invoked as part of a client transaction, this transaction is suspended, and a new transaction is created for the method. Once the method completes, the client transaction is resumed. If the method is called outside any transactions, a new transaction is created for the method.

`TransactionAttributeType.SUPPORTS`	If the method is invoked as part of a client transaction, it is executed as part of this transaction. If the method is invoked outside a transaction, no new transaction is created for the method.

Although the default transaction attribute is reasonable in most cases, it is good to be able to override this default if necessary. For example, as transactions have a performance impact, being able to turn off transactions for a method that does not need them is beneficial. For a case like this, we would decorate our method as illustrated in the following code snippet:

```
@TransactionAttribute(value=TransactionAttributeType.NEVER)
public void doitAsFastAsPossible()
{
   //performance critical code goes here.
}
```

Other transaction attribute types can be declared by annotating the methods with the corresponding constant in the `TransactionAttributeType` enum.

If we wish to override the default transaction attribute consistently across all methods in a session bean, we can decorate the session bean class with the `@TransactionAttribute` annotation; the value of its `value` attribute will be applied to every method in the session bean.

Container-managed transactions are automatically rolled back whenever an exception is thrown inside an EJB method. Additionally, we can programmatically roll back a container-managed transaction by invoking the `setRollbackOnly()` method on an instance of `javax.ejb.EJBContext` corresponding to the session bean in question. The following example is a new version of the session bean we saw earlier in this chapter, modified to roll back transactions if necessary:

```
package net.ensode.javaeebook;

//imports omitted

@Stateless
public class CustomerDaoRollbackBean implements CustomerDaoRollback
{
   @Resource
   private EJBContext ejbContext;

   @PersistenceContext
   private EntityManager entityManager;
```

```
public void saveNewCustomer(Customer customer)
{
  if (customer == null || customer.getCustomerId() != null)
  {
    ejbContext.setRollbackOnly();
  }
  else
  {
    customer.setCustomerId(getNewCustomerId());
    entityManager.persist(customer);
  }
}

public void updateCustomer(Customer customer)
{
  if (customer == null || customer.getCustomerId() == null)
  {
    ejbContext.setRollbackOnly();
  }
  else
  {
    entityManager.merge(customer);
  }
}
//Additional method omitted for brevity.

}
```

In this version of the DAO session bean, we deleted the `saveCustomer()` method and made the `saveNewCustomer()` and `updateCustomer()` methods public. Each of these methods now checks to see if the `customerId` field is set correctly for the operation we are trying to perform (`null` for inserts and not `null` for updates). It also checks to make sure the object to be persisted is not `null`. If any of the checks results in invalid data, the method simply rolls back the transaction by invoking the `setRollBackOnly()` method on the injected instance of `EJBContext` and does not update the database.

Bean-managed transactions

As we have seen, container-managed transactions make it ridiculously easy to write code that is wrapped in a transaction. There is nothing special that we need to do to make them that way; as a matter of fact, some developers are sometimes not even aware that they are writing code that will be transactional in nature when they develop session beans. Container-managed transactions cover most typical use cases that we will encounter. However they do have a limitation; each method can be wrapped in a single transaction or without a transaction. With container-managed transactions, it is not possible to implement a method that generates more than one transaction, but this can be accomplished by using bean-managed transactions:

```
package net.ensode.javaeebook;

import java.sql.Connection;
import java.sql.PreparedStatement;
import java.sql.ResultSet;
import java.sql.SQLException;
import java.util.List;

import javax.annotation.Resource;
import javax.ejb.Stateless;
import javax.ejb.TransactionManagement;
import javax.ejb.TransactionManagementType;
import javax.persistence.EntityManager;
import javax.persistence.PersistenceContext;
import javax.sql.DataSource;
import javax.transaction.UserTransaction;

@Stateless
@TransactionManagement(value = TransactionManagementType.BEAN)
public class CustomerDaoBmtBean implements CustomerDaoBmt
{
  @Resource
  private UserTransaction userTransaction;

  @PersistenceContext
  private EntityManager entityManager;

  @Resource(name = "jdbc/__CustomerDBPool")
  private DataSource dataSource;

  public void saveMultipleNewCustomers(
      List<Customer> customerList)
  {
    for (Customer customer : customerList)
```

```java
        {
          try
          {
            userTransaction.begin();
            customer.setCustomerId(getNewCustomerId());
            entityManager.persist(customer);
            userTransaction.commit();
          }
          catch (Exception e)
          {
            e.printStackTrace();
          }
        }
      }

      private Long getNewCustomerId()
      {
        Connection connection;
        Long newCustomerId = null;
        try
        {
          connection = dataSource.getConnection();
          PreparedStatement preparedStatement =
              connection.prepareStatement("select " +
              "max(customer_id)+1 as new_customer_id " +
              "from customers");

          ResultSet resultSet = preparedStatement.executeQuery();

          if (resultSet != null && resultSet.next())
          {
            newCustomerId = resultSet.getLong("new_customer_id");
          }

          connection.close();
        }
        catch (SQLException e)
        {
          e.printStackTrace();
        }

        return newCustomerId;
      }
    }
```

In this example, we implemented a method named `saveMultipleNewCustomers()`. This method takes a `List` of customers as its sole parameter. The intention of this method is to save as many elements in the `ArrayList` as possible. An exception while saving one of the entities should not stop the method from attempting to save the remaining elements. This behavior is not possible using container-managed transactions, since an exception thrown when saving one of the entities will roll back the whole transaction; the only way to achieve this behavior is through bean-managed transactions.

As can be seen in the example, we declare that the session bean uses bean-managed transactions by decorating the class with the `@TransactionManagement` annotation and using `TransactionManagementType.BEAN` as the value for its `value` attribute (the only other valid value for this attribute is `TransactionManagementType.CONTAINER`, but since this is the default value, it is not necessary to specify it).

To be able to programmatically control transactions, we inject an instance of `javax.transaction.UserTransaction`, which is then used in the `for` loop inside the `saveMultipleNewCustomers()` method to begin and commit transactions in each iteration of the loop.

If we need to roll back a bean-managed transaction, we can do it by simply calling the `rollback()` method on the appropriate instance of `javax.transaction.UserTransaction`.

Before moving on, it is worth noting that, even though all the examples in this section were session beans, the concepts explained apply to message-driven beans as well.

Enterprise JavaBean life cycles

Enterprise JavaBeans go through different states in their life cycle. Each type of EJB has different states. States specific to each type of EJB are discussed in the next sections.

Stateful session bean life cycle

We can annotate methods in session beans so that they are automatically invoked by the EJB container at certain points in the bean's life cycle. For example, we could have a method invoked right after the bean is created or right before it is destroyed.

Before explaining the annotations available to implement life cycle methods, a brief explanation of the session bean life cycle is in order. The life cycle of a stateful session bean is different from the life cycle of a stateless or singleton session bean.

A stateful session bean life cycle contains three states: **Does Not Exist**, **Ready**, and **Passive**:

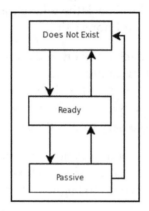

Before a stateful session bean is deployed, it is in the **Does Not Exist** state. Upon successful deployment, the EJB container does any required dependency injection on the bean and it goes into the **Ready** state. At this point, the bean is ready to have its methods called by a client application.

When a stateful session bean is in the **Ready** state, the EJB container may decide to passivate it, that is, to move it from the main memory to secondary storage, when this happens the bean goes into the **Passive** state.

If an instance of a stateful session bean hasn't been accessed for a period of time, the EJB container will set the bean to the **Does Not Exist** state. How long a bean will stay in memory before being destroyed varies from application server to application server, and is usually configurable. By default, GlassFish will send a stateful session bean to the **Does Not Exist** state after 90 minutes of inactivity. When deploying our code to GlassFish, this default can be changed by going to the GlassFish administration console; expanding the **Configuration** node in the tree at the right-hand side; expanding the **server-config** node; clicking on the **EJB Container** node; scrolling down towards the bottom of the page and modifying the value of the **Removal Timeout** text field; and then finally clicking on either of the **Save** buttons (the top right or bottom right of the main page):

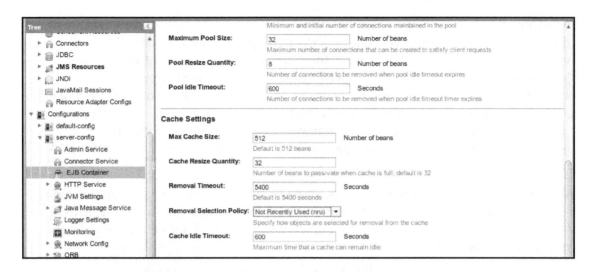

However, this technique sets the timeout value for all stateful session beans. If we need to modify the timeout value for a specific session bean, we need to include a `glassfish-ejb-jar.xml` deployment descriptor in the JAR file containing the session bean. In this deployment descriptor, we can set the timeout value as the value of the `<removal-timeout-in-seconds>` element:

```xml
<?xml version="1.0" encoding="UTF-8"?>
<!DOCTYPE glassfish-ejb-jar PUBLIC "-//GlassFish.org//DTD GlassFish
Application Server 3.1 EJB 3.1//EN"
"http://glassfish.org/dtds/glassfish-ejb-jar_3_1-1.dtd">
<glassfish-ejb-jar>
  <enterprise-beans>
    <ejb>
      <ejb-name>MyStatefulSessionBean</ejb-name>
      <bean-cache>
          <removal-timeout-in-seconds>
              600
          </removal-timeout-in-seconds>
      </bean-cache>
    </ejb>
  </enterprise-beans>
</glassfish-ejb-jar>
```

Even though we are no longer required to create an `ejb-jar.xml` for our session beans (this was necessary in previous versions of the J2EE specification), we can still write one if we want to. The `<ejb-name>` element in the `glassfish-ejb-jar.xml` deployment descriptor must match the value of the element of the same name in `ejb-jar.xml`. If we choose not to create an `ejb-jar.xml`, then this value must match the name of the EJB class. The timeout value for the stateful session bean must be the value of the `<removal-timeout-in-seconds>` element; as the name of the element suggests, the unit of time to use is seconds. In the preceding example, we set the timeout value to 600 seconds, or 10 minutes.

Any methods in a stateful session bean decorated with the `@PostActivate` annotation will be invoked just after the stateful session bean has been activated. Similarly, any method decorated with the `@PrePassivate` annotation will be invoked just before the stateful session bean is passivated.

When a stateful session bean that is in the **Ready** state times out and is sent to the **Does not Exist** state, any method decorated with the `@PreDestroy` annotation is executed. If the session bean is in the **Passive** state and it times out, methods decorated with the `@PreDestroy` annotation are not executed. Additionally, if a client of the stateful session bean executes any method decorated with the `@Remove` annotation, any methods decorated with the `@PreDestroy` annotation are executed and the bean is marked for garbage collection.

The `@PostActivate`, `@PrePassivate`, and `@Remove` annotations are valid only for stateful session beans. The `@PreDestroy` and `@PostConstruct` annotations are valid for stateful session beans, stateless session beans, and message-driven beans.

Stateless and singleton session bean life cycles

A stateless or singleton session bean life cycle contains only the **Does Not Exist** and **Ready** states:

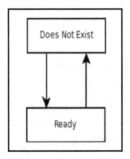

Stateless and singleton session beans are never passivated. A stateless or singleton session bean's methods can be decorated with the `@PostConstruct` and the `@PreDestroy` annotations. Just like in stateful session beans, any methods decorated with the `@PostConstruct` annotation will be executed when the session bean goes from the **Does Not Exist** to the **Ready** State, and any methods decorated with the `@PreDestroy` annotation will be executed when a stateless session bean goes from the **Ready** state to the **Does Not Exist** state. Stateless and singleton session beans are never passivated, therefore any `@PrePassivate` and `@PostActivate` annotations in a stateless session bean are simply ignored by the EJB container.

Most application servers allow us to configure how long to wait before an idle stateless or singleton session bean is destroyed. If using GlassFish, we can control how the life cycle of stateless session beans (and message-driven beans) is managed via the administration web console:

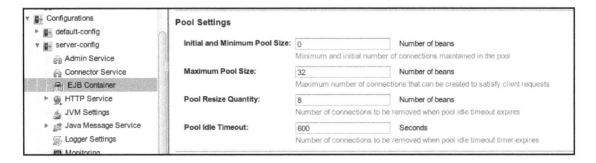

The settings shown in the preceding screenshot allow us to control the stateless session bean life cycle:

- **Initial and Minimum Pool Size** refers to the minimum number of beans in the pool
- **Maximum Pool Size** refers to the maximum number of beans in the pool
- **Pool Resize Quantity** refers to how many beans will be removed from the pool when the pool idle timeout expires
- **Pool Idle Timeout** refers to the number of seconds of inactivity to wait before removing beans from the pool

The preceding settings affect all poolable (stateless session beans and message-driven beans) EJBs. Just like with stateful session beans, these settings can be overridden on a case-by-case basis, by adding a GlassFish-specific `glassfish-ejb.jar.xml` deployment descriptor:

```xml
<?xml version="1.0" encoding="UTF-8"?>


<!DOCTYPE glassfish-ejb-jar PUBLIC "-//GlassFish.org//DTD GlassFish
Application Server 3.1 EJB 3.1//EN"
"http://glassfish.org/dtds/glassfish-ejb-jar_3_1-1.dtd">
<glassfish-ejb-jar>
    <enterprise-beans>
        <ejb>
            <ejb-name>MyStatelessSessionBean</ejb-name>
            <bean-pool>
                <steady-pool-size>10</steady-pool-size>
                <max-pool-size>60</max-pool-size>
                <resize-quantity>5</resize-quantity>
                <pool-idle-timeout-in-seconds>
                    900
                </pool-idle-timeout-in-seconds>
            </bean-pool>
        </ejb>
    </enterprise-beans>
</glassfish-ejb-jar>
```

`glassfish-ejb-jar.xml` contains XML tags that are equivalent to the corresponding settings in the web console:

- `<steady-pool-size>` corresponds to **Initial and Minimum Pool Size** in the GlassFish web console

- `<max-pool-size>` corresponds to **Maximum Pool Size** in the GlassFish web console
- `<resize-quantity>` corresponds to **Pool Resize Quantity** in the GlassFish web console
- `<pool-idle-timeout-in-seconds>` corresponds to **Pool Idle Timeout** in the GlassFish web console

Message-driven bean life cycle

Just like stateless session beans, message-driven beans contain only the **Does Not Exist** and **Ready** states:

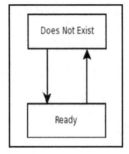

A message-driven bean can have methods decorated with the `@PostConstruct` and `@PreDestroy` methods. Methods decorated with the `@PostConstruct` are executed just before the bean goes to the **Ready** state. Methods decorated with the `@PreDestroy` annotation are executed just before the bean goes to the **Does Not Exist** state.

EJB timer service

Stateless session beans and message-driven beans can have a method that is executed periodically at regular intervals of time. This can be accomplished by using the EJB timer service. The following example illustrates how to take advantage of this feature:

```
package net.ensode.javaeebook;

//imports omitted

@Stateless
public class EjbTimerExampleBean implements EjbTimerExample
```

```
{
  private static Logger logger =
Logger.getLogger(EjbTimerExampleBean.class
      .getName());
  @Resource
  TimerService timerService;

  public void startTimer(Serializable info)
  {
    Timer timer = timerService.createTimer
      (new Date(), 5000, info);
  }

  public void stopTimer(Serializable info)
  {
    Timer timer;
    Collection timers = timerService.getTimers();

    for (Object object : timers)
    {
      timer = ((Timer) object);

      if (timer.getInfo().equals(info))
      {
        timer.cancel();
        break;
      }
    }
  }

  @Timeout
  public void logMessage(Timer timer)
  {
    logger.info("This message was triggered by :" +
        timer.getInfo() + " at "
        + System.currentTimeMillis());
  }
}
```

In the preceding example, we inject an implementation of the `javax.ejb.TimerService` interface by decorating an instance variable of this type with the `@Resource` annotation. We can then create a timer by invoking the `createTimer()` method of this `TimerService` instance.

There are several overloaded versions of the `createTimer()` method. The one we chose to use takes an instance of `java.util.Date` as its first parameter; this parameter is used to indicate the first time the timer should expire ("trfgo off"). In the example, we chose to use a brand new instance of the `Date` class, which makes the timer expire immediately. The second parameter of the `createTimer()` method is the amount of time to wait, in milliseconds, before the timer expires again. In the preceding example, the timer will expire every five seconds. The third parameter of the `createTimer()` method can be an instance of any class implementing the `java.io.Serializable` interface. Since a single EJB can have several timers executing concurrently, this third parameter is used to uniquely identify each of the timers. If we don't need to identify the timers, null can be passed as a value for this parameter.

The EJB method invoking `TimerService.createTimer()` must be called from an EJB client. Placing this call in an EJB method (decorated with the `@PostConstruct` annotation to start the timer automatically when the bean is placed in the **Ready** state) will result in an `IllegalStateException` being thrown.

We can stop a timer by invoking its `cancel()` method. There is no way to directly obtain a single timer associated with an EJB; what we need to do is invoke the `getTimers()` method on the instance of `TimerService` that is linked to the EJB. This method will return a collection containing all the timers associated with the EJB; we can then iterate through the collection and cancel the correct one by invoking its `getInfo()` method. This method will return the `Serializable` object we passed as a parameter to the `createTimer()` method.

Finally, any EJB method decorated with the `@Timeout` annotation will be executed when a timer expires. Methods decorated with this annotation must return void and take a single parameter of type `javax.ejb.Timer`. In our example, the method simply writes a message to the server log.

The following class is a standalone client for the preceding EJB:

```
package net.ensode.javaeebook;

import javax.ejb.EJB;
```

```
public class Client
{
  @EJB
  private static EjbTimerExample ejbTimerExample;

  public static void main(String[] args)
  {
    try
    {
      System.out.println("Starting timer 1...");
      ejbTimerExample.startTimer("Timer 1");
      System.out.println("Sleeping for 2 seconds...");
      Thread.sleep(2000);
      System.out.println("Starting timer 2...");
      ejbTimerExample.startTimer("Timer 2");
      System.out.println("Sleeping for 30 seconds...");
      Thread.sleep(30000);
      System.out.println("Stopping timer 1...");
      ejbTimerExample.stopTimer("Timer 1");
      System.out.println("Stopping timer 2...");
      ejbTimerExample.stopTimer("Timer 2");
      System.out.println("Done.");
    }
    catch (InterruptedException e)
    {
      e.printStackTrace();
    }
  }
}
```

The example simply starts a timer, waits for a couple of seconds, and then starts a second timer. It then sleeps for 30 seconds and then stops both timers. After deploying the EJB and executing the client, we should see some entries like this in the server log:

```
[2013-08-26T20:44:55.180-0400] [glassfish 4.0] [INFO] []
[net.ensode.javaeebook.EjbTimerExampleBean] [tid: _ThreadID=147
_ThreadName=__ejb-thread-pool1] [timeMillis: 1377564295180] [levelValue:
800] [[
   This message was triggered by :Timer 1 at 1377564295180]]
[2013-08-26T20:44:57.203-0400] [glassfish 4.0] [INFO] []
[net.ensode.javaeebook.EjbTimerExampleBean] [tid: _ThreadID=148
_ThreadName=__ejb-thread-pool2] [timeMillis: 1377564297203] [levelValue:
800] [[
   This message was triggered by :Timer 2 at 1377564297203]]
[2013-08-26T20:44:58.888-0400] [glassfish 4.0] [INFO] []
[net.ensode.javaeebook.EjbTimerExampleBean] [tid: _ThreadID=149
_ThreadName=__ejb-thread-pool3] [timeMillis: 1377564298888] [levelValue:
```

```
800] [[
      This message was triggered by :Timer 1 at 1377564298888]]
    [2013-08-26T20:45:01.156-0400] [glassfish 4.0] [INFO] []
[net.ensode.javaeebook.EjbTimerExampleBean] [tid: _ThreadID=150
_ThreadName=__ejb-thread-pool4] [timeMillis: 1377564301156] [levelValue:
800] [[
      This message was triggered by :Timer 2 at 1377564301156]]
```

These entries are created each time one of the timer expires.

Calendar-based EJB timer expressions

The example in the previous section has one disadvantage: the `startTimer()` method in the session bean must be invoked from a client in order to start the timer. This restriction makes it difficult to have the timer start as soon as the bean is deployed.

Java EE 6 introduced calendar-based EJB timer expressions. Calendar-based expressions allow one or more methods in our session beans to be executed at a certain date and time. For example, we could configure one of our methods to be executed every night at 8:10 pm, which is exactly what our next example does:

```
package com.ensode.javaeebook.calendarbasedtimer;

import java.util.logging.Logger;
import javax.ejb.Stateless;
import javax.ejb.LocalBean;
import javax.ejb.Schedule;

@Stateless
@LocalBean
public class CalendarBasedTimerEjbExampleBean {

  private static Logger logger = Logger.getLogger(
      CalendarBasedTimerEjbExampleBean.class.getName());

  @Schedule(hour = "20", minute = "10")
  public void logMessage() {
    logger.info("This message was triggered at:"
        + System.currentTimeMillis());
  }
}
```

As we can see in the preceding example, we set up the time when the method will be executed via the `javax.ejb.Schedule` annotation. In this particular example, we set up our method to be executed at 8:10 pm by setting the `hour` attribute of the `@Schedule` annotation to `"20"`, and its minute attribute to `"10"` (since the value of the hour attribute is 24 hour-based, hour 20 is equivalent to 8:00 pm).

The `@Schedule` annotation has several other attributes that allow a lot of flexibility in specifying when the method should be executed. We could, for instance, have a method executed on the third Friday of every month, or on the last day of the month, and so on and so forth.

The following table lists all the attributes in the `@Schedule` annotation that allow us to control when the annotated method will be executed:

Attribute	Description	Example values	Default value
dayOfMonth	The day of the month	`"3"`: The third day of the month `"Last"`: The last day of the month `"-2"`: Two days before the end of the month `"1st Tue"`: The first Tuesday of the month	`"*"`
dayOfWeek	The day of the week	`"3"`: Every Wednesday `"Thu"`: Every Thursday	`"*"`
hour	Hour of the day (24 hour-based)	`"14"`: 2:00 pm	`"0"`
minute	Minute of the hour	`"10"`: Ten minutes after the hour	`"0"`
month	Month of the year	`"2"`: February `"March"`: March	`"*"`
second	Second of the minute	`"5"`: Five seconds after the minute	`"0"`
timezone	Timezone ID	`"America/New York"`	`""`
year	Four digit year	`"2010"`	`"*"`

In addition to single values, most attributes accept the asterisk (*) as a wild card, meaning that the annotated method will be executed every unit of time (every day, hour, and so on).

Additionally, we can specify more than one value by separating the values with commas; for example, if we needed a method to be executed every Tuesday and Thursday, we could annotate the method as `@Schedule(dayOfWeek="Tue, Thu")`.

We can also specify a range of values, with the first value and last value separated by a dash (-); to execute a method from Monday through Friday, we could use `@Schedule(dayOfWeek="Mon-Fri")`.

Additionally, we could specify that we need the method to be executed every *n* units of time (for example, every day, every 2 hours, every 10 minutes, and so on). To do something like this, we could use `@Schedule(hour="*/12")`, which would execute the method every 12 hours.

As we can see, the `@Schedule` annotation provides a lot of flexibility when it comes to specifying when we need our methods executed. Plus, it provides the advantage of not needing a client call to activate the scheduling. Additionally, it has the advantage of using a cron-like syntax; therefore, developers familiar with this Unix tool will feel right at home using this annotation.

EJB security

Enterprise JavaBeans allow us to declaratively decide which users can access their methods. For example, some methods might only be available to users in certain roles. A typical scenario is that only users with the administrator role can add, delete, or modify other users in the system.

The following example is a slightly modified version of the DAO session bean we saw earlier in this chapter. In this version, some methods that were previously private are made public. Additionally, the session bean was modified to allow only users in certain roles to access its methods:

```
package net.ensode.javaeebook;

// imports omitted

@Stateless
@RolesAllowed("appadmin")
public class CustomerDaoBean implements CustomerDao
{
```

```java
@PersistenceContext
private EntityManager entityManager;

@Resource(name = "jdbc/__CustomerDBPool")
private DataSource dataSource;

public void saveCustomer(Customer customer)
{
  if (customer.getCustomerId() == null)
  {
    saveNewCustomer(customer);
  }
  else
  {
    updateCustomer(customer);
  }
}

public Long saveNewCustomer(Customer customer)
{
  entityManager.persist(customer);

  return customer.getCustomerId();
}

public void updateCustomer(Customer customer)
{
  entityManager.merge(customer);
}

@RolesAllowed({ "appuser", "appadmin" })
public Customer getCustomer(Long customerId)
{
  Customer customer;

  customer = entityManager.find(Customer.class, customerId);

  return customer;
}

public void deleteCustomer(Customer customer)
{
  entityManager.remove(customer);
}
```

As we can see, we declare what roles have access to the methods by using the `@RolesAllowed` annotation. This annotation can take either a single string or an array of strings as a parameter. When a single string is used as a parameter for this annotation, only users with the role specified by the parameter can access the method. If an array of strings is used as a parameter, users with any of the roles specified by the array's elements can access the method.

The `@RolesAllowed` annotation can be used to decorate an EJB class, in which case its values apply to all the methods in the EJB, or to one or more methods; in this second case its values apply only to the method the annotation is decorating. If, like in our example, both the EJB class and one or more of its methods are decorated with the `@RolesAllowed` annotation, the method level annotation takes precedence.

The procedure to create roles varies from application server to application server; when using GlassFish, application roles need to be mapped to a security realm's group name (refer to `Chapter 9`, *Securing Java EE Applications* for details). This mapping, along with what realm to use, is set in the `glassfish-ejb-jar.xml` deployment descriptor:

```xml
<?xml version="1.0" encoding="UTF-8"?>
<!DOCTYPE glassfish-ejb-jar PUBLIC "-//GlassFish.org//DTD GlassFish
Application Server 3.1 EJB 3.1//EN"
"http://glassfish.org/dtds/glassfish-ejb-jar_3_1-1.dtd">
<glassfish-ejb-jar>
    <security-role-mapping>
        <role-name>appuser</role-name>
        <group-name>appuser</group-name>
    </security-role-mapping>
    <security-role-mapping>
        <role-name>appadmin</role-name>
        <group-name>appadmin</group-name>
    </security-role-mapping>
    <enterprise-beans>
        <ejb>
            <ejb-name>CustomerDaoBean</ejb-name>
            <ior-security-config>
                <as-context>
                    <auth-method>username_password</auth-method>
                    <realm>file</realm>
                    <required>true</required>
                </as-context>
            </ior-security-config>
        </ejb>
    </enterprise-beans>
</glassfish-ejb-jar>
```

The `<security-role-mapping>` element of `glassfish-ejb-jar.xml` does the mapping between application roles and the security realm's group. The value of the `<role-name>` sub element must contain the application role; this value must match the value used in the `@RolesAllowed` annotation. The value of the `<group-name>` sub-element must contain the name of the security group in the security realm used by the EJB. In the preceding example, we map two application roles to the corresponding groups in the security realm. Although in this particular example the name of the application role and the security group match, this does not need to be the case.

 Automatically matching roles to security groups: When using GlassFish, it is possible to automatically match any application roles to identically-named security groups in the security realm. This can be accomplished by logging in to the GlassFish web console, clicking on the **Configuration** node, clicking on **Security**, clicking on the checkbox labeled **Default Principal To Role Mapping,** and finally saving this configuration change.

As can be seen in the example, the security realm to use for authentication is defined in the `<realm>` sub-element of the `<as-context>` element. The value of this sub-element must match the name of a valid security realm in the application server. Other sub-elements of the `<as-context>` element include `<auth-method>`; the only valid value for this element is `username_password`, and `<required>`, whose only valid values are `true` and `false`.

Client authentication

If the client code accessing a secured EJB is part of a web application whose user has already authenticated, then the user's credentials will be used to determine whether the user should be allowed to access the method they are trying to execute.

When using GlassFish as our application server, standalone clients must be executed through the `appclient` utility. The following code illustrates a typical client for the secured session bean:

```
package net.ensode.javaeebook;

import javax.ejb.EJB;

public class Client
{
   @EJB
   private static CustomerDao customerDao;

   public static void main(String[] args)
```

```
        {
          Long newCustomerId;

          Customer customer = new Customer();
          customer.setFirstName("Mark");
          customer.setLastName("Butcher");
          customer.setEmail("butcher@phony.org");

          System.out.println("Saving New Customer...");
          newCustomerId = customerDao.saveNewCustomer(customer);

          System.out.println("Retrieving customer...");
          customer = customerDao.getCustomer(newCustomerId);
          System.out.println(customer);
        }
    }
```

As we can see, the code does nothing to authenticate the user. The session bean is simply injected into the code via the `@EJB` annotation and it is used as usual. How this is handled varies depending on what application server we are using. GlassFish's `appclient` utility takes care of authenticating the user, after invoking the client code via the `appclient` utility:

```
appclient -client ejbsecurityclient.jar
```

The `appclient` utility will present the user with a login window when it attempts to invoke a secure method on the EJB:

Assuming the credentials are correct and that the user has the appropriate permissions, the EJB code will execute and we should see the expected output from the preceding `Client` class:

```
Saving New Customer...
Retrieving customer...
customerId = 29
firstName = Mark
lastName = Butcher
email = butcher@phony.org
```

Summary

In this chapter, we covered how to implement business logic via stateless and stateful session beans. Additionally, we covered how to implement message-driven beans to consume JMS messages.

We also explained how to take advantage of the transactional nature of EJBs to simplify implementing the DAO pattern.

Additionally, we explained the concept of container-managed transactions, and how to control them by using the appropriate annotations. We also explained how to implement bean-managed transactions, for cases in which container-managed transactions are not enough to satisfy our requirements.

Life cycles for the different types of Enterprise JavaBean were covered, including an explanation on how to have EJB methods automatically invoked by the EJB container at certain points in the life cycle.

We also covered how to have EJB methods invoked periodically by the EJB container by taking advantage of the EJB timer service.

Finally, we looked at how to make sure EJB methods are only invoked by authorized users by annotating EJB classes and/or methods with the appropriate EJB security annotations.

5
Contexts and Dependency Injection

Contexts and Dependency Injection (**CDI**) was added to the Java EE specification in Java EE 6. Java EE 8 includes a new version of CDI, which adds new features such as asynchronous events and event ordering. CDI provides several advantages that were previously unavailable to Java EE developers, such as allowing any JavaBean to be used as a JSF managed bean, including stateless and stateful session beans. As its name implies, CDI simplifies dependency injection in Java EE applications.

In this chapter, we will cover the following topics:

- Named beans
- Dependency injection
- Scopes
- Qualifiers
- CDI events

Named beans

CDI provides us with the ability to name our beans via the `@Named` annotation. Named beans allow us to easily inject our beans into other classes that depend on them (see the next section), and to easily refer to them from JSF pages via the unified expression language.

The following example shows the `@Named` annotation in action:

```
package net.ensode.javaee8book.cdidependencyinjection.beans;

import javax.enterprise.context.RequestScoped;
import javax.inject.Named;

@Named
@RequestScoped
public class Customer {

  private String firstName;
  private String lastName;

  public String getFirstName() {
    return firstName;
  }

  public void setFirstName(String firstName) {
    this.firstName = firstName;
  }

  public String getLastName() {
    return lastName;
  }

  public void setLastName(String lastName) {
    this.lastName = lastName;
  }
}
```

As we can see, all we need to do to name our class is to decorate it with the `@Named` annotation. By default, the name of the bean will be the class name with its first letter switched to lowercase; in our example, the name of the bean would be `customer`. If we wish to use a different name, we can do so by setting the `value` attribute of the `@Named` annotation. For example, if we had wanted to use the name `customerBean` for the bean above, we could have done so by modifying the `@Named` annotation as follows:

```
@Named(value="customerBean")
```

Or simply:

```
@Named("customerBean")
```

Since the `value` attribute name does not need to be specified, if we don't use an attribute name, then `value` is implied.

This name can be used to access our bean from JSF pages using the unified expression language:

```xml
<?xml version='1.0' encoding='UTF-8' ?>
<!DOCTYPE html PUBLIC "-//W3C//DTD XHTML 1.0 Transitional//EN"
"http://www.w3.org/TR/xhtml1/DTD/xhtml1-transitional.dtd">
<html xmlns="http://www.w3.org/1999/xhtml"
      xmlns:h="http://xmlns.jcp.org/jsf/html">
  <h:head>
    <title>Enter Customer Information</title>
  </h:head>
  <h:body>
    <h:form>
      <h:panelGrid columns="2">
        <h:outputLabel for="firstName" value="First
          Name"/>
        <h:inputText id="firstName"
          value="#{customer.firstName}"/>
        <h:outputLabel for="lastName" value="Last
          Name"/>
        <h:inputText id="lastName"
          value="#{customer.lastName}"/>
        <h:panelGroup/>
      </h:panelGrid>
    </h:form>
  </h:body>
</html>
```

As we can see, named beans are accessed from JSF pages exactly as standard JSF managed beans are. This allows JSF to access any named bean, decoupling the Java code from the JSF API.

When deployed and executed, our simple application looks like this:

Dependency injection

Dependency injection is a technique for supplying external dependencies to a Java class. Java EE 5 introduced dependency injection via the @Resource annotation, however, this annotation is limited to injecting resources such as database connections, JMS resources, and so on. CDI includes the @Inject annotation, which can be used to inject instances of Java classes into any dependent objects.

JSF applications typically follow the **Model-View-Controller** (**MVC**) design pattern. As such, often some JSF managed beans take the role of controllers in the pattern, while others take the role of the model. This approach typically requires the controller managed bean to have access to one or more of the model-managed beans. CDI's dependency injection capabilities make injecting beans into one another very simple, as illustrated in the following example:

```
package net.ensode.javaee8book.cdidependencyinjection.ejb;

import java.util.logging.Logger;
import javax.inject.Inject;
import javax.inject.Named;

@Named
@RequestScoped
public class CustomerController {

  private static final Logger logger = Logger.getLogger(
      CustomerController.class.getName());
  @Inject
  private Customer customer;

  public String saveCustomer() {

    logger.info("Saving the following information \n" + customer.
        toString());

    //If this was a real application, we would have code to save
    //customer data to the database here.

    return "confirmation";
  }
}
```

Notice that all we had to do to initialize our `Customer` instance was to decorate it with the `@Inject` annotation. When the bean is constructed by the application server, an instance of the `Customer` bean is automatically injected into this field. Notice that the injected bean is used in the `saveCustomer()` method.

Qualifiers

In some instances, the type of bean we wish to inject into our code may be an interface or a Java superclass, but we may be interested in injecting a specific subclass or a class implementing the interface. For cases like this, CDI provides qualifiers we can use to indicate the specific type we wish to inject into our code.

A CDI qualifier is an annotation that must be decorated with the `@Qualifier` annotation. This annotation can then be used to decorate the specific subclass or interface implementation we wish to qualify. Additionally, the injected field in the client code needs to be decorated with the qualifier as well.

Suppose our application could have a special kind of customer; for example, frequent customers could be given the status of premium customers. To handle those premium customers, we could extend our `Customer` named bean and decorate it with the following qualifier:

```
package net.ensode.javaee8book.cdidependencyinjection.qualifiers;

import static java.lang.annotation.ElementType.TYPE;
import static java.lang.annotation.ElementType.FIELD;
import static java.lang.annotation.ElementType.PARAMETER;
import static java.lang.annotation.ElementType.METHOD;
import static java.lang.annotation.RetentionPolicy.RUNTIME;
import java.lang.annotation.Retention;
import java.lang.annotation.Target;
import javax.inject.Qualifier;

@Qualifier
@Retention(RUNTIME)
@Target({METHOD, FIELD, PARAMETER, TYPE})
public @interface Premium {
}
```

As we mentioned before, qualifiers are standard annotations; they typically have retention of runtime and can target methods, fields, parameters, or types, as illustrated in the above example. The only difference between a qualifier and a standard annotation is that qualifiers are decorated with the @Qualifier annotation.

Once we have our qualifier in place, we need to use it to decorate the specific subclass or interface implementation:

```java
package net.ensode.javaee8book.cdidependencyinjection.beans;

import javax.enterprise.context.RequestScoped;
import javax.inject.Named;
import
net.ensode.javaee8book.cdidependencyinjection.qualifiers.Premium;

@Named
@RequestScoped
@Premium
public class PremiumCustomer extends Customer {

  private Integer discountCode;

  public Integer getDiscountCode() {
    return discountCode;
  }

  public void setDiscountCode(Integer discountCode) {
    this.discountCode = discountCode;
  }
}
```

Once we have decorated the specific instance we need to qualify, we can use our qualifiers in the client code to specify the exact type of dependency we need:

```java
package net.ensode.javaee8book.cdidependencyinjection.beans;

import java.util.Random;
import java.util.logging.Logger;
import javax.enterprise.context.RequestScoped;
import javax.inject.Inject;
import javax.inject.Named;
import
net.ensode.javaee8book.cdidependencyinjection.qualifiers.Premium;

@Named
@RequestScoped
public class CustomerController {
```

```
private static final Logger logger = Logger.getLogger(
    CustomerController.class.getName());
@Inject
@Premium
private Customer customer;

public String saveCustomer() {

  PremiumCustomer premiumCustomer = (PremiumCustomer) customer;

  premiumCustomer.setDiscountCode(generateDiscountCode());

  logger.info("Saving the following information \n"
      + premiumCustomer.getFirstName() + " "
      + premiumCustomer.getLastName()
      + ", discount code = "
      + premiumCustomer.getDiscountCode());

  //If this was a real application, we would have code to save
  //customer data to the database here.
  return "confirmation";
}

public Integer generateDiscountCode() {
  return new Random().nextInt(100000);
}
}
```

Since we used our @Premium qualifier to decorate the customer field, an instance of PremiumCustomer is injected into that field, as this class is also decorated with the @Premium qualifier.

As far as our JSF pages go, we simply access our named bean as usual, using its name:

```
<?xml version='1.0' encoding='UTF-8' ?>
<!DOCTYPE html PUBLIC "-//W3C//DTD XHTML 1.0 Transitional//EN"
"http://www.w3.org/TR/xhtml1/DTD/xhtml1-transitional.dtd">
<html xmlns="http://www.w3.org/1999/xhtml"
    xmlns:h="http://xmlns.jcp.org/jsf/html">
  <h:head>
      <title>Enter Customer Information</title>
  </h:head>
  <h:body>
      <h:form>
          <h:panelGrid columns="2">
              <h:outputLabel for="firstName" value="First Name"/>
              <h:inputText id="firstName"
```

```
                    value="#{premiumCustomer.firstName}"/>
          <h:outputLabel for="lastName" value="Last Name"/>
          <h:inputText id="lastName"
              value="#{premiumCustomer.lastName}"/>
          <h:outputLabel for="discountCode" value="Discount
          Code"/>
          <h:inputText id="discountCode"
              value="#{premiumCustomer.discountCode}"/>
          <h:panelGroup/>
          <h:commandButton value="Submit"
              action="#{customerController.saveCustomer}"/>
        </h:panelGrid>
      </h:form>
    </h:body>
  </html>
```

In this example, we are using the default name for our bean, which is the class name with the first letter switched to lowercase.

Our simple application renders and acts just like a "plain" JSF application, as far as the user is concerned:

Named bean scopes

Just like JSF managed beans, CDI named beans are scoped. This means that CDI beans are contextual objects. When a named bean is needed, either because of injection or because it is referred from a JSF page, CDI looks for an instance of the bean in the scope it belongs to and injects it into the dependent code. If no instance is found, one is created and stored in the appropriate scope for future use. The different scopes are the context in which the bean exists.

The following table lists the different valid CDI scopes:

Scope	Annotation	Description
Request	`@RequestScoped`	request-scoped beans are shared through the duration of a single request. A single request could refer to an HTTP request, an invocation to a method in an EJB, a web service invocation, or sending a JMS message to a message-driven bean.
Conversation	`@ConversationScoped`	The conversation scope can span multiple requests but is typically shorter than the session scope.
Session	`@SessionScoped`	session-scoped beans are shared across all requests in an HTTP session. Each user of an application gets their own instance of a session scoped bean.
Application	`@ApplicationScoped`	application-scoped beans live through the whole application lifetime. Beans in this scope are shared across user sessions.
Dependent	`@Dependent`	dependent-scoped beans are not shared; any time a dependent scoped bean is injected, a new instance is created.

As we can see, CDI includes most scopes supported by JSF, and also adds a couple of its own. CDI's **request scope** differs from JSF's request scope, in which a request does not necessarily refer to an HTTP request; it could simply be an invocation on an EJB method, a web service invocation, or sending a JMS message to a message-driven bean.

The **conversation scope** does not exist in JSF. This scope is similar to JSF's flow scope, since it is longer than the request scope but shorter than the session scope, and typically spans three or more pages. Classes wishing to access a conversation-scoped bean must have an instance of `javax.enterprise.context.Conversation` injected. At the point where we want to start the conversation, the `begin()` method must be invoked on this object. At the point where we want to end the conversation, the `end()` method must be invoked on it.

CDI's **session scope** behaves just like its JSF counterpart. The lifecycle of session-scoped beans are tied to the life of an HTTP session.

CDI's **application scope** also behaves just like the equivalent scope in JSF. Application-scoped beans are tied to the life of an application. A single instance of each application-scoped bean exists per application, which means that the same instance is accessible to all HTTP sessions.

Just like the conversation scope, CDI's **dependent scope** does not exist in JSF. New dependent scope beans are instantiated every time it is needed; usually when it is injected into a class that depends on it.

Suppose we wanted to have a user enter some data that would be stored in a single named bean, but that bean has several fields. Therefore, we would like to split the data entry into several pages. This is a fairly common situation and one that was not easy to handle using previous versions of Java EE (JSF 2.2 added Faces Flows to solve this problem; refer to Chapter 2, *JavaServer Faces*), or the servlet API for that matter. The reason this situation was not easy to manage using those technologies is that you could either put a class in the request scope, in which case the class would be destroyed after every single request, losing its data in the process, or in the session scope, in which the class would stick around in memory long after it was needed. For cases like this, CDI's conversation scope is a good solution:

```
package net.ensode..javaee8book.conversationscope.model;

import java.io.Serializable;
import javax.enterprise.context.ConversationScoped;
import javax.inject.Named;
import org.apache.commons.lang3.builder.ReflectionToStringBuilder;

@Named
@ConversationScoped
public class Customer implements Serializable {

    private String firstName;
    private String middleName;
    private String lastName;
    private String addrLine1;
    private String addrLine2;
    private String addrCity;
    private String state;
    private String zip;
    private String phoneHome;
    private String phoneWork;
    private String phoneMobile;
```

```java
public String getAddrCity() {
    return addrCity;
}

public void setAddrCity(String addrCity) {
    this.addrCity = addrCity;
}

public String getAddrLine1() {
    return addrLine1;
}

public void setAddrLine1(String addrLine1) {
    this.addrLine1 = addrLine1;
}

public String getAddrLine2() {
    return addrLine2;
}

public void setAddrLine2(String addrLine2) {
    this.addrLine2 = addrLine2;
}

public String getFirstName() {
    return firstName;
}

public void setFirstName(String firstName) {
    this.firstName = firstName;
}

public String getLastName() {
    return lastName;
}

public void setLastName(String lastName) {
    this.lastName = lastName;
}

public String getMiddleName() {
    return middleName;
}

public void setMiddleName(String middleName) {
    this.middleName = middleName;
}
```

```java
    public String getPhoneHome() {
        return phoneHome;
    }

    public void setPhoneHome(String phoneHome) {
        this.phoneHome = phoneHome;
    }

    public String getPhoneMobile() {
        return phoneMobile;
    }

    public void setPhoneMobile(String phoneMobile) {
        this.phoneMobile = phoneMobile;
    }

    public String getPhoneWork() {
        return phoneWork;
    }

    public void setPhoneWork(String phoneWork) {
        this.phoneWork = phoneWork;
    }

    public String getState() {
        return state;
    }

    public void setState(String state) {
        this.state = state;
    }

    public String getZip() {
        return zip;
    }

    public void setZip(String zip) {
        this.zip = zip;
    }

    @Override
    public String toString() {
        return ReflectionToStringBuilder.reflectionToString(this);
    }
}
```

We declare that our bean is conversation scoped by decorating it with the
@ConversationScoped annotation. Conversation-scoped beans also need to implement
java.io.Serializable. Other than those two requirements, there is nothing special
about our code; it is a simple JavaBean with private properties and corresponding getter
and setter methods.

 We are using the Apache commons-lang library in our code to easily
implement a toString() method for our bean. commons-lang has
several utility methods like this that implement frequently needed,
tedious to code functionality. commons-lang is available in the central
Maven repositories and at http://commons.apache.org/lang.

In addition to having our conversation-scoped bean injected, our client code must also have
an instance of javax.enterprise.context.Conversation injected, as illustrated in the
following example:

```
package net.ensode.javaee8book.conversationscope.controller;

import java.io.Serializable;
import javax.enterprise.context.Conversation;
import javax.enterprise.context.RequestScoped;
import javax.inject.Inject;
import javax.inject.Named;
import net.ensode.javaee8book.conversationscope.model.Customer;

@Named
@RequestScoped
public class CustomerInfoController implements Serializable {

    @Inject
    private Conversation conversation;
    @Inject
    private Customer customer;

    public String customerInfoEntry() {
        conversation.begin();
        System.out.println(customer);
        return "page1";
    }

    public String navigateToPage1() {
        System.out.println(customer);
        return "page1";
    }
```

```
public String navigateToPage2() {
    System.out.println(customer);
    return "page2";
}

public String navigateToPage3() {
    System.out.println(customer);
    return "page3";
}

public String navigateToConfirmationPage() {
    System.out.println(customer);
    conversation.end();
    return "confirmation";
}
}
```

Conversations can be either **long-running** or **transient**. Transient conversations end at the end of a request, while long-running conversations span multiple requests. In most cases, we use long-running conversations to hold a reference to a conversation-scoped bean across multiple HTTP requests in a web application.

A long-running conversation starts when the `begin()` method is invoked in the injected `Conversation` instance, and it ends when we invoke the `end()` method on the same object.

JSF pages simply access our CDI beans as usual:

```
<?xml version='1.0' encoding='UTF-8' ?>
<!DOCTYPE html PUBLIC "-//W3C//DTD XHTML 1.0 Transitional//EN"
"http://www.w3.org/TR/xhtml1/DTD/xhtml1-transitional.dtd">
<html xmlns="http://www.w3.org/1999/xhtml"
    xmlns:h="http://xmlns.jcp.org/jsf/html">
    <h:head>
        <title>Customer Information</title>
    </h:head>
    <h:body>
        <h3>Enter Customer Information (Page 1 of 3)</h3>
        <h:form>
            <h:panelGrid columns="2">
                <h:outputLabel for="firstName" value="First Name"/>
                <h:inputText id="firstName" value="#
                {customer.firstName}"/>
                <h:outputLabel for="middleName" value="Middle
                Name"/>
                <h:inputText id="middleName" value="#
                {customer.middleName}"/>
                <h:outputLabel for="lastName" value="Last Name"/>
```

```
                <h:inputText id="lastName" value="#
                 {customer.lastName}"/>
                <h:panelGroup/>
                <h:commandButton value="Next"
                action="#
                {customerInfoController.navigateToPage2}"/>
            </h:panelGrid>
        </h:form>
    </h:body>
</html>
```

As we navigate from one page to the next, we keep the same instance of our conversation-scoped bean; therefore, all user entered data remains. When the `end()` method is called on our conversation bean, the conversation ends and our conversation-scoped bean is destroyed.

Keeping our bean in the conversation scope simplifies the task of implementing *wizard-style* user interfaces, where data can be entered across several pages:

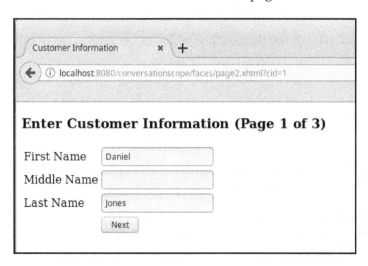

In our example, after clicking the **Next** button on the first page, we can see our partially populated bean in the application server log:

```
INFO:
net.ensode..javaee8book.conversationscope.model.Customer@6e1c51b4[f
irstName=Daniel,middleName=,lastName=Jones,addrLine1=,addrLine2=,ad
drCity=,state=AL,zip=<null>,phoneHome=<null>,phoneWork=<null>,phone
Mobile=<null>]
```

At this point, the second page in our simple wizard is displayed:

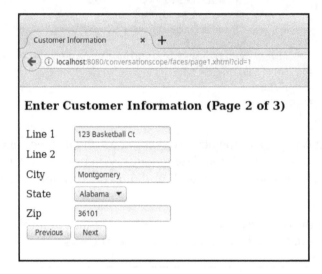

When we click **Next**, we can see that additional fields are populated in our conversation-scoped bean:

```
INFO:
net.ensode.javaee8book.conversationscope.model.Customer@6e1c51b4[fi
rstName=Daniel,middleName=,lastName=Jones,addrLine1=123 Basketball
Ct,addrLine2=,addrCity=Montgomery,state=AL,zip=36101,phoneHome=<nul
l>,phoneWork=<null>,phoneMobile=<null>]
```

When we submit the third page in our wizard (not shown), additional bean properties corresponding to the fields on that page are populated.

When we are at the point where we don't need to keep the customer information in memory anymore, we need to call the end() method on the Conversation bean that was injected into our code. This is exactly what we do in our code before displaying the confirmation page:

```
public String navigateToConfirmationPage() {
        System.out.println(customer);
        conversation.end();
        return "confirmation";
    }
```

After the request to show the confirmation page is completed, our conversation-scoped bean is destroyed, since we invoked the end() method in our injected Conversation class.

We should note that, since the conversation, scope requires an instance of `javax.enterprise.context.Conversation` to be injected, this scope requires that the action in the command button or link used to navigate between pages be an expression resolving to a named bean method. Using static navigation won't work, since the `Conversation` instance won't be injected anywhere.

CDI events

CDI provides event handling facilities. Events allow loosely-coupled communication between different CDI beans. A CDI bean can fire an event, then one or more event listeners handle the event.

Firing CDI events

The following example is a new version of the `CustomerInfoController` class we discussed in the previous section. The class has been modified to fire an event every time the user navigates to a new page:

```
package net.ensode.javaee8book.cdievents.controller;

import java.io.Serializable;
import javax.enterprise.context.Conversation;
import javax.enterprise.context.RequestScoped;
import javax.enterprise.event.Event;
import javax.inject.Inject;
import javax.inject.Named;
import net.ensode.javaee8book.cdievents.event.NavigationInfo;
import net.ensode.javaee8book.cdievents.model.Customer;

@Named
@RequestScoped
public class CustomerInfoController implements Serializable {

    @Inject
    private Conversation conversation;
    @Inject
    private Customer customer;
    @Inject
    private Event<NavigationInfo> navigationInfoEvent;

    public String customerInfoEntry() {
        conversation.begin();
```

```
        NavigationInfo navigationInfo = new NavigationInfo();
        navigationInfo.setPage("1");
        navigationInfo.setCustomer(customer);

        navigationInfoEvent.fire(navigationInfo);
        return "page1";
    }

    public String navigateToPage1() {
        NavigationInfo navigationInfo = new NavigationInfo();
        navigationInfo.setPage("1");
        navigationInfo.setCustomer(customer);

        navigationInfoEvent.fire(navigationInfo);

        return "page1";
    }

    public String navigateToPage2() {
        NavigationInfo navigationInfo = new NavigationInfo();
        navigationInfo.setPage("2");
        navigationInfo.setCustomer(customer);

        navigationInfoEvent.fire(navigationInfo);
        return "page2";
    }

    public String navigateToPage3() {
        NavigationInfo navigationInfo = new NavigationInfo();
        navigationInfo.setPage("3");
        navigationInfo.setCustomer(customer);

        navigationInfoEvent.fire(navigationInfo);
        return "page3";
    }

    public String navigateToConfirmationPage() {
        NavigationInfo navigationInfo = new NavigationInfo();
        navigationInfo.setPage("confirmation");
        navigationInfo.setCustomer(customer);

        navigationInfoEvent.fire(navigationInfo);
        conversation.end();
        return "confirmation";
    }
}
```

As we can see, to create an event, we inject an instance of `javax.enterprise.event.Event`. This class uses generics, therefore, we need to specify its type; the type of the `Event` class can be any class implementing `java.io.Serializable`. In our case, we are passing an instance of a simple POJO we wrote as the type parameter. Our POJO is called `NavigationInfo` and has two properties: one `Customer`type, and a `String` containing the page the user is navigating to. Recall from the previous sections that each of the methods on our `CustomerInfoController` class triggers navigation from one page in the application to another. In this version of the controller, a CDI event is fired every time we navigate to a new page. In each case, we create a new instance of `NavigationInfo`, populate it, then fire the event by invoking the `fire()` method on our instance of `javax.enterprise.event.Event`.

Handling CDI events

To handle CDI events, the CDI bean handling the event needs to implement an `observer` method. The `observer` method accepts a parameter of the type that was used to fire the event, that is, the generic type used to create the event that was fired. In our example, the generic type of our event is an instance of a class named `NavigationInfo`, as can be seen in the declaration of our event in the preceding section. To handle the event, the observer method needs to annotate the corresponding parameter with the `@Observes` annotation, as illustrated in the following example:

```
package net.ensode.javaee8book.cdievents.eventlistener;

import java.io.Serializable;
import javax.enterprise.context.SessionScoped;
import javax.enterprise.event.Observes;
import net.ensode.javaee8book.cdievents.event.NavigationInfo;

@SessionScoped
public class NavigationEventListener implements Serializable {

    public void handleNavigationEvent(
        @Observes NavigationInfo navigationInfo) {
        System.out.println("Navigation event fired");
        System.out.println("Page: " + navigationInfo.getPage());
        System.out.println("Customer: " +
         navigationInfo.getCustomer());
    }
}
```

In this example event handler, the `handleNavigationEvent()` method takes an instance of `NavigationInfo` as a parameter. Notice that this parameter is annotated with `@Observes`; this causes the method to be invoked automatically by CDI every time a `NavigationInfo` type event is fired.

 In our example, we have only one event listener, but in practice, we can have as many event listeners as we need.

Asynchronous events

CDI 2.0 introduced the ability to fire events asynchronously. Firing events asynchronously can help with performance, since various observer methods can be invoked concurrently. Firing an event asynchronously is very similar to firing an event synchronously, the only difference is that, instead of invoking the `fire()` method in our `Event` instance, we invoke its `fireAsync()` method. The following example illustrates how to do this:

```
public class EventSource{
   @Inject Event<MyEvent> myEvent;
   public void fireEvent(){
      myEvent.fireAsync(myEvent);
   }
}
```

Observer methods to handle asynchronous events are identical to their synchronous counterparts.

Event ordering

Another new feature introduced in CDI 2.0 is the ability to specify in which order our `observer` methods handle CDI events. This can be accomplished via the `@Priority` annotation, as illustrated in the following example:

```
import javax.annotation.Priority;
import javax.enterprise.context.SessionScoped;
import javax.enterprise.event.Observes;
import javax.interceptor.Interceptor;

@SessionScoped
public class EventHandler{
    void handleIt (
```

```
    @Observes @Priority(Interceptor.Priority.APPLICATION)
      MyEvent me) {
  //handle the event
    }
  }
```

The `@Priority` annotation takes an argument of type `int`. This argument specifies the priority for the `observer` method. The highest priority is defined by the `APPLICATION` constant defined in the `Interceptor.Priority` class. This is the priority we gave to the `observer` method in our example. Lower priority values take precedence; the default priority is `Interceptor.Priority.APPLICATION + 100`.

Summary

In this chapter, we provided an introduction to Contexts and Dependency Injection (CDI). We covered how JSF pages can access CDI named beans as if they were JSF managed beans. We also covered how CDI makes it easy to inject dependencies into our code via the `@Inject` annotation. Additionally, we explained how we can use qualifiers to determine which specific implementation of a dependency to inject into our code. Finally, we covered all the scopes that a CDI bean can be placed into, which include equivalents to all the JSF scopes, plus an additional two not included in JSF, namely, the conversation scope and the dependent scope.

6
JSON Processing with JSON-P and JSON-B

JSON, or the **JavaScript Object Notation**, is a human-readable data interchange format. As its name implies, JSON is derived from JavaScript. Java EE 7 introduced **JSON-P**, the Java API for JSON processing. Java EE 8 introduced an additional JSON API, namely, the Java API for **JSON Binding (JSON-B)**. In this chapter, we will cover both JSON-P and JSON-B.

JSON-P includes two APIs for processing JSON, the **Model API** and the **Streaming API**, both of which will be covered in this chapter. JSON-B transparently populates Java objects from JSON strings, as well as easily generating JSON strings from Java objects.

In this chapter, we will cover the following topics:

- The JSON-P Model API:
    - Generating JSON data with the Model API
    - Parsing JSON data with the Model API
- The JSON-P Streaming API:
    - Generating JSON data with the Streaming API
    - Parsing JSON data with the Streaming API
- Populating Java objects from JSON with JSON-B
- Generating JSON strings from Java objects with JSON-B

The JSON-P Model API

The JSON-P Model API allows us to generate an in-memory representation of a JSON object. This API is more flexible than the Streaming API discussed later in this chapter, however, it is slower and requires more memory, which can be a concern when handling large volumes of data.

Generating JSON data with the Model API

At the heart of the JSON-P Model API is the `JsonObjectBuilder` class. This class has several overloaded `add()` methods, which can be used to add properties and their corresponding values to generated JSON data.

The following code sample illustrates how to generate JSON data using the Model API:

```
package net.ensode.javaee8book.jsonpobject;

//other imports omitted for brevity.
import javax.inject.Named;
import javax.json.Json;
import javax.json.JsonObject;
import javax.json.JsonReader;
import javax.json.JsonWriter;

@Named
@SessionScoped
public class JsonpBean implements Serializable{

  private String jsonStr;

  @Inject
  private Customer customer;

  public String buildJson() {
    JsonObjectBuilder jsonObjectBuilder =
        Json.createObjectBuilder();
    JsonObject jsonObject = jsonObjectBuilder.
        add("firstName", "Scott").
        add("lastName", "Gosling").
        add("email", "sgosling@example.com").
        build();

    StringWriter stringWriter = new StringWriter();
```

```
try (JsonWriter jsonWriter = Json.createWriter(stringWriter))
{
    jsonWriter.writeObject(jsonObject);
}

setJsonStr(stringWriter.toString());

return "display_json";

    }
    //getters and setters omitted for brevity
}
```

As can be seen in the preceding example, we generate an instance of `JsonObject` by invoking the `add()` method on an instance of `JsonObjectBuilder`. In the preceding example, we see how we can add `String` values to our `JsonObject` by invoking the `add()` method on `JsonObjectBuilder`. The first parameter of the `add()` method is the property name of the generated JSON object, and the second parameter corresponds to the value of said property. The return value of the `add()` method is another instance of `JsonObjectBuilder`, therefore, invocations to the `add()` method can be chained, as shown in the preceding example.

 The preceding example is a CDI-named bean corresponding to a larger JSF application. Other parts of the application are not shown because they are not relevant to the discussion. The complete sample application can be obtained as part of this book's example code download.

Once we have added all the desired properties, we need to invoke the `build()` method of `JsonObjectBuilder`, which returns an instance of a class implementing the `JsonObject` interface.

In many cases, we will want to generate a `String` representation of the JSON object we created so that it can be processed by another process or service. We can do this by creating an instance of a class implementing the `JsonWriter` interface by invoking the static `createWriter()` method of the `Json` class and passing an instance of `StringWriter` as its sole parameter. Once we have an instance of the `JsonWriter` implementation, we need to invoke its `writeObject()` method, passing our `JsonObject` instance as its sole parameter.

At this point, our `StringWriter` instance will have the `String` representation of our JSON object as its value, so invoking its `toString()` method will return a `String` containing our JSON object.

Our specific example will generate a JSON string that looks like this:

```
{"firstName":"Scott","lastName":"Gosling","email":"
sgosling@example.com "}
```

Although, in our example, we added only `String` objects to our JSON object, we are not limited to this type of value; `JsonObjectBuilder` has several overloaded versions of its `add()` method, allowing us to add several different types of values to our JSON objects.

The following table summarizes all of the available versions of the `add()` method:

add(String **name**, BigDecimal **value**)	Adds a `BigDecimal` value to our JSON object.
add(String **name**, BigInteger **value**)	Adds a `BigInteger` value to our JSON object.
add(String **name**, JsonArrayBuilder **value**)	Adds an array to our JSON object. A `JsonArrayBuilder` implementation allows us to create JSON arrays.
add(String **name**, JsonObjectBuilder **value**)	Adds another JSON object to our original JSON object (property values for JSON objects can be other JSON objects). The added `JsonObject` implementation is built from the provided `JsonObjectBuilder` parameter.
add(String **name**, JsonValue **value**)	Adds another JSON object to our original JSON object (property values for JSON objects can be other JSON objects).
add(String **name**, String **value**)	Adds a `String` value to our JSON object.
add(String **name**, boolean **value**)	Adds a `boolean` value to our JSON object.
add(String **name**, double **value**)	Adds a `double` value to our JSON object.
add(String **name**, int **value**)	Adds an `int` value to our JSON object.
add(String **name**, long **value**)	Adds a `long` value to our JSON object.

In all cases, the first parameter of the `add()` method corresponds to the name of the property in our JSON object, and the second parameter corresponds to the value of the property.

Parsing JSON data with the Model API

In the last section, we saw how to generate JSON data from our Java code with the object model API. In this section, we will see how we can read and parse existing JSON data. The following code sample illustrates how to do this:

```java
package net.ensode.javaee8book.jsonpobject;

//other imports omitted
import javax.json.Json;
import javax.json.JsonObject;
import javax.json.JsonReader;
import javax.json.JsonWriter;

@Named
@SessionScoped
public class JsonpBean implements Serializable{

  private String jsonStr;

  @Inject
  private Customer customer;


  public String parseJson() {
    JsonObject jsonObject;
    try (JsonReader jsonReader = Json.createReader(
        new StringReader(jsonStr))) {
          jsonObject = jsonReader.readObject();
        }
    customer.setFirstName(
      jsonObject.getString("firstName"));
    customer.setLastName(
      jsonObject.getString("lastName"));
    customer.setEmail(jsonObject.getString("email"));
    return "display_parsed_json";
  }

  //getters and setters omitted

}
```

To parse an existing JSON string, we need to create a `StringReader` object, passing the `String` object containing the JSON to be parsed as a parameter. We then pass the resulting `StringReader` instance to the static `createReader()` method of the `Json` class. This method invocation will return an instance of `JsonReader`. We can then obtain an instance of `JsonObject` by invoking the `readObject()` method on it.

In the preceding example, we used the `getString()` method to obtain the values of all properties in our JSON object. The first and only argument for this method is the name of the property we wish to retrieve. Unsurprisingly, the return value is the value of the property.

In addition to the `getString()` method, there are several other similar methods to obtain values of other types. The following table summarizes these methods:

`get(Object key)`	Retrieves an instance of a class implementing the `JsonValue` interface.
`getBoolean(String name)`	Retrieves a `boolean` value corresponding to the given key.
`getInt(String name)`	Retrieves a `int` value corresponding to the given key.
`getJsonArray(String name)`	Retrieves the instance of a class implementing the `JsonArray` interface corresponding to the given key.
`getJsonNumber(String name)`	Retrieves the instance of a class implementing the `JsonNumber` interface corresponding to the given key.
`getJsonObject(String name)`	Retrieves the instance of a class implementing the `JsonObject` interface corresponding to the given key.
`getJsonString(String name)`	Retrieves the instance of a class implementing the `JsonString` interface corresponding to the given key.
`getString(String name)`	Retrieves a `String` corresponding to the given key.

In all cases, the `String` parameter of the method corresponds to the key name, and the return value is the JSON property value we wish to retrieve.

The JSON-P Streaming API

The JSON-P Streaming API allows sequential reading of a JSON object from a stream (a subclass of `java.io.OutputStream` or a subclass of `java.io.Writer`). It is faster and more memory efficient than the Model API, however, the trade-off is that it is more limited, since the JSON data needs to be read sequentially and we cannot access specific JSON properties directly the way the Model API allows.

Generating JSON data with the Streaming API

The JSON Streaming API has a `JsonGenerator` class that we can use to generate JSON data and write it to a stream. This class has several overloaded `write()` methods, which can be used to add properties and their corresponding values to the generated JSON data.

The following code sample illustrates how to generate JSON data using the Streaming API:

```
package net.ensode.javaee8book.jsonpstreaming;

//other imports omitted
import javax.json.Json;
import javax.json.stream.JsonGenerator;
import javax.json.stream.JsonParser;
import javax.json.stream.JsonParser.Event;

@Named
@SessionScoped
public class JsonpBean implements Serializable {

  private String jsonStr;

  @Inject
  private Customer customer;

  public String buildJson() {
    StringWriter stringWriter = new StringWriter();
    try (JsonGenerator jsonGenerator =
      Json.createGenerator(stringWriter)) {
      jsonGenerator.writeStartObject().
        write("firstName", "Larry").
        write("lastName", "Gates").
        write("email", "lgates@example.com").
        writeEnd();
    }
    setJsonStr(stringWriter.toString());
```

```
            return "display_json";
    }

    //getters and setters omitted
    }
```

We create an instance of `JsonGenerator` by invoking the `createGenerator()` static method of the `Json` class. The JSON-P API provides two overloaded versions of this method: one takes an instance of a class that extends `java.io.Writer` (such as `StringWriter`, which we used in our example), and the other one takes an instance of a class that extends `java.io.OutputStream`.

Before we can start adding properties to the generated JSON stream, we need to invoke the `writeStartObject()` method on `JsonGenerator`. This method writes the JSON start object character (represented by an opening curly brace ("{") in JSON strings), and returns another instance of `JsonGenerator`, allowing us to chain write() invocations to add properties to our JSON stream.

The `write()` method on `JsonGenerator` allows us to add properties to the JSON stream we are generating. Its first parameter is a `String` corresponding to the name of the property we are adding, and the second parameter is the value of the property.

In our example, we are adding only `String` values to the JSON stream we are creating, however, we are not limited to Strings; the JSON-P Streaming API provides several overloaded `write()` methods that allow us to add several different types of data to our JSON stream. The following table summarizes all of the available versions of the `write()` method:

`write(String name, BigDecimal value)`	Writes a `BigDecimal` value to our JSON stream.
`write(String name, BigInteger value)`	Writes a `BigInteger` value to our JSON stream
`write(String name, JsonValue value)`	Writes a JSON object to our JSON stream (property values for JSON streams can be other JSON objects)
`write(String name, String value)`	Writes a `String` value to our JSON stream
`write(String name, boolean value)`	Writes a `boolean` value to our JSON stream
`write(String name, double value)`	Writes a `double` value to our JSON stream

| write(String name, int value) | Writes an int value to our JSON stream |
| write(String name, long value) | Writes a long value to our JSON stream |

In all cases, the first parameter of the write() method corresponds to the name of the property we are adding to our JSON stream, and the second parameter corresponds to the value of the property.

Once we are done adding properties to our JSON stream, we need to invoke the writeEnd() method on JsonGenerator. This method adds the JSON end object character (represented by a closing curly brace (}) in JSON strings).

At this point, our stream or reader is populated with the JSON data we generated. What we do with it depends on our application logic. In our example, we simply invoked the toString() method of our StringReader to obtain the String representation of the JSON data we created.

Parsing JSON data with the Streaming API

In this section, we will cover how to parse the JSON data we receive from a stream. Please refer to the following code:

```
package net.ensode.javaee8book.jsonpstreaming;

//other imports omitted
import javax.json.Json;
import javax.json.stream.JsonGenerator;
import javax.json.stream.JsonParser;
import javax.json.stream.JsonParser.Event;

@Named
@SessionScoped
public class JsonpBean implements Serializable {

  private String jsonStr;

  @Inject
  private Customer customer;

  public String parseJson() {

    StringReader stringReader = new StringReader(jsonStr);
```

```java
        JsonParser jsonParser = Json.createParser(stringReader);

        Map<String, String> keyValueMap = new HashMap<>();
        String key = null;
        String value = null;

        while (jsonParser.hasNext()) {
            JsonParser.Event event = jsonParser.next();

            if (event.equals(Event.KEY_NAME)) {
                key = jsonParser.getString();
            } else if (event.equals(Event.VALUE_STRING)) {
                value = jsonParser.getString();
            }

            keyValueMap.put(key, value);
        }

        customer.setFirstName(keyValueMap.get("firstName"));
        customer.setLastName(keyValueMap.get("lastName"));
        customer.setEmail(keyValueMap.get("email"));

        return "display_parsed_json";
    }

    //getters and setters omitted

}
```

The first thing we need to do to read JSON data using the Streaming API is to create an instance of `JsonParser` by invoking the static `createJsonParser()` method on the `Json` class. There are two overloaded versions of the `createJsonParser()` method: one takes an instance of a class that extends `java.io.InputStream`, the other one takes an instance of a class that extends `java.io.Reader`. In our example, we use the latter, passing an instance of `java.io.StringReader`, which is a subclass of `java.io.Reader`.

The next step is to loop through the JSON data to obtain the data to be parsed. We can achieve this by invoking the `hasNext()` method on `JsonParser`, which returns true if there is more data to be read, and false otherwise.

We then need to read the next piece of data in our stream. The `JsonParser.next()` method returns an instance of `JsonParser.Event`, which indicates the type of data that we just read. In our example, we check only for key names (that is, `firstName`, `lastName`, and `email`), and the corresponding string values. We check for the type of data we just read by comparing the event returned by `JsonParser.next()` against several values defined in the `Event` enum defined in `JsonParser`.

The following table summarizes all of the possible events that can be returned from `JsonParser.next()`:

`Event.START_OBJECT`	Indicates the start of a JSON object.
`Event.END_OBJECT`	Indicates the end of a JSON object.
`Event.START_ARRAY`	Indicates the start of an array.
`Event.END_ARRAY`	Indicates the end of an array.
`Event.KEY_NAME`	Indicates the name of a JSON property was read; we can obtain the key name by invoking `getString()` on `JsonParser`.
`Event.VALUE_TRUE`	Indicates that a Boolean value of `true` was read.
`Event.VALUE_FALSE`	Indicates that a Boolean value of `false` was read.
`Event.VALUE_NULL`	Indicates that a `null` value was read.
`Event.VALUE_NUMBER`	Indicates that a `numeric` value was read.
`Event.VALUE_STRING`	Indicates that a `string` value was read.

As shown in the example, `String` values can be retrieved by invoking `getString()` on `JsonParser`. Numeric values can be retrieved in several different formats; the following table summarizes the methods in `JsonParser` that can be used to retrieve numeric values:

`getInt()`	Retrieves the numeric value as an `int`.
`getLong()`	Retrieves the numeric value as a `long`.
`getBigDecimal()`	Retrieves the numeric value as an instance of `java.math.BigDecimal`.

`JsonParser` also provides a convenience `isIntegralNumber()` method, which returns `true` if the numeric value can be safely cast to an `int` or a `long`.

What we do with the values we obtain from the stream depends on our application logic. In our example, we place them on a `Map`, then use said `Map` to populate a Java class.

JSON pointer

JSON-P 1.1, introduced in Java EE 8, introduces support for JSON Pointer. JSON Pointer is an **Internet Engineering Task Force** (**IETF**) standard that defines a string syntax to identify a specific value within a JSON document, similar to what XPath provides for XML documents.

The syntax for JSON Pointer is straightforward, for example, suppose we have the following JSON document:

```
{
  "dateOfBirth": "1997-03-03",
  "firstName": "David",
  "lastName": "Heffelfinger",
  "middleName": "Raymond",
  "salutation": "Mr"
}
```

If we would like to obtain the value of the `lastName` property of the document, the JSON Pointer expression to use would be `"/lastName"`.

If our JSON document consisted of an array, then we would have to prefix the property with the index in the array, for example, to obtain the `lastName` property of the second element in the following JSON array:

```
[
  {
    "dateOfBirth": "1997-01-01",
    "firstName": "David",
    "lastName": "Delabassee",
    "salutation": "Mr"
  },
  {
    "dateOfBirth": "1997-03-03",
    "firstName": "David",
    "lastName": "Heffelfinger",
    "middleName": "Raymond",
    "salutation": "Mr"
  }
]
```

The JSON Pointer expression to do so would be `"/1/lastName"`. The `"/1"` at the beginning of the expression refers to the element index in the array. Just as in Java, JSON arrays are 0 indexed, therefore, in this example, we are obtaining the value of the `lastName` property in the second element of the array. Let's now look at an example of how we would use the new JSON-P JSON Pointer API to perform this task:

```
package net.ensode.javaee8book.jsonpointer;
//imports omitted

@Path("jsonpointer")
public class JsonPointerDemoService {

  private String jsonString; //initialization omitted

  @GET
  public String jsonPointerDemo() {
    initializeJsonString(); //method body omitted for brevity
    JsonReader jsonReader = Json.createReader
        (new StringReader(jsonString));
    JsonArray jsonArray = jsonReader.readArray();
    JsonPointer jsonPointer = Json.createPointer("/1/lastName");
    return jsonPointer.getValue(jsonArray).toString();
  }
}
```

The preceding code sample is a RESTful web service written using Java EE's JAX-RS API (see `Chapter 10`, *RESTful Web Services with JAX-RS* for details). In order to read property values from a JSON document, we first need to create an instance of `javax.json.JsonReader` by invoking the static `createReader()` method on `javax.json.Json`. The `createReader()` method takes an instance of any class implementing the `java.io.Reader` interface as an argument. In our example, we are creating a new instance of `java.io.StringReader` on the fly, and passing our JSON string as a parameter to its constructor.

 There is an overloaded version of `JSON.createReader()` that takes an instance of any class implementing `java.io.InputStream`.

In our example, our JSON document consists of an array of objects, therefore, we populate an instance of `javax.json.JsonArray` by invoking the `readArray()` method on the `JsonReader` object we created (if our JSON document had consisted of a single JSON object, we would have invoked `JsonReader.readObject()` instead).

Now that we have populated our `JsonArray` variable, we create an instance of `javax.json.JsonPointer` and initialize it with the JSON Pointer expression we want to use to obtain the value we are searching for. Remember that we are looking for the value of the `lastName` property in the second element of the array, therefore, the appropriate JSON Pointer expression is `/1/lastName`.

Now that we have created an instance of `JsonPointer` with the appropriate JSON Pointer expression, we simply invoke its `getValue()` method, passing our `JsonArray` object as a parameter, then invoke `toString()` on the result. The return value of this invocation will be the value of the `lastName` property on the JSON document ("Heffelfinger", in our example).

JSON Patch

JSON-P 1.1 also introduced support for JSON Patch, another **Internet Engineering Task Force** standard, this one providing a series of operations that can be applied to a JSON document. JSON Patch allows us to perform partial updates on a JSON object.

The following operations are supported by JSON Patch:

JSON Patch Operation	Description
add	Adds an element to a JSON document.
remove	Removes an element from a JSON document.
replace	Replaces a value in a JSON document with a new value.
move	Moves a value in a JSON document from its current location in the document to a new position.
copy	Copies a value in a JSON document to a new location in the document.
test	Verifies that the value in a specific location in a JSON document is equal to the specified value.

JSON-P supports all of the preceding JSON Patch operations, which rely on JSON Pointer expressions to locate the source and target locations in JSON documents.

The following example illustrates how we can use JSON Patch with JSON-P 1.1:

```
package net.ensode.javaee8book.jsonpatch;

//imports omitted for brevity

@Path("jsonpatch")
public class JsonPatchDemoService {

  private String jsonString;

  @GET
  public Response jsonPatchDemo() {
    initializeJsonString(); //method declaration omitted
    JsonReader jsonReader = Json.createReader(
        new StringReader(jsonString));
    JsonArray jsonArray = jsonReader.readArray();
    JsonPatch jsonPatch = Json.createPatchBuilder()
            .replace("/1/dateOfBirth", "1977-01-01")
            .build();
    JsonArray modifiedJsonArray =jsonPatch.apply(jsonArray);

    return Response.ok(modifiedJsonArray.toString(),
    MediaType.APPLICATION_JSON).build();
  }
}
```

In this example, let's assume we are dealing with the same JSON document we used in our previous example: an array of two individual JSON objects, each with a dateOfBirth property (among other properties).

In our example, we create an instance of JsonArray, as before, then modify the dateOfBirth of the second element in the array. In order to do this, we create an instance of javax.json.JsonPatchBuilder via the static createPatchBuilder() method in the javax.json.Json class. In our example, we are replacing the value of one of the properties with a new value. We use the replace() method of our JsonPatch instance to accomplish this; the first argument in the method is a JSON Pointer expression indicating the location of the property we are going to modify, the second argument is the new value for the property. As its name implies JsonPatchBuilder follows the Builder design pattern, meaning that most of its methods return another instance of JsonPatchBuilder; this allows us to chain method calls on the resulting instances of JsonPatchBuilder (in our example, we are performing only one operation, but this doesn't have to be the case).

Once we are done specifying the operation(s) to perform on our JSON object, we create an instance of `javax.json.JsonPatch` by invoking the `build()` method on `JsonPatchBuilder`.

Once we have created the patch, we apply it to our JSON object (an instance of `JsonArray`, in our example), by invoking its `patch()` method, passing the JSON object as a parameter.

In our example of how to replace the value of a JSON property with another via JSON Patch support in JSON-P 1.1, JSON-P supports all operations currently supported by JSON Patch. The API is straightforward. For details on how to use other JSON Patch operations with JSON-P, consult the Java EE 8 API documentation at `https://javaee.github.io/javaee-spec/javadocs/`.

Populating Java objects from JSON with JSON-B

A common programming task is to populate Java objects from JSON strings. It is such a common tasks that several libraries have been created to transparently populate Java objects from JSON, freeing application developers from having to manually code this functionality. There are some non-standard Java libraries that accomplish this task, such as Jackson (`https://github.com/FasterXML/jackson`), JSON-simple (`https://github.com/fangyidong/json-simple`), and Gson (`https://github.com/google/gson`). Java EE 8 introduces a new API providing this functionality, namely the Java API for JSON Binding (JSON-B). In this section, we will cover how to transparently populate a Java object from a JSON string.

The following example shows a RESTful web service written using the Java API for RESTful Web Services (JAX-RS). The service responds to HTTP POST requests in its `addCustomer()` method. This method takes a `String` as a parameter and this string is expected to contain valid JSON. Please refer to the following code:

```
package net.ensode.javaee8book.jaxrs21example.service;

import net.ensode.javaee8book.jaxrs21example.dto.Customer;
import java.util.logging.Level;
import java.util.logging.Logger;
import javax.json.bind.Jsonb;
import javax.json.bind.JsonbBuilder;
import javax.ws.rs.POST;
import javax.ws.rs.Consumes;
import javax.ws.rs.Path;
```

```
import javax.ws.rs.core.MediaType;
import javax.ws.rs.core.Response;

@Path("/customercontroller")
public class CustomerControllerService {

private static final Logger LOG =
Logger.getLogger(CustomerControllerService.class.getName());

@POST
@Consumes(MediaType.APPLICATION_JSON)
public Response addCustomer(String customerJson) {
  Response response;
  Jsonb jsonb = JsonbBuilder.create();

  Customer customer = jsonb.fromJson(customerJson,
      Customer.class);
  LOG.log(Level.INFO, "Customer object populated from JSON");
  LOG.log(Level.INFO, String.format("%s %s %s %s %s",
  customer.getSalutation(),
  customer.getFirstName(),
  customer.getMiddleName(),
  customer.getLastName(),
  customer.getDateOfBirth()));
  response = Response.ok("{}").build();
  return response;
  }


}
```

The JSON-B implementation provided by our application server provides an instance of a class implementing the JsonbBuilder interface. This class provides a static create() method that we can use to obtain an instance of Jsonb.

Once we have an instance of Jsonb, we can use it to parse a JSON string and automatically populate a Java object. This is done via its fromJson() method. The fromJson() method takes a String containing the JSON data we need to parse as its first parameter, and the type of the object we wish to populate as its second parameter. In our example, we are populating a simple Customer class containing fields such as firstName, middleName, lastName, and dateOfBirth. JSON-B will look for JSON property names matching the property names in the Java object and automatically populate the Java object with the corresponding JSON properties. It couldn't be more simple than that.

Once we have populated our Java object, we can do whatever we need to do with it. In our example, we simply log the properties of the Java object to verify that it was populated correctly.

Generating JSON strings from Java objects with JSON-B

In addition to populating Java objects from JSON data, JSON-B can also generate JSON strings from Java objects. The following example illustrates how to do this:

```
package net.ensode.javaee8book.jsonbjavatojson.service;

//imports omitted for brevity

@Path("/customersearchcontroller")
public class CustomerSearchControllerService {
  private final List<Customer> customerList = new ArrayList<>();

  @GET
  @Path("{firstName}")
  public Response getCustomerByFirstName(@PathParam("firstName")
  String firstName) {
    List<Customer> filteredCustomerList;
    String jsonString;
    initializeCustomerList(); //method declaration omitted

    Jsonb jsonb = JsonbBuilder.create();

    filteredCustomerList = customerList.stream().filter(
        customer -> customer.getFirstName().equals(firstName)).
        collect(Collectors.toList());

    jsonString = jsonb.toJson(filteredCustomerList);

    return Response.ok(jsonString).build();
  }
}
```

In this example, we are converting a `List` of `Customer` objects to JSON.

 We chose a `List` for the example to illustrate that JSON-B supports this functionality, but of course, we could also convert a single object to its JSON representation.

Just as before, we create an instance of `javax.json.bind.Jsonb` by invoking the static `javax.json.bind.JsonbBuilder.create()` method. Once we have our `Jsonb` instance, we simply invoke its `toJson()` method to convert the list of objects to its equivalent JSON representation.

Summary

In this chapter, we covered the Java API for JSON Processing (JSON-P). We illustrated how to generate and parse JSON data via JSON-P's model and Streaming APIs. Additionally, we covered new JSON-P 1.1 features, such as support for JSON Pointer and JSON Patch. Finally, we covered how to seamlessly populate Java objects from JSON, and how to easily generate JSON strings from Java objects via the new JSON-B API.

7
WebSocket

Traditionally, web applications have been developed using the request/response model followed by the HTTP protocol. In this traditional request/response model, the request is always initiated by the client, then the server sends a response back to the client.

There has never been a way for the server to send data to the client independently, that is, without having to wait for a request, until now. The WebSocket protocol allows fully duplex, two-way communication between the client (browser) and the server.

Java EE 7 introduced the Java API for WebSocket, which allows us to develop WebSocket endpoints in Java.

In this chapter, we will cover the following topics:

- Developing WebSocket server endpoints
- Developing WebSocket clients in JavaScript
- Developing WebSocket clients in Java

Developing a WebSocket server endpoint

There are two ways we can implement a WebSocket server endpoint via the Java API for WebSocket. We can either develop an endpoint programmatically, in which case we need to extend the `javax.websocket.Endpoint` class, or by decorating **Plain Old Java Objects (POJOs)** with WebSocket specific annotations. These two approaches are very similar, therefore, we will only be discussing the annotation approach in detail, and will briefly explain how to develop WebSocket server endpoints programmatically later in the chapter.

In this chapter, we will develop a simple web-based chat application, taking full advantage of the Java API for WebSocket.

Developing an annotated WebSocket server endpoint

The following Java class illustrates how we can develop a WebSocket server endpoint by annotating a Java class:

```java
package net.ensode.javaeebook.websocketchat.serverendpoint;

import java.io.IOException;
import java.util.logging.Level;
import java.util.logging.Logger;
import javax.websocket.OnClose;
import javax.websocket.OnMessage;
import javax.websocket.OnOpen;
import javax.websocket.Session;
import javax.websocket.server.ServerEndpoint;

@ServerEndpoint("/websocketchat")
public class WebSocketChatEndpoint {

    private static final Logger LOG =
    Logger.getLogger(WebSocketChatEndpoint.class.getName());

    @OnOpen
    public void connectionOpened() {
        LOG.log(Level.INFO, "connection opened");
    }

    @OnMessage
    public synchronized void processMessage(Session session, String
        message) {
        LOG.log(Level.INFO, "received message: {0}", message);

        try {
            for (Session sess : session.getOpenSessions()) {
                if (sess.isOpen()) {
                    sess.getBasicRemote().sendText(message);
                }
            }
        } catch (IOException ioe) {
            LOG.log(Level.SEVERE, ioe.getMessage());
        }
    }

    @OnClose
    public void connectionClosed() {
```

```
                        LOG.log(Level.INFO, "connection closed");
            }


        }
```

The class level `@ServerEndpoint` annotation indicates that the class is a WebSocket server endpoint. The **URI (Uniform Resource Identifier)** of the server endpoint is the value specified between the parenthesis following the annotation (`"/websocketchat"`, in this example). WebSocket clients will use this URI to communicate with our endpoint.

The `@OnOpen` annotation is used to decorate a method that needs to be executed whenever a WebSocket connection is opened from any of the clients. In our example, we are simply sending some output to the server log, but of course any valid server-side Java code can be placed here.

Any method annotated with the `@OnMessage` annotation will be invoked whenever our server endpoint receives a message from any of the clients. Since we are developing a chat application, our code simply broadcasts the message it receives to all connected clients.

In our example, the `processMessage()` method is annotated with `@OnMessage`, and it takes two parameters: an instance of a class implementing the `javax.websocket.Session` interface, and a `String` containing the message that was received. Since we are developing a chat application, our WebSocket server endpoint simply broadcasts the received message to all connected clients.

The `getOpenSessions()` method of the `Session` interface returns a set of `Session` objects representing all open sessions. We iterate through this set to broadcast the received message back to all connected clients by invoking the `getBasicRemote()` method on each `Session` instance, then invoking the `sendText()` method on the resulting `RemoteEndpoint.Basic` implementation returned by this call.

The `getOpenSessions()` method on the `Session` interface returns all the open sessions at the time the method was invoked. It is possible for one or more of the sessions to have closed after the method was invoked, therefore, it is recommended to invoke the `isOpen()` method on a `Session` implementation before attempting to send data back to the client.

Finally, we need to decorate a method with the `@OnClose` annotation if we need to handle the event when a client disconnects from the server endpoint. In our example, we simply log a message to the server log.

There is one additional annotation that we didn't use in our example. The `@OnError` annotation is used to decorate a method that needs to be invoked in the event of an error in sending or receiving data to or from the client.

As we can see, developing an annotated WebSocket server endpoint is straightforward; we simply need to add a few annotations and the application server will invoke our annotated methods as necessary.

If we wish to develop a WebSocket server endpoint programmatically, we need to write a Java class that extends `javax.websocket.Endpoint`. This class has `onOpen()`, `onClose()`, and `onError()` methods, which are called at appropriate times during the endpoint's lifecycle. There is no method equivalent to the `@OnMessage` annotation to handle incoming messages from clients; the `addMessageHandler()` method needs to be invoked in the `Session`, passing an instance of a class implementing the `javax.websocket.MessageHandler` interface (or one of its subinterfaces) as its sole parameter.

In general, it is easier and more straightforward to develop annotated WebSocket endpoints, as opposed to their programmatic counterparts, therefore, we recommend the annotated approach whenever possible.

Developing WebSocket clients

Most WebSocket clients are implemented as web pages taking advantage of the JavaScript WebSocket API. We will cover how to do this in the next section.

The Java API for WebSocket provides a client API that allows us to develop WebSocket clients as standalone Java applications. We will be covering this capability later in the chapter.

Developing JavaScript client-side WebSocket code

In this section, we will cover how to develop client-side JavasScript code to interact with the WebSocket endpoint we developed in the previous section.

The client page for our WebSocket example is implemented as a JSF page using HTML5 friendly markup (as explained in `Chapter 2`, *JavaServer Faces*).

Our client page consists of a text area, where we can see what users of our application are saying (it is, after all, a chat application), and an input text we can use to send a message to other users:

The markup for our client page looks like this:

```
<?xml version="1.0" encoding="UTF-8"?>
<!DOCTYPE html>
<html xmlns="http://www.w3.org/1999/xhtml"
xmlns:jsf="http://xmlns.jcp.org/jsf">
<head>
<title>WebSocket Chat</title>
<meta name="viewport" content="width=device-width"/>
<script type="text/javascript">
var websocket;
function init() {
websocket = new WebSocket(
'ws://localhost:8080/websocketchat/websocketchat');

websocket.onopen = function(event) {
websocketOpen(event)
};
websocket.onmessage = function(event) {
websocketMessage(event)
};
websocket.onerror = function(event) {
websocketError(event)
```

```
};

}

function websocketOpen(event) {
console.log("webSocketOpen invoked");
}

function websocketMessage(event) {
console.log("websocketMessage invoked");
document.getElementById('chatwindow').value += '\r' +
event.data;
}

function websocketError(event) {
console.log("websocketError invoked");
}

function sendMessage() {
var userName =
document.getElementById('userName').value;
var msg =
document.getElementById('chatinput').value;

websocket.send(userName + ": " + msg);
}

function closeConnection(){
websocket.close();
}

window.addEventListener("load", init);
</script>
</head>
<body>
<form jsf:prependId="false">
<input type="hidden" id="userName"
value="#{user.userName}"/>
<table border="0">
<tbody>
<tr>
<td>
<label for="chatwindow">
Chat Window
</label>
</td>
<td>
<textArea id="chatwindow" rows="10"/>
```

```
</td>
</tr>
<tr>
<td>
<label for="chatinput">
Type Something Here
</label>
</td>
<td>
<input type="text" id="chatinput"/>
<input id="sendBtn" type="button" value="Send"
 onclick="sendMessage()"/>
</td>
</tr>
<tr>
<td></td>
<td>
<input type="button" id="exitBtn" value="Exit"
 onclick="closeConnection()"/>
</td>
</tr>
</tbody>
</table>
</form>
</body>
</html>
```

The last line of our JavaScript code (`window.addEventListener("load", init);`) sets our JavaScript `init()` function to be executed as soon as the page loads.

In the `init()` function, we initialize a new JavaScript WebSocket object, passing the URI of our server endpoint as a parameter. This lets our JavaScript code know the location of our server endpoint.

The JavaScript WebSocket object has a number of function types, used to handle different events, such as opening the connection, receiving a message, and handling errors. We need to set these types to our own JavaScript functions so that we can handle these events, which is what we do in our `init()` function, right after invoking the constructor for the JavaScript WebSocket object. In our example, the functions we assigned to the WebSocket object simply delegate their functionality to standalone JavaScript functions.

Our `websocketOpen()` function is called whenever the WebSocket connection is opened. In our example, we simply send a message to the browser's JavaScript console.

Our `webSocketMessage()` function is invoked whenever the browser receives a web socket message from our WebSocket endpoint. In our example, we update the contents of the text area with the ID `chatWindow` with the contents of the message.

Our `websocketError()` function is called whenever there is a WebSocket related error. In our example, we simply send a message to the browser's JavaScript console.

Our JavaScript `sendMessage()` function sends a message to the WebSocket server endpoint, containing both the username and the contents of the text input with the ID `chatinput`. This function is called when the user clicks on the button with the ID `sendBtn`.

Our `closeConnection()` JavaScript function closes the connection to our WebSocket server endpoint. This function is called when the user clicks on the button with the ID `exitBtn`.

As we can see from this example, writing client-side JavaScript code to interact with WebSocket endpoints is fairly straightforward.

Developing WebSocket clients in Java

Although developing web-based WebSocket clients is currently the most common way of developing WebSocket clients, the Java API for WebSocket provides a client API we can use to develop WebSocket clients in Java.

In this section, we will be developing a simple WebSocket client using the client API of the Java API for WebSocket. The final product looks like this:

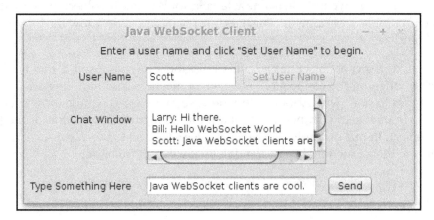

However, we won't be covering the GUI code (developed using the Swing framework), since it is not relevant to the discussion. The complete code for the example, including the GUI code, can be downloaded from the Packt Publishing website.

Just as with WebSocket server endpoints, Java WebSocket clients can be developed either programmatically or by using annotations. Once again, we will cover only the annotation approach; developing a programmatic client is very similar to the way programmatic server endpoints are developed, which is to say, programmatic clients must extend `javax.websocket.Endpoint` and override the appropriate methods.

Without further ado, here is the code for our Java WebSocket client:

```java
package net.ensode.websocketjavaclient;

import java.io.IOException;
import java.net.URI;
import java.net.URISyntaxException;
import javax.websocket.ClientEndpoint;
import javax.websocket.CloseReason;
import javax.websocket.ContainerProvider;
import javax.websocket.DeploymentException;
import javax.websocket.OnClose;
import javax.websocket.OnError;
import javax.websocket.OnMessage;
import javax.websocket.OnOpen;
import javax.websocket.Session;
import javax.websocket.WebSocketContainer;

@ClientEndpoint
public class WebSocketClient {

    private String userName;
    private Session session;
    private final WebSocketJavaClientFrame
webSocketJavaClientFrame;

    public WebSocketClient(WebSocketJavaClientFrame
        webSocketJavaClientFrame) {
        this.webSocketJavaClientFrame = webSocketJavaClientFrame;

        try {
            WebSocketContainer webSocketContainer =
                ContainerProvider.getWebSocketContainer();
            webSocketContainer.connectToServer(this,
                new URI(
        "ws://localhost:8080/websocketchat/websocketchat"));
```

```
                } catch (DeploymentException |
                        IOException | URISyntaxException ex) {
                ex.printStackTrace();
            }

        }

    @OnOpen
    public void onOpen(Session session) {
        System.out.println("onOpen() invoked");
        this.session = session;
    }

    @OnClose
    public void onClose(CloseReason closeReason) {
        System.out.println("Connection closed, reason: "
                + closeReason.getReasonPhrase());
    }

    @OnError
    public void onError(Throwable throwable) {
        System.out.println("onError() invoked");
        throwable.printStackTrace();
    }

    @OnMessage
    public void onMessage(String message, Session session) {
        System.out.println("onMessage() invoked");
          webSocketJavaClientFrame.getChatWindowTextArea().
            setText(
            webSocketJavaClientFrame.getChatWindowTextArea().
            getText() + "\n" + message);
    }

    public void sendMessage(String message) {
        try {
            System.out.println("sendMessage() invoked, message = "
              + message);
            session.getBasicRemote().sendText(userName + ": " +
            message);
        } catch (IOException ex) {
            ex.printStackTrace();
        }
    }

    public String getUserName() {
        return userName;
    }
```

```
        public void setUserName(String userName) {
            this.userName = userName;
        }

    }
```

The class-level `@ClientEndPoint` annotation denotes our class as a WebSocket client; all Java WebSocket clients must be annotated with this annotation.

The code to establish a connection to the WebSocket server endpoint is in our class constructor. First, we need to invoke `ContainerProvider.getWebSocketContainer()` to obtain an instance of `javax.websocket.WebSocketContainer`. We then establish the connection by invoking the `connectToServer()` method on our `WebSocketContainer` instance, passing a class annotated with `@ClientEndpoint` as the first parameter (in our example, we use this because the connection code is inside our WebSocket Java client code), and a URI object containing the WebSocket server endpoint URI as the second parameter.

After the connection is established, we are ready to respond to WebSocket events. Alert readers may have noticed that the exact same annotations we used to develop our server endpoint are used again in our client code.

Any method annotated with the `@OnOpen` annotation will be invoked automatically when the connection to the WebSocket server endpoint is established. The method must return void and can have an optional parameter of type `javax.websocket.Session`. In our example, we send some output to the console and initialize a class variable with the `Session` instance we received as a parameter.

Methods annotated with the `@OnClose` annotation are invoked whenever the WebSocket session is closed. The annotated method can have an optional `javax.websocket.Session` parameter and an optional `CloseReason`parameter. In our example, we chose to use only the `CloseReason` optional parameter, since this class has a handy `getReasonPhrase()` method that provides a short explanation of why the session was closed.

The `@OnError` annotation is used to decorate any methods that will be called when an error occurs. Methods annotated with `@OnError` must have a `java.lang.Throwable` parameter (the parent class of `java.lang.Exception`), and can have an optional `type  session` parameter. In our example, we simply send the stack trace of the `Throwable` parameter to `stderr`.

Methods annotated with @OnMessage are invoked whenever an incoming WebSocket message is received. @OnMessage methods can have different parameters depending on the type of message received and how we wish to handle it. In our example, we used the most common case, receiving a text message. In this particular case, we need a String parameter, which will hold the contents of the message, and an optional Session parameter.

 Refer to the JavaDoc documentation for @OnMessage at http://docs.oracle.com/javaee/7/api/javax/websocket/OnMessage.html for information on how to handle other types of messages.

In our example, we simply update the **Chat Window** text area, appending the received message to its contents.

To send a WebSocket message, we invoke the getBasicRemote() method on our Session instance, then invoke the sendText() method on the resulting R.emoteEndpoint. A basic implementation is returned by this call (if this looks familiar, it is because we did the exact same thing in the WebSocket server endpoint code). In our example, we do this in the sendMessage() method.

Additional information about the Java API for WebSocket

In this chapter, we covered the bulk of the functionality provided by the Java API for WebSocket. For additional information, refer to the user guide for Tyrus, the Java API for WebSocket reference implementation, at https://tyrus.java.net/documentation/1.3.1/user-guide.html.

Summary

In this chapter, we covered the Java API for WebSocket, a Java EE API for developing WebSocket server endpoints and clients. We first saw how to develop WebSocket server endpoints by taking advantage of the Java API for WebSocket. Then, we covered how to develop web-based WebSocket clients using JavaScript. Finally, we explained how to develop WebSocket client applications in Java.

8
Java Messaging Service

The **Java Messaging API** (**JMS**) provides a mechanism for Java EE applications to send messages to each other. Java EE 7 introduced JMS 2.0, which greatly simplified the development of applications involving messaging functionality.

JMS applications do not communicate directly; instead, message producers send messages to a destination, and message consumers receive messages from that destination.

A message destination is a message queue when the **Point-To-Point** (**PTP**) messaging domain is used, or a message topic when the Publish/Subscribe (pub/sub) messaging domain is used.

In this chapter, we will cover the following topics:

- Working with message queues
- Working with message topics

Most application servers need to be configured in order for JMS applications to work properly. The Appendix, *Configuring and deploying to GlassFish*, includes instructions for configuring GlassFish. Consult your application server documentation for instructions on configuring other Java EE 8 compliant application servers.

Message queues

As we mentioned earlier, Message queues are used when our JMS code uses the Point-To-Point (PTP) Messaging Domain. For the PTP Messaging Domain, there is usually one message producer and one message consumer. The message producer and the message consumer don't need to be running concurrently in order to communicate. The messages placed in the message queue by the message producer will stay in the message queue until the message consumer executes and requests the messages from the queue.

Sending messages to a message queue

The following example illustrates how to add messages to a message queue:

```java
package net.ensode.javaee8book.jmsptpproducer;

import java.util.logging.Level;
import java.util.logging.Logger;
import javax.annotation.Resource;
import javax.enterprise.context.RequestScoped;
import javax.inject.Named;
import javax.jms.ConnectionFactory;
import javax.jms.JMSContext;
import javax.jms.JMSProducer;
import javax.jms.Queue;

@Named
@RequestScoped
public class MessageSender {

    @Resource
    private ConnectionFactory connectionFactory;
    @Resource(mappedName = "jms/JavaEE8BookQueue")
    private Queue queue;

    private static final Logger LOG =
        Logger.getLogger(MessageSender.class.getName());

    public void produceMessages() {

        JMSContext jmsContext = connectionFactory.createContext();
        JMSProducer jmsProducer = jmsContext.createProducer();

        String msg1 = "Testing, 1, 2, 3. Can you hear me?";
        String msg2 = "Do you copy?";
```

```
String msg3 = "Good bye!";

LOG.log(Level.INFO, "Sending the following message: {0}",
    msg1);
jmsProducer.send(queue, msg1);
LOG.log(Level.INFO, "Sending the following message: {0}",
    msg2);
jmsProducer.send(queue, msg2);
LOG.log(Level.INFO, "Sending the following message: {0}",
msg3);
jmsProducer.send(queue, msg3);

    }
  }
```

The produceMessages() method in the MessageSender class performs all the necessary steps to send messages to a message queue.

The first thing this method does is create an instance of javax.jms.JMSContext by invoking the createContext() method on the injected instance of javax.jms.ConnectionFactory. Notice that the mappedName attribute of the @Resource annotation decorating the connection factory object matches the JNDI name of the connection factory we set up in the GlassFish web console. Behind the scenes, a JNDI lookup is made using this name to obtain the connection factory object.

Next, we create an instance of javax.jms.JMSProducer by invoking the createProducer() method on the JMSContext instance we just created.

After obtaining an instance of JMSProducer, the code sends a series of text messages by invoking its send() method. This method takes the message destination as its first parameter, and a String containing the message text as its second parameter.

There are several overloaded versions of the send() method in JMSProducer. The one we used in our example is a convenience method that creates an instance of javax.jms.TextMessage and sets its text to the String we provide as the second parameter in the method invocation.

Although the above example sends only text messages to the queue, we are not limited to this type of message. The JMS API provides several types of messages that can be sent and received by JMS applications. All message types are defined as interfaces in the javax.jms package.

The following table lists all of the available message types:

Message Type	Description
BytesMessage	Allows sending an array of bytes as a message. JMSProducer has a convenience send() method that takes an array of bytes as one of its parameters. This method creates an instance of javax.jms.BytesMessage on the fly as the message is being sent.
MapMessage	Allows sending an implementation of java.util.Map as a message. JMSProducer has a convenience send() method that takes Map as one of its parameters. This method creates an instance of javax.jms.MapMessage on the fly as the message is being sent.
ObjectMessage	Allows sending any Java object implementing java.io.Serializable as a message. JMSProducer has a convenience send() method that takes an instance of a class implementing java.io.Serializable as its second parameter. This method creates an instance of javax.jms.ObjectMessage on the fly as the message is being sent.
StreamMessage	Allows sending an array of bytes as a message. Differs from BytesMessage in that it stores the type of each primitive type added to the stream.
TextMessage	Allows sending a java.lang.String as a message. As seen in their above example, JMSProducer has a convenience send() method that takes a String as its second parameter, this method creates an instance of javax.jms.TextMessage on the fly as the message is being sent.

 For more information on all of the above message types, consult the JavaDoc documentation at
https://javaee.github.io/javaee-spec/javadocs/.

Retrieving messages from a message queue

Of course, there is no point in sending messages from a queue if nothing is going to receive them. The following example illustrates how to retrieve messages from a JMS message queue:

```
package net.ensode.javaee8book.jmsptpconsumer;
```

```
import java.io.Serializable;
import java.util.logging.Level;
import java.util.logging.Logger;
import javax.annotation.Resource;
import javax.enterprise.context.RequestScoped;
import javax.inject.Named;
import javax.jms.ConnectionFactory;
import javax.jms.JMSConsumer;
import javax.jms.JMSContext;
import javax.jms.Queue;

@Named
@RequestScoped
public class MessageReceiver implements Serializable{

    @Resource
    private ConnectionFactory connectionFactory;
    @Resource(mappedName = "jms/JavaEE8BookQueue")
    private Queue queue;
    private static final Logger LOG =
     Logger.getLogger(MessageReceiver.class.getName());

    public void receiveMessages() {
        String message;
        boolean goodByeReceived = false;

        JMSContext jmsContext = connectionFactory.createContext();
        JMSConsumer jMSConsumer = jmsContext.createConsumer(queue);

        LOG.log(Level.INFO, "Waiting for messages...");
        while (!goodByeReceived) {
            message = jMSConsumer.receiveBody(String.class);

            if (message != null) {
                LOG.log(Level.INFO,
                 "Received the following message: {0}", message);
                if (message.equals("Good bye!")) {
                    goodByeReceived = true;
                }
            }
        }
    }
}
```

Just as in the previous example, an instance of `javax.jms.ConnectionFactory` and an instance of `javax.jms.Queue` are injected by using the @Resource annotation.

In our code, we get an instance of `javax.jms.JMSContext` by invoking the `createContext()` method of `ConnectionFactory`, just as in the previous example.

In this example, we obtain an instance of `javax.jms.JMSConsumer` by calling the `createConsumer()` method on our `JMSContext` instance.

Messages are received by invoking the `receiveBody()` method on our instance of `JMSConsumer`. This method takes the type of the message we are expecting as its sole parameter (`String.class` in our example) and returns an object of the type specified in its parameter (an instance of `java.lang.String` in our example).

In this particular example, we placed this method call in a `while` loop, since we are expecting a message that will let us know that no more messages are coming. Specifically, we are looking for a message containing the text `Good bye!` Once we receive said message, we break out of the loop and continue processing. In this particular case, there is no more processing to do, therefore, execution ends after we break out of the loop.

After executing the code, we should see the following output in the server log:

```
Waiting for messages...
Received the following message: Testing, 1, 2, 3. Can you hear me?
Received the following message: Do you copy?
Received the following message: Good bye!
```

This, of course, assumes that the previous example was already executed and placed messages in the message queue.

 A disadvantage of processing JMS messages as discussed in this section is that message processing is synchronous. In a Java EE environment, we can process JMS messages asynchronously by employing message-driven beans, as discussed in `Chapter 4`, *Enterprise JavaBeans*.

Browsing message queues

JMS provides a way to browse message queues without actually removing messages from those queues. The following example illustrates how to do this:

```
package net.ensode.javaee8book.jmsqueuebrowser;

import java.util.Enumeration;
import java.util.logging.Level;
import java.util.logging.Logger;
```

```
import javax.annotation.Resource;
import javax.enterprise.context.RequestScoped;
import javax.inject.Named;
import javax.jms.ConnectionFactory;
import javax.jms.JMSContext;
import javax.jms.JMSException;
import javax.jms.Queue;
import javax.jms.QueueBrowser;
import javax.jms.TextMessage;

@Named
@RequestScoped
public class MessageQueueBrowser {

    @Resource
    private ConnectionFactory connectionFactory;
    @Resource(mappedName = "jms/JavaEE8BookQueue")
    private Queue queue;
    private static final Logger LOG =
    Logger.getLogger(MessageQueueBrowser.class.getName());

    public void browseMessages() {
        try {
            Enumeration messageEnumeration;
            TextMessage textMessage;
            JMSContext jmsContext =
        connectionFactory.createContext();
            QueueBrowser browser = jmsContext.createBrowser(queue);
            messageEnumeration = browser.getEnumeration();

            if (messageEnumeration != null) {
                if (!messageEnumeration.hasMoreElements()) {
                    LOG.log(Level.INFO, "There are no messages "
                            + "in the queue.");
                } else {
                    LOG.log(Level.INFO,
                            "The following messages are in the
                            queue:");
                    while (messageEnumeration.hasMoreElements()) {
                        textMessage = (TextMessage)
                         messageEnumeration.nextElement();
                        LOG.log(Level.INFO, textMessage.getText());
                    }
                }
            }
        } catch (JMSException e) {
            LOG.log(Level.SEVERE, "JMS Exception caught", e);
        }
```

```
        }

        public static void main(String[] args) {
            new MessageQueueBrowser().browseMessages();
        }
    }
```

As we can see, the procedure to browse messages in a message queue is straightforward. We obtain a JMS connection factory, a JMS queue, and a JMS context in the usual way, then invoke the `createBrowser()` method on the JMS context object. This method returns an implementation of the `javax.jms.QueueBrowser` interface. This interface contains a `getEnumeration()` method that we can invoke to obtain an `Enumeration` containing all of the messages in the queue. To examine the messages in the queue, we simply traverse this enumeration and obtain the messages one by one. In the above example, we simply invoke the `getText()` method of each message in the queue.

Message topics

Message topics are used when our JMS code uses the Publish/Subscribe (pub/sub) messaging domain. When using this messaging domain, the same message can be sent to all subscribers to the topic.

Sending messages to a message topic

The following example illustrates how to send messages to a message topic:

```
package net.ensode.javaee8book.jmspubsubproducer;

import java.util.logging.Level;
import java.util.logging.Logger;
import javax.annotation.Resource;
import javax.enterprise.context.RequestScoped;
import javax.inject.Named;
import javax.jms.ConnectionFactory;
import javax.jms.JMSContext;
import javax.jms.JMSProducer;
import javax.jms.Topic;

@Named
@RequestScoped
public class MessageSender {
```

```
@Resource
private ConnectionFactory connectionFactory;
@Resource(mappedName = "jms/JavaEE8BookTopic")
private Topic topic;
private static final Logger LOG =
    Logger.getLogger(MessageSender.class.getName());

public void produceMessages() {
    JMSContext jmsContext = connectionFactory.createContext();
    JMSProducer jmsProducer = jmsContext.createProducer();

    String msg1 = "Testing, 1, 2, 3. Can you hear me?";
    String msg2 = "Do you copy?";
    String msg3 = "Good bye!";

    LOG.log(Level.INFO, "Sending the following message: {0}",
        msg1);
    jmsProducer.send(topic, msg1);
    LOG.log(Level.INFO, "Sending the following message: {0}",
        msg2);
    jmsProducer.send(topic, msg2);
    LOG.log(Level.INFO, "Sending the following message: {0}",
        msg3);
    jmsProducer.send(topic, msg3);

}
}
```

As we can see, the preceding code is nearly identical to the MessageSender class we saw when we discussed Point-To-Point messaging. As a matter of fact, the only lines of code that are different are the ones that are highlighted. The JMS API was designed this way so that application developers do not have to learn two different APIs for the PTP and pub/sub domains.

Since the code is nearly identical to the corresponding example in the *Message queues* section, we will only explain the differences between the two examples. In this example, instead of declaring an instance of a class implementing javax.jms.Queue, we declare an instance of a class implementing javax.jms.Topic. We then pass this instance of javax.jms.Topic as the first method of the send() method of our JMSProducer object, along with the message we wish to send.

Receiving messages from a message topic

Just as sending messages to a message topic is almost identical to sending messages to a message queue, receiving messages from a message topic is almost identical to receiving messages from a message queue:

```java
package net.ensode.javaee8book.jmspubsubconsumer;

import java.util.logging.Level;
import java.util.logging.Logger;
import javax.annotation.Resource;
import javax.enterprise.context.RequestScoped;
import javax.inject.Named;
import javax.jms.ConnectionFactory;
import javax.jms.JMSConsumer;
import javax.jms.JMSContext;
import javax.jms.Topic;

@Named
@RequestScoped
public class MessageReceiver {

    @Resource
    private ConnectionFactory connectionFactory;
    @Resource(mappedName = "jms/JavaEE8BookTopic")
    private Topic topic;
    private static final Logger LOG =
        Logger.getLogger(MessageReceiver.class.getName());

    public void receiveMessages() {
        String message;
        boolean goodByeReceived = false;

        JMSContext jmsContext = connectionFactory.createContext();
        JMSConsumer jMSConsumer = jmsContext.createConsumer(topic);

        LOG.log(Level.INFO, "Waiting for messages...");
        while (!goodByeReceived) {
            message = jMSConsumer.receiveBody(String.class);

            if (message != null) {
                System.out.print(
                "Received the following message: ");
                LOG.log(Level.INFO, message);
                if (message.equals("Good bye!")) {
                    goodByeReceived = true;
                }
```

```
                              }
                        }
                  }
            }
```

Once again, the differences between this code and the corresponding code for PTP are trivial. Instead of declaring an instance of a class implementing `javax.jms.Queue`, we declare a class implementing `javax.jms.Topic`, and we use the `@Resource` annotation to inject an instance of this class into our code, using the JNDI name we used when configuring our application server. We then obtain an instance of `JMSContext` and `JMSConsumer`, as before, then receive the messages from the topic by invoking the `receiveBody()` method on `JMSConsumer`.

Using the pub/sub messaging domain as illustrated in this section has the advantage that messages can be sent to several message consumers. This can be easily tested by concurrently executing two instances of the `MessageReceiver` class we developed in this section, then executing the `MessageSender` class we developed in the previous section. We should see console output for each instance, indicating that both instances received all messages.

Creating durable subscribers

The disadvantage of using the pub/sub messaging domain is that message consumers must be executing when the messages are sent to the topic. If a message consumer is not executing at the time, it will not receive the messages, whereas, in PTP, messages are kept in the queue until the message consumer executes. Fortunately, the JMS API provides a way to use the pub/sub messaging domain and keep messages in the topic until all subscribed message consumers execute and receive the message. This can be accomplished by creating durable subscribers to a JMS Topic.

In order to be able to service durable subscribers, we need to set the `ClientId` property of our JMS connection factory. Each durable subscriber must have a unique client ID, therefore, a unique connection factory must be declared for each potential durable subscriber.

The procedure to set the `ClientId` property of a JMS connection factory varies depending on the application server being used. The *Appendix*, *Configuring and deploying to GlassFish* has instructions on setting this property on GlassFish. Consult your application server documentation for instructions on setting this property when using other Java EE compliant application servers.

Invalid ClientId Exception? Only one JMS client can connect to a topic for a specific client ID. If more than one JMS client attempts to obtain a JMS connection using the same connection factory, a JMSException stating that the Client ID is already in use will be thrown. The solution is to create a connection factory for each potential client that will be receiving messages from the durable topic.

Once we have set up our application server to be able to provide durable subscriptions, we are ready to write some code to take advantage of them:

```java
package net.ensode.javaee8book.jmspubsubdurablesubscriber;

import java.util.logging.Level;
import java.util.logging.Logger;
import javax.annotation.Resource;
import javax.enterprise.context.ApplicationScoped;
import javax.inject.Named;
import javax.jms.ConnectionFactory;
import javax.jms.JMSConsumer;
import javax.jms.JMSContext;
import javax.jms.Topic;

@Named
@ApplicationScoped
public class MessageReceiver {

    @Resource(mappedName =
      "jms/JavaEE8BookDurableConnectionFactory")
    private ConnectionFactory connectionFactory;
    @Resource(mappedName = "jms/JavaEE8BookTopic")
    private Topic topic;
    private static final Logger LOG =
      Logger.getLogger(MessageReceiver.class.getName());

    public void receiveMessages() {
        String message;
        boolean goodByeReceived = false;

        JMSContext jmsContext = connectionFactory.createContext();
        JMSConsumer jMSConsumer =
        jmsContext.createDurableConsumer(topic, "Subscriber1");

        LOG.log(Level.INFO, "Waiting for messages...");
        while (!goodByeReceived) {
            message = jMSConsumer.receiveBody(String.class);
```

```
          if (message != null) {
            LOG.log(Level.INFO,
              "Received the following message: {0}", message);
            if (message.equals("Good bye!")) {
               goodByeReceived = true;
            }
          }
        }
      }

    }
```

As we can see, the preceding code is not much different from previous examples whose purpose was to retrieve messages. There are only two differences from previous examples: The instance of `ConnectionFactory` we are injecting is set up to handle durable subscriptions, and instead of calling the `createConsumer()` method on the JMS context object, we are calling `createDurableConsumer()`. The `createDurableConsumer()` method takes two arguments: a JMS `Topic` object to retrieve messages from, and a `String` designating a name for this subscription. This second parameter must be unique for all subscribers to the durable topic.

Summary

In this chapter, we covered how to set up JMS connection factories, JMS message queues, and JMS message topics in GlassFish, by using the GlassFish web console. We also covered how to send messages to a message queue via the `javax.jms.JMSProducer` interface. Additionally, we covered how to receive messages from a message queue via the `javax.jms.JMSConsumer` interface. We also covered how to asynchronously receive messages from a message queue by implementing the `javax.jms.MessageListener` interface and saw how to use the above interfaces to send and receive messages to and from a JMS message topic. We also looked at how to browse messages in a message queue without removing those messages from the queue via the `javax.jms.QueueBrowser` interface. Finally, we saw how to set up and interact with durable subscriptions to JMS topics.

9
Securing Java EE Applications

Java EE 8 introduces a new security API that standardizes application security across all Java EE 8 compliant application servers. The API includes standardized access to identity stores, which allow a uniform way of retrieving user credentials from a relational or LDAP database, as well as allowing us to implement access to custom identity stores. The new Java EE 8 API includes support for authentication mechanisms, allowing us to authenticate users in a standard way. Several authentication mechanisms are supported such as basic HTTP authentication, client certificates, HTML forms, and more.

In this chapter, we will cover the following topics:

- Identity stores
- Authentication mechanisms

Identity stores

Identity stores provide access to a persistence storage system, such as a relational or **LDAP (Lightweight Directory Access Protocol)** database, where user credentials are stored. The Java EE Security API supports relational and LDAP databases directly, and it allows us to integrate with custom identity stores, if necessary.

Setting up an identity store stored in a relational database

To authenticate a secured resource, such as a Servlet or JAX-RS RESTful web service, against credentials stored in a relational database, we need to annotate an application-scoped CDI bean with the `@DatabaseIdentityStoreDefinition` annotation, as illustrated in the following example.

```
package
net.ensode.javaee8book.httpauthdatabaseidentitystore.security;

import javax.enterprise.context.ApplicationScoped;
import
javax.security.enterprise.identitystore.DatabaseIdentityStoreDefini
tion;

@DatabaseIdentityStoreDefinition(
        dataSourceLookup = "jdbc/userAuth",
        callerQuery = "select password from users where name = ?",
        groupsQuery = "select g.GROUP_NAME from "
            + "USER_GROUPS ug, users u, "
            + "GROUPS g where u.USERNAME=? "
            + "and ug.USER_ID = u.user_id "
            + "and g.GROUP_ID= ug.GROUP_ID"
)
@ApplicationScoped
public class ApplicationConfig {

}
```

In our example, the JNDI name for the JDBC connection for the relational database containing user credentials is `jdbc/userAuth`, which is the value we provided to the `dataSourceLookup` attribute of the `@DatabaseIdentityStoreDefinition` annotation.

The `callerQuery` parameter of `@DatabaseIdentityStoreDefinition` is used to specify the SQL query used to retrieve the username and password for the user we are authenticating. The values retrieved from the database must match the values provided by the user (via an authentication mechanism, covered later in this chapter).

Most secured applications have different types of users separated into roles, for example, an application could have "regular" users plus administrators. Administrators would be allowed to perform certain actions that regular users would not. For example, administrators could be able to reset user passwords and add or remove users from the system. The `groupsQuery` attribute of `@DatabaseIdentityStoreDefinition` allows us to retrieve all roles for the user.

Setting up an identity store stored in an LDAP database

To secure resources against credentials stored in an LDAP database, we need to annotate the resource to be secured (such as a servlet or JAX-RS RESTful web service) with the `@LdapIdentityStoreDefinition` annotation, the following example illustrates how to do this:

```
package
net.ensode.javaee8book.httpauthdatabaseidentitystore.servlet;
import java.io.IOException;
import javax.security.enterprise.identitystore.
LdapIdentityStoreDefinition;
import javax.servlet.ServletException;
import javax.servlet.annotation.WebServlet;
import javax.servlet.http.HttpServlet;
import javax.servlet.http.HttpServletRequest;
import javax.servlet.http.HttpServletResponse;

@LdapIdentityStoreDefinition(
        url = "ldap://myldapserver:33389/",
        callerBaseDn = "ou=caller,dc=packtpub,dc=com",
        groupSearchBase = "ou=group,dc=packtpub,dc=com")
@WebServlet(name = "ControllerServlet", urlPatterns =
 {"/controller"})
public class ControllerServlet extends HttpServlet {

    @Override
    protected void doGet(
    HttpServletRequest req, HttpServletResponse res)
            throws ServletException, IOException {
        System.out.println("doGet() invoked");
    }
}
```

The `url` attribute of `@LdapIdentityStoreDefinition` is used to specify the URL of the LDAP server containing user credentials for our application, its `callerBaseDn` attribute is used to specify the LDAP base-distinguished name to verify user credentials supplied by the user. Finally, its `groupSearchBase` attribute is used to retrieve the roles for the user.

Custom identity stores

In some cases, we may need to integrate our application security with an identity store not directly supported by the security API, for example, we may have a requirement to integrate with an existing commercial security product. For cases like this, the Java EE security API allows us to roll our own identity store definition.

To handle custom identity stores, we need to create an application-scoped CDI bean; the bean must implement the `IdentityStore` interface, as illustrated in the following example:

```
package net.ensode.javaee8book.security.basicauthexample;

import java.util.Arrays;
import java.util.HashSet;
import java.util.Set;
import javax.annotation.PostConstruct;
import javax.enterprise.context.ApplicationScoped;
import javax.security.enterprise.credential.Credential;
import
javax.security.enterprise.credential.UsernamePasswordCredential;
import
javax.security.enterprise.identitystore.CredentialValidationResult;
import javax.security.enterprise.identitystore.IdentityStore;

@ApplicationScoped
public class DummyIdentityStore implements IdentityStore {

  Set<String> adminRoleSet;
  Set userRoleSet;
  Set userAdminRoleSet;

  @PostConstruct
  public void init() {
    adminRoleSet = new HashSet<>(Arrays.asList("admin"));
    userRoleSet = new HashSet<>(Arrays.asList("user"));
    userAdminRoleSet = new HashSet<>(Arrays.asList("user",
      "admin"));
  }
```

```
@Override
public CredentialValidationResult validate(Credential credential)
 {
  UsernamePasswordCredential usernamePasswordCredential =
         (UsernamePasswordCredential) credential;

  CredentialValidationResult credentialValidationResult;

  if (usernamePasswordCredential.compareTo(
         "david", "secret")) {
    credentialValidationResult =
          new CredentialValidationResult("david",
          adminRoleSet);
  }
  else if (usernamePasswordCredential.compareTo("alan",
       "iforgot")) {
    credentialValidationResult =
          new CredentialValidationResult("alan",
            userAdminRoleSet);
  }
  else {
    credentialValidationResult =
      CredentialValidationResult.INVALID_RESULT;
  }

  return credentialValidationResult;
 }
}
```

The `validate()` method is defined in the `IdentityStore` interface provided by the security API; in our example, we implement this method so that we can implement custom validation for our application.

In our example, we are hardcoding valid credentials into the code, do not do this for real applications!

The `validate()` method defined in the `IdentityStore` interface accepts an instance of a class implementing the `Credential` interface as its sole argument. In the body of our method, we cast it down to `UserNamePasswordCredential`, then we invoke its `compareTo()` method, passing the expected username and password. If the provided credentials match either one of the expected sets of credentials, then we allow the user to successfully log in; we do this by returning an instance of `CredentialValidationResult` containing the username and a `Set` containing all the roles that the user has in our application.

If the supplied credentials don't match either of the expected credentials, then we prevent the user from logging in by returning `CredentialValidationResult.INVALID_RESULT`.

Authentication mechanisms

Authentication mechanisms provide a way for the user to provide their credentials so that they can be authenticated against an identity store.

The Java EE 8 Security API provides support for basic HTTP authentication, a standard authentication mechanism supported by most web browsers, as well as form authentication, where users provide their credentials via an HTML form. Form authentication, by default, submits a form to a security servlet provided by the Java EE implementation. If we need more flexibility or to better align with other Java EE technologies, the security API provides custom form authentication as well, which allows us, as application developers, to have more control over how to authenticate users attempting to access our application.

Basic authentication mechanism

Basic authentication mechanisms can be achieved by annotating the resource to secure (that is, a servlet or JAX-RS RESTful web service) with the `@BasicAuthenticationMechanismDefinition` annotation:

```
package net.ensode.javaee8book.security.basicauthexample;

import java.io.IOException;
import javax.annotation.security.DeclareRoles;
import
javax.security.enterprise.authentication.mechanism.http.BasicAuthen
ticationMechanismDefinition;
import javax.servlet.ServletException;
import javax.servlet.annotation.HttpConstraint;
```

```java
import javax.servlet.annotation.ServletSecurity;
import javax.servlet.annotation.WebServlet;
import javax.servlet.http.HttpServlet;
import javax.servlet.http.HttpServletRequest;
import javax.servlet.http.HttpServletResponse;

@BasicAuthenticationMechanismDefinition(
        realmName = "Book Realm"
)
@WebServlet(name = "SecuredServlet",
     urlPatterns = {"/securedServlet"})
@DeclareRoles({"user", "admin"})
@ServletSecurity(
        @HttpConstraint(rolesAllowed = "admin"))
public class SecuredServlet extends HttpServlet {

    @Override
    protected void doGet(HttpServletRequest request,
        HttpServletResponse response)
            throws ServletException, IOException {
        response.getOutputStream().
            print("Congratulations, login successful.");
    }
}
```

The value of the `realmName` attribute of the `@BasicAuthenticationMechanismDefinition` annotation will be sent to the browser in the `WWW-Authenticate` response header.

Using basic authentication will cause the browser to pop up a window asking for a **User Name** and a **Password**:

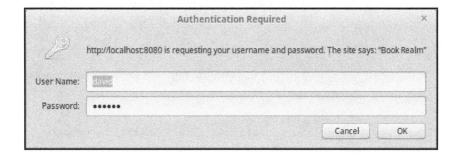

Once the user enters the correct credentials, then access is granted to the protected resource:

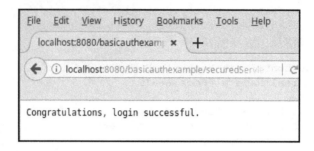

Form authentication mechanism

Another way we can authenticate our users is to develop an HTML form to collect the user's credentials, then delegate authentication to the Java EE Security API. The first step when following this approach is to develop an HTML page where the user can log in to the application, as illustrated in the following example:

```html
<!DOCTYPE html>
<html>
    <head>
        <meta http-equiv="Content-Type" content="text/html;
charset=UTF-8">
        <title>Login</title>
    </head>
    <body>
        <p>Please enter your username and password to access the
            application</p>
        <form method="POST" action="j_security_check">
            <table cellpadding="0" cellspacing="0" border="0">
                <tr>
                    <td align="right">Username: </td>
                    <td>
                        <input type="text" name="j_username">
                    </td>
                </tr>
                <tr>
                    <td align="right">Password: </td>
                    <td>
                        <input type="password"
                        name="j_password">
                    </td>
                </tr>
                <tr>
```

```
                    <td></td>
                    <td><input type="submit" value="Login"></td>
                </tr>
            </table>
        </form>
    </body>
</html>
```

As seen in the example, the HTML form used for logging in must submit an HTTP POST request, the value for its `action` attribute must be `j_security_check`. `j_security_check` maps to a servlet provided by the Java EE Security API, we don't need to develop any validation logic ourselves. The form must have a couple of input fields, one for the username and one for the password, names for these fields must be `j_username` and `j_password`, respectively; the security servlet provided by the Java EE API will retrieve these values and authenticate the user automatically.

Additionally, we need to provide an HTML page where the user will be redirected if login fails. The page can have any valid HTML markup; in our example, we simply provide an error message and a link to direct the user back to the login page so that they can try to log in again:

```
<!DOCTYPE html>
<html>
    <head>
        <meta http-equiv="Content-Type" content="text/html;
         charset=UTF-8">
        <title>Login Error</title>
    </head>
    <body>
        There was an error logging in.
        <br />
        <a href="login.html">Try again</a>
    </body>
</html>
```

On the server side, all we need to do is annotate the secured resource with the `@FormAuthenticationMechanismDefinition` annotation, which will let the Java EE Security API know we are using form-based authentication, and what HTML pages to use to log in or to display when logging in fails:

```
package net.ensode.javaee8book.httpauthdbidentitystore;

import java.io.IOException;
import javax.annotation.security.DeclareRoles;
import
javax.security.enterprise.authentication.mechanism.http.FormAuthent
```

```
icationMechanismDefinition;
import
javax.security.enterprise.authentication.mechanism.http.LoginToCont
inue;
import
javax.security.enterprise.identitystore.DatabaseIdentityStoreDefini
tion;
import javax.security.enterprise.identitystore.Pbkdf2PasswordHash;
import javax.servlet.ServletException;
import javax.servlet.annotation.HttpConstraint;
import javax.servlet.annotation.ServletSecurity;
import javax.servlet.annotation.WebServlet;
import javax.servlet.http.HttpServlet;
import javax.servlet.http.HttpServletRequest;
import javax.servlet.http.HttpServletResponse;

@FormAuthenticationMechanismDefinition(
        loginToContinue = @LoginToContinue(
                loginPage = "/login.html",
                errorPage = "/loginerror.html"
        )
)

@DatabaseIdentityStoreDefinition(
        dataSourceLookup = "java:global/authDS",
        callerQuery = "select password from users where USERNAME =
         ?",
        groupsQuery = "select g.GROUP_NAME from USER_GROUPS ug,
        users u, GROUPS g where ug.USER_ID = u.user_id and
        g.GROUP_ID= ug.GROUP_ID and u.USERNAME=?",
        hashAlgorithm = Pbkdf2PasswordHash.class,
        hashAlgorithmParameters = {
            "Pbkdf2PasswordHash.Iterations=3072",
            "Pbkdf2PasswordHash.Algorithm=PBKDF2WithHmacSHA512",
            "Pbkdf2PasswordHash.SaltSizeBytes=64"
        }
)
@DeclareRoles({"user", "admin"})
@WebServlet("/securedServlet")
@ServletSecurity(
        @HttpConstraint(rolesAllowed = {"admin"}))
public class SecuredServlet extends HttpServlet {

    @Override
    protected void doGet(HttpServletRequest request,
     HttpServletResponse response)
            throws ServletException, IOException {
        response.getWriter().write("Congratulations, login
```

```
                successful.");
        }
    }
```

The @FormAuthenticationMechanismDefinition annotation has a required loginToContinue attribute; the value of this attribute must be an instance of the @LoginToContinue annotation. @LoginToContinue has two required attributes, loginPage and errorPage; the value of these attributes must indicate the path for the login page, and the path of the page to display in case of authentication failure, respectively.

After building and deploying our code, then attempting to access a protected resource, the user is automatically redirected to our login page:

If the user enters the correct credentials, then access to the protected resource is granted:

If invalid credentials are entered, then the user is directed to our error page:

Custom form authentication mechanism

Another way we can authenticate users in our application is to use a custom form authentication mechanism; this type of authentication mechanism is useful when we want to integrate our application with a web framework, such as JSF. In our next example, we will illustrate how to do just that, integrating the Java EE Security API with JSF, via custom form authentication.

To use custom form authentication in our applications, we need to use the aptly named @CustomFormAuthenticationMechanismDefinition annotation, as illustrated in the following example:

```
package net.ensode.javaee8book.httpauthdbidentitystore;

import java.io.IOException;
import javax.annotation.security.DeclareRoles;
import
javax.security.enterprise.authentication.mechanism.http.CustomFormA
uthenticationMechanismDefinition;
import
javax.security.enterprise.authentication.mechanism.http.LoginToCont
inue;
import
javax.security.enterprise.identitystore.DatabaseIdentityStoreDefini
tion;
import javax.security.enterprise.identitystore.Pbkdf2PasswordHash;
import javax.servlet.ServletException;
import javax.servlet.annotation.HttpConstraint;
import javax.servlet.annotation.ServletSecurity;
import javax.servlet.annotation.WebServlet;
import javax.servlet.http.HttpServlet;
```

```
import javax.servlet.http.HttpServletRequest;
import javax.servlet.http.HttpServletResponse;

@CustomFormAuthenticationMechanismDefinition(
    loginToContinue = @LoginToContinue(
        loginPage="/faces/login.xhtml",
        errorPage=""
    )
)

@DatabaseIdentityStoreDefinition(
        dataSourceLookup = "java:global/authDS",
        callerQuery = "select password from users where USERNAME =
        ?",
        groupsQuery = "select g.GROUP_NAME from USER_GROUPS ug, "
                + "users u, GROUPS g where ug.USER_ID = u.user_id "
                + "and g.GROUP_ID= ug.GROUP_ID and u.USERNAME=?",
                 hashAlgorithm = Pbkdf2PasswordHash.class,
        hashAlgorithmParameters = {
            "Pbkdf2PasswordHash.Iterations=3072",
            "Pbkdf2PasswordHash.Algorithm=PBKDF2WithHmacSHA512",
            "Pbkdf2PasswordHash.SaltSizeBytes=64"
        }
)
@DeclareRoles({"user", "admin"})
@WebServlet("/securedServlet")
@ServletSecurity(
        @HttpConstraint(rolesAllowed = {"admin"}))
public class SecuredServlet extends HttpServlet {

    @Override
    protected void doGet(HttpServletRequest request,
     HttpServletResponse response)
            throws ServletException, IOException {
        response.getWriter().write("Congratulations, login
        successful.");
    }
}
```

Just like the @FormAuthenticationMechanismDefinition annotation we saw previously, the @CustomFormAuthenticationMechanismDefinition annotation has a loginToContinue attribute that takes an instance of the @LoginToContinue annotation as its value. In this case, since we are integrating with JSF, the value of the loginPage attribute of @LoginToContinue must point to the path of a Facelets page used for the user to log in. When using JSF to authenticate the user, it is expected that the login page will display an error message if authentication fails, therefore we need to leave the errorPage attribute of @LoginToContinue blank.

Our login page is a standard Facelets page that collects user credentials and redirects to a CDI bean that acts as a controller:

```xml
<?xml version='1.0' encoding='UTF-8' ?>
<!DOCTYPE html PUBLIC "-//W3C//DTD XHTML 1.0 Transitional//EN"
"http://www.w3.org/TR/xhtml1/DTD/xhtml1-transitional.dtd">
<html xmlns="http://www.w3.org/1999/xhtml"
      xmlns:h="http://xmlns.jcp.org/jsf/html">
    <h:head>
        <title>Login</title>
    </h:head>
    <h:body>
        <h:form>
            <h:messages/>
            <h:panelGrid columns="2">
                <h:outputLabel for="userName"
                    value="User Name:"/>
                <h:inputText id="userName"
                    value="#{user.userName}"/>
                <h:outputLabel for="password"
                    value="Password: "/>
                <h:inputSecret id="password"
                    value="#{user.password}"/>
                <h:panelGroup/>
                <h:commandButton
                    action="#{loginController.login()}"
                    value="Login"/>
            </h:panelGrid>
        </h:form>
    </h:body>
</html>
```

Our login page has input fields for username and password; it stores those values into a CDI named bean (not shown as it is trivial) via value-binding expressions. When the user clicks on the **Login** button, controls go to a `LoginController` CDI named bean that performs the actual authentication:

```
package net.ensode.javaee8book.httpauthdbidentitystore.customauth;

import javax.enterprise.context.RequestScoped;
import javax.faces.application.FacesMessage;
import javax.faces.context.ExternalContext;
import javax.faces.context.FacesContext;
import javax.inject.Inject;
import javax.inject.Named;
import javax.security.enterprise.AuthenticationStatus;
import javax.security.enterprise.SecurityContext;
import javax.security.enterprise.authentication.mechanism.http.Authenticat
ionParameters;
import javax.security.enterprise.credential.UsernamePasswordCredential;
import javax.servlet.http.HttpServletRequest;
import javax.servlet.http.HttpServletResponse;

@Named
@RequestScoped
public class LoginController {

    @Inject
    private SecurityContext securityContext;

    @Inject
    private User user;

    public void login() {
        FacesContext facesContext =
        FacesContext.getCurrentInstance();
        ExternalContext externalContext =
            facesContext.getExternalContext();
        HttpServletRequest httpServletRequest =
            (HttpServletRequest) externalContext.getRequest();
        HttpServletResponse httpServletResponse =
            (HttpServletResponse) externalContext.getResponse();
        UsernamePasswordCredential uNamePasswordCredential =
            new UsernamePasswordCredential(user.getUserName(),
            user.getPassword());

        AuthenticationParameters authenticationParameters =
```

```
            AuthenticationParameters.withParams().credential(
            uNamePasswordCredential);

        AuthenticationStatus authenticationStatus =
            securityContext.authenticate(httpServletRequest,
            httpServletResponse, authenticationParameters);

    if (authenticationStatus.equals(
        AuthenticationStatus.SEND_CONTINUE)) {
        facesContext.responseComplete();
    } else if (authenticationStatus.equals(
        AuthenticationStatus.SEND_FAILURE)) {
        FacesMessage facesMessage = new FacesMessage(
            "Login error");
        facesContext.addMessage(null, facesMessage);
    }

    }
}
```

In our `LoginController` class, we need to inject an instance of `javax.security.enterprise.SecurityContext`, since we will need it for authentication. Our `login()` method is where we implement the authentication logic. The first thing we need to do is create an instance of `UsernamePasswordCredential`, passing the user-entered username and password as parameters to its constructor.

We then create an instance of `javax.security.enterprise.authentication.mechanism.http.AuthenticationParameters`, by invoking the static `withParams()` method on `AuthenticationParameters`, then invoking the `credential()` method on the resulting instance of `AuthenticationParameters`. We then pass the instance of `UserNamePasswordCredential` we just created as a parameter; this returns yet another instance of `AuthenticationParameters`, which we can use to actually validate the user-entered credentials.

We validate user-entered credentials by invoking the `authenticate()` method on our `SecurityContext` instance, passing the HTTP Request and Response objects as parameters, as well as the instance of `AuthenticationParameters` containing the user-entered credentials. This method invocation will return an instance of `AuthenticationStatus`, we need to check the returned instance to determine whether the user entered valid credentials.

If `SecurityContext.authenticate()` returns `AuthenticationStatus.SEND_CONTINUE`, then the user-entered credentials were valid and we can allow the user to access the requested resource. If, instead, the method returns `AuthenticationStatus.SEND_FAILURE`, then the user-entered credentials were invalid, and we need to prevent the user from accessing the protected resource.

After deploying and running our application, when a user attempts to access a protected resource, they are automatically redirected to a login page, which in this case, since we are using custom form authentication, is implemented using JSF:

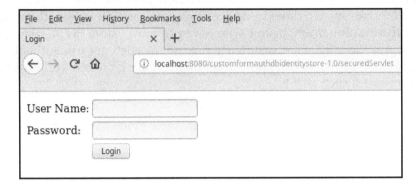

Entering correct credentials will direct the user to the protected resource (not shown) while entering incorrect credentials directs the user back to the login page, which should show an appropriate error message:

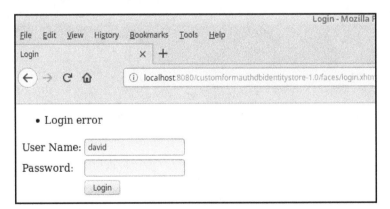

Summary

In this chapter, we covered the new Security API introduced in Java EE 8. We covered how we can access different types of identity stores to retrieve user credentials, such as relational databases or LDAP databases. We also covered how the security API provides the ability to integrate with custom identity stores, in case we need to access one that is not directly supported.

Additionally, we saw how we can use different authentication mechanisms to allow access to our secured Java EE applications. This included how to implement the basic authentication mechanism provided by all web browsers, as well as how to implement form-based authentication mechanisms, where we provide custom HTML pages used for authentication. Additionally, we saw how we can use the custom form authentication mechanism provided by the security API so that we can integrate our application security with a web framework such as JSF.

10
RESTful Web Services with JAX-RS

Representational State Transfer (**REST**) is an architectural style in which web services are viewed as resources and can be identified by **Uniform Resource Identifiers** (**URIs**).

Web services developed using this styles are known as RESTful web services.

JAX-RS became part of Java EE in version 6 of the Java EE specification, although it had been available as a standalone API before then. In this chapter, we will cover how to develop RESTful web services through the JAX-RS API.

The following topics will be covered in this chapter:

- An introduction to RESTful web services and JAX-RS
- Developing a simple RESTful web service
- Developing a RESTful web service client
- Path parameters
- Query parameters
- Server-Sent events

An introduction to RESTful web services and JAX-RS

RESTful web services are very flexible. They can consume several types of different MIME types, although they are typically written to consume and/or produce XML or **JSON** (**JavaScript Object Notation**).

Web services must support one or more of the following four HTTP methods:

- **GET** - By convention, a `GET` request is used to retrieve an existing resource
- **POST** - By convention, a `POST` request is used to update an existing resource
- **PUT** - By convention, a `PUT` request is used to create a new resource
- **DELETE** - By convention, a `DELETE` request is used to delete an existing resource

We develop a RESTful web service with JAX-RS by creating a class with annotated methods that are invoked when our web service receives one of the above HTTP requests. Once we have developed and deployed our RESTful web service, we need to develop a client that will send requests to our service. JAX-RS includes a standard client-side API that we can use to develop RESTful web service clients.

Developing a simple RESTful web service

In this section, we will develop a simple web service to illustrate how we can make methods in our service respond to different HTTP request methods.

Developing a RESTful web service using JAX-RS is simple and straightforward. Each of our RESTful web services needs to be invoked via its **Unique Resource Identifier** (**URI**). This URI is specified by the `@Path` annotation, which we need to use to decorate our RESTful web service resource class.

When developing RESTful web services, we need to develop methods that will be invoked when our web service receives an HTTP request. We need to implement methods to handle one or more of the four types of request that RESTful web services handle: GET, `POST`, `PUT`, and/or `DELETE`.

The JAX-RS API provides four annotations that we can use to decorate methods in our web service. These annotations are appropriately named `@GET`, `@POST`, `@PUT`, and `@DELETE`. Decorating a method in our web service with one of these annotations will make it respond to the corresponding HTTP method.

Additionally, each method in our service must produce and/or consume a specific MIME type. The MIME type to be produced needs to be specified with the `@Produces` annotation. Similarly, the MIME type to be consumed must be specified with the `@Consumes` annotation.

The following example illustrates the concepts we have just explained:

 Please note that this example does not *really* do anything; the purpose of the example is to illustrate how to make different methods in our RESTful web service resource class respond to different HTTP methods.

```java
package com.ensode.javaee8book.jaxrsintro.service;

import javax.ws.rs.Consumes;
import javax.ws.rs.DELETE;
import javax.ws.rs.GET;
import javax.ws.rs.POST;
import javax.ws.rs.PUT;
import javax.ws.rs.Path;
import javax.ws.rs.Produces;
import javax.ws.rs.core.MediaType;

@Path("customer")
public class CustomerResource {

  @GET  @Produces("text/xml")
  public String getCustomer() {
     //in a "real" RESTful service, we would retrieve data from a
database
     //then return an XML representation of the data.

     System.out.println("--- " + this.getClass().getCanonicalName()
         + ".getCustomer() invoked");

     return "<customer>\n"
         + "<id>123</id>\n"
         + "<firstName>Joseph</firstName>\n"
         + "<middleName>William</middleName>\n"
         + "<lastName>Graystone</lastName>\n"
         + "</customer>\n";
  }

  /**
   * Create a new customer
   * @param customer XML representation of the customer to create
```

```
      */
      @PUT   @Consumes("text/xml")
      public void createCustomer(String customerXML) {
        //in a "real" RESTful service, we would parse the XML
        //received in the customer XML parameter, then insert
        //a new row into the database.

        System.out.println("--- " + this.getClass().getCanonicalName()
            + ".createCustomer() invoked");

        System.out.println("customerXML = " + customerXML);
      }

      @POST   @Consumes(MediaType.TEXT_XML)
      public void updateCustomer(String customerXML) {
        //in a "real" RESTful service, we would parse the XML
        //received in the customer XML parameter, then update
        //a row in the database.

        System.out.println("--- " + this.getClass().getCanonicalName()
            + ".updateCustomer() invoked");

        System.out.println("customerXML = " + customerXML);
      }

      @DELETE   @Consumes("text/xml")
      public void deleteCustomer(String customerXML) {
        //in a "real" RESTful service, we would parse the XML
        //received in the customer XML parameter, then delete
        //a row in the database.

        System.out.println("--- " + this.getClass().getCanonicalName()
            + ".deleteCustomer() invoked");

        System.out.println("customerXML = " + customerXML);
      }
    }
```

Notice that this class is annotated with the @Path annotation. This annotation designates the Uniform Resource Identifier (URI) for our RESTful web service. The complete URI for our service will include the protocol, server name, port, context root, the REST resources path (see the next subsection), and the value passed to this annotation.

Assuming that our web service was deployed to a server called example.com using the HTTP protocol on port 8080, has a context root of `jaxrsintro`, and a REST resources path of `"resources"`, then the complete URI for our service would be:

```
http://example.com:8080/jaxrsintro/resources/customer
```

Since web browsers generate a `GET` request when pointed to a URL, we can test the GET method of our service simply by pointing the browser to our service's URI.

Notice that each of the methods in our class is annotated with one of the `@GET`, `@POST`, `@PUT`, or `@DELETE` annotations. These annotations make our methods respond to the corresponding HTTP method.

Additionally, if our method returns data to the client, we declare the MIME type of the data to be returned in the `@Produces` annotation. In our example, only the `getCustomer()` method returns data to the client. We wish to return data in XML format, therefore we set the value of the `@Produces` annotation to the JAX-RS provided constant `MediaType.TEXT_XML`, which has a value of `"text/xml"`. Similarly, if our method needs to consume data from the client, we need to specify the MIME type of the data to be consumed. This is done via the `@Consumes` annotation. All methods except `getCustomer()` in our service consume data. In all cases, we expect the data to be in XML format, therefore, we again specify `MediaType.TEXT_XML` as the MIME type to be consumed.

Configuring the REST resources path for our application

As briefly mentioned in the previous section, before successfully deploying a RESTful web service developed using JAX-RS, we need to configure the REST resources path for our application. We can do this by developing a class that extends `javax.ws.rs.core.Application` and decorating it with the `@ApplicationPath`, annotation.

Configuring via the @ApplicationPath annotation

When developing applications against modern versions of Java EE, in many cases, it isn't necessary to write a `web.xml` deployment descriptor; JAX-RS is no different. We can configure the REST resources path in Java code via an annotation.

To configure our REST resources path without having to rely on a `web.xml` deployment descriptor, all we need to do is write a class that extends `javax.ws.ApplicationPath`, and decorate it with the `@ApplicationPath` annotation. The value passed to this annotation is the REST resources `path` for our services.

The following code sample illustrates this process:

```
package com.ensode.javaee8book..jaxrsintro.service.config;

import javax.ws.rs.ApplicationPath;
import javax.ws.rs.core.Application;

@ApplicationPath("resources")
public class JaxRsConfig extends Application {
}
```

Notice that the class does not have to implement any methods; it simply needs to extend `javax.ws.rs.Application` and be decorated with the `@ApplicationPath` annotation. The class must be public, may have any name, and may be placed in any package.

Testing our web service

As we mentioned earlier, web browsers send a GET request to any URLs we point them to. Therefore, the easiest way to test GET requests to our service is to simply point the browser to our service's URI:

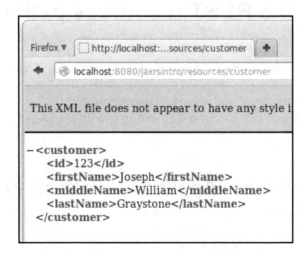

Web browsers only support GET and POST requests. To test a POST request through the browser, we would have to write a web application containing an HTML form having an action attribute value of our service's URI. Although trivial for a single service, it can become cumbersome to do this for every RESTful web service we develop.

Thankfully, there is an open source command-line utility called curl we can use to test our web services. curl is included with most Linux distributions, and can be easily downloaded for Windows, mac OS X, and several other platforms, at http://curl.haxx.se/.

curl can send all four request method types (GET, POST, PUT, and DELETE) to our service. Our server's response will simply be displayed on the command-line console. Curl takes an -X command-line option, which allows us to specify which request method to send. To send a GET request, we simply need to type the following into the command line:

```
curl -XGET
http://localhost:8080/jaxrsintro/resources/customer
```

Which results in the following output:

```
<customer>
<id>123</id>
<firstName>Joseph</firstName>
<middleName>William</middleName>
<lastName>Graystone</lastName>
</customer>
```

Which, unsurprisingly, is the same output we saw when we pointed our browser to the service's URI.

The default request method for curl is GET, therefore, the -X parameter in our example above is redundant; we could have achieved the same result by invoking the following command from the command line:

```
curl http://localhost:8080/jaxrsintro/resources/customer
```

After submitting either of the above two commands and examining the application server log, we should see the output of the System.out.println() statements we added to the getCustomer() method:

```
INFO: --- com.ensode.jaxrsintro.service.CustomerResource.getCustomer()
invoked
```

For all other request method types, we need to send some data to our service. This can be accomplished with the `--data` command-line argument to `curl`:

```
curl -XPUT -HContent-type:text/xml --data
"<customer><id>321</id><firstName>Amanda</firstName><middleName>Zoe</middle
Name><lastName>Adams</lastName></customer>"
http://localhost:8080/jaxrsintro/resources/customer
```

As can be seen in the preceding example, we need to specify the MIME type via curl's `-H` command-line argument using the format seen in the preceding example.

We can verify that the preceding command worked as expected by inspecting the application server log:

```
INFO: --- com.ensode.jaxrsintro.service.CustomerResource.createCustomer()
invoked
INFO: customerXML =
<customer><id>321</id><firstName>Amanda</firstName><middleName>Zoe</middleN
ame><lastName>Adams</lastName></customer>
```

We can test other `request` method types just as easily:

```
curl -XPOST -HContent-type:text/xml --data
"<customer><id>321</id><firstName>Amanda</firstName><middleName>Tamara</mid
dleName><lastName>Adams</lastName></customer>"
http://localhost:8080/jaxrsintro/resources/customer
```

Which results in the following output in the application server log:

```
INFO: --- com.ensode.jaxrsintro.service.CustomerResource.updateCustomer()
invoked
INFO: customerXML =
<customer><id>321</id><firstName>Amanda</firstName><middleName>Tamara</midd
leName><lastName>Adams</lastName></customer>
```

We can test the `delete` method by executing the following command:

```
curl -XDELETE -HContent-type:text/xml --data
"<customer><id>321</id><firstName>Amanda</firstName><middleName>Tamara</mid
dleName><lastName>Adams</lastName></customer>"
http://localhost:8080/jaxrsintro/resources/customer
```

Resulting in the following output in the application server log:

```
INFO: --- com.ensode.jaxrsintro.service.CustomerResource.deleteCustomer()
invoked
INFO: customerXML =
<customer><id>321</id><firstName>Amanda</firstName><middleName>Tamara</midd
leName><lastName>Adams</lastName></customer>
```

Converting data between Java and XML with JAXB

In our previous example, we were processing "raw" XML received as a parameter, as well as returning "raw" XML to our client. In a real application, we would more than likely parse the XML received from the client and use it to populate a Java object. Additionally, any XML that we need to return to the client would have to be constructed from a Java object.

Converting data from Java to XML and back is such a common use case that the Java EE specification provides an API to do it. This API is the **Java API for XML Binding** (**JAXB**).

JAXB makes converting data from Java to XML transparent and trivial; all we need to do is decorate the class we wish to convert to XML with the `@XmlRootElement` annotation. The following code example illustrates how to do this:

```java
package com.ensode.javaee8book.jaxrstest.entity;

import java.io.Serializable;
import javax.xml.bind.annotation.XmlRootElement;

@XmlRootElement
public class Customer implements Serializable {

  private Long id;
  private String firstName;
  private String middleName;
  private String lastName;

  public Customer() {
  }

  public Customer(Long id, String firstName,
      String middleInitial, String lastName) {
    this.id = id;
    this.firstName = firstName;
    this.middleName = middleInitial;
```

```
      this.lastName = lastName;
    }

    //getters and setters omitted for brevity

    @Override
    public String toString() {
      return "id = " + getId() + "\nfirstName = " + getFirstName()
          + "\nmiddleName = " + getMiddleName() + "\nlastName = "
          + getLastName();
    }
}
```

As we can see, other than the @XmlRootElement annotation at the class level, there is nothing unusual about the above Java class.

Once we have a class that we have decorated with the @XmlRootElement annotation, we need to change the parameter type of our web service from String to our custom class:

```
package com.ensode.javaee8book.jaxbxmlconversion.service;

import com.ensode.jaxbxmlconversion.entity.Customer;
import javax.ws.rs.Consumes;
import javax.ws.rs.DELETE;
import javax.ws.rs.GET;
import javax.ws.rs.POST;
import javax.ws.rs.PUT;
import javax.ws.rs.Path;
import javax.ws.rs.Produces;

@Path("customer")
public class CustomerResource {

  private Customer customer;

  public CustomerResource() {
    //"fake" the data, in a real application the data
    //would come from a database.
    customer = new Customer(1L, "David",
        "Raymond", "Heffelfinger");
  }

  @GET
  @Produces("text/xml")
  public Customer getCustomer() {
    //in a "real" RESTful service, we would retrieve data from a
    database
```

```
        //then return an XML representation of the data.

        System.out.println("--- " + this.getClass().getCanonicalName()
            + ".getCustomer() invoked");

        return customer;
    }

    @POST
    @Consumes("text/xml")
    public void updateCustomer(Customer customer) {
        //in a "real" RESTful service, JAXB would parse the XML
        //received in the customer XML parameter, then update
        //a row in the database.

        System.out.println("--- " + this.getClass().getCanonicalName()
            + ".updateCustomer() invoked");


        System.out.println("---- got the following customer: "
            + customer);
    }

    @PUT
    @Consumes("text/xml")
    public void createCustomer(Customer customer) {
        //in a "real" RESTful service, we would insert
        //a new row into the database with the data in the
        //customer parameter

        System.out.println("--- " + this.getClass().getCanonicalName()
            + ".createCustomer() invoked");

        System.out.println("customer = " + customer);

    }

    @DELETE
    @Consumes("text/xml")
    public void deleteCustomer(Customer customer) {
        //in a "real" RESTful service, we would delete a row
        //from the database corresponding to the customer parameter
        System.out.println("--- " + this.getClass().getCanonicalName()
            + ".deleteCustomer() invoked");

        System.out.println("customer = " + customer);
    }
}
```

As we can see, the difference between this version of our RESTful web service and the previous one is that all parameter types and return values have been changed from `String` to `Customer`. JAXB takes care of converting our parameters and return types to and from XML as appropriate. When using JAXB, an object of our custom class is automatically populated with data from the XML data sent from the client, similarly, return values are transparently converted to XML.

Developing a RESTful web service client

Although curl allows us to quickly test our RESTful web services and it is a developer-friendly tool, it is not exactly user-friendly; we shouldn't expect to have our user enter curl commands in their command line to use our web service. For this reason, we need to develop a client for our services. JAX-RS includes a standard client-side API that we can use to easily develop RESTful web service clients.

The following example illustrates how to use the JAX-RS client API:

```java
package com.ensode.javaee8book..jaxrsintroclient;

import com.ensode.jaxbxmlconversion.entity.Customer;
import javax.ws.rs.client.Client;
import javax.ws.rs.client.ClientBuilder;
import javax.ws.rs.client.Entity;

public class App {

    public static void main(String[] args) {
        App app = new App();
        app.insertCustomer();
    }

    public void insertCustomer() {
        Customer customer = new Customer(234L, "Tamara", "A",
                "Graystone");
        Client client = ClientBuilder.newClient();
        client.target(
"http://localhost:8080/jaxbxmlconversion/resources/customer").
            request().put(
            Entity.entity(customer, "text/xml"),
            Customer.class);
    }
}
```

The first thing we need to do is create an instance of `javax.ws.rs.client.Client` by invoking the static `newClient()` method on the `javax.ws.rs.client.ClientBuilder` class.

We then invoke the `target()` method on our `Client` instance, passing the URI of our RESTful web service as a parameter. The `target()` method returns an instance of a class implementing the `javax.ws.rs.client.WebTarget` interface.

At this point, we invoke the `request()` method on our `WebTarget` instance. This method returns an implementation of the `javax.ws.rs.client.Invocation.Builder` interface.

In this particular example, we are sending an HTTP PUT request to our RESTful web service, therefore, at this point, we invoke the `put()` method of our `Invocation.Builder` implementation. The first parameter of the `put()` method is an instance of `javax.ws.rs.client.Entity`. We can create one on the fly by invoking the static `entity()` method on the `Entity` class. The first parameter for this method is the object we wish to pass to our RESTful web service, and the second parameter is the string representation of the MIME type of the data we will be passing to the RESTful web service. The second parameter of the `put()` method is the type of response the client expects from the service. After we invoke the `put()` method, an HTTP PUT request is sent to our RESTful web service and the method we decorated with the `@Put` annotation (`createCustomer()`, in our example) is invoked. There are similar `get()`, `post()`, and `delete()` methods which we can invoke to send the corresponding HTTP requests to our RESTful web service.

Query and path parameters

In our previous examples, we were working with a RESTful web service to manage a single customer object. In real life, this would obviously not be very helpful. A common case is to develop a RESTful web service to handle a collection of objects (customers, in our example). To determine which specific object in the collection we are working with, we can pass parameters to our RESTful web services. There are two types of parameters we can use, **Query** and **Path** parameters.

Query parameters

We can add parameters to methods that will handle HTTP requests in our web service. Parameters decorated with the @QueryParam annotation will be retrieved from the request URL.

The following example illustrates how to use query parameters in our JAX-RS RESTful web services:

```
package com.ensode.javaee8book.queryparams.service;

import com.ensode.queryparams.entity.Customer;
import javax.ws.rs.Consumes;
import javax.ws.rs.DELETE;
import javax.ws.rs.GET;
import javax.ws.rs.POST;
import javax.ws.rs.PUT;
import javax.ws.rs.Path;
import javax.ws.rs.Produces;
import javax.ws.rs.QueryParam;

@Path("customer")
public class CustomerResource {

  private Customer customer;

  public CustomerResource() {
    customer = new Customer(1L, "Samuel",
        "Joseph", "Willow");
  }

  @GET
  @Produces("text/xml")
  public Customer getCustomer(@QueryParam("id") Long id) {
    //in a "real" RESTful service, we would retrieve data from a
    database
    //using the supplied id.

    System.out.println("--- " + this.getClass().getCanonicalName()
        + ".getCustomer() invoked, id = " + id);

    return customer;
  }

  /**
   * Create a new customer
   * @param customer XML representation of the customer to create
```

```
    */
@PUT
@Consumes("text/xml")
public void createCustomer(Customer customer) {
  //in a "real" RESTful service, we would parse the XML
  //received in the customer XML parameter, then insert
  //a new row into the database.

  System.out.println("--- " + this.getClass().getCanonicalName()
      + ".createCustomer() invoked");

  System.out.println("customer = " + customer);


}


@POST
@Consumes("text/xml")
public void updateCustomer(Customer customer) {
  //in a "real" RESTful service, we would parse the XML
  //received in the customer XML parameter, then update
  //a row in the database.

  System.out.println("--- " + this.getClass().getCanonicalName()
      + ".updateCustomer() invoked");

  System.out.println("customer = " + customer);

  System.out.println("customer= " + customer);
}

@DELETE
@Consumes("text/xml")
public void deleteCustomer(@QueryParam("id") Long id) {
  //in a "real" RESTful service, we would invoke
  //a DAO and delete the row in the database with the
  //primary key passed as the "id" parameter.

  System.out.println("--- " + this.getClass().getCanonicalName()
      + ".deleteCustomer() invoked, id = " + id);

  System.out.println("customer = " + customer);
  }
}
```

Notice that all we had to do was decorate the parameters with the @QueryParam annotation. This annotation allows JAX-RS to retrieve any query parameters matching the value of the annotation and assign its value to the parameter variable.

We can add a parameter to the web service's URL, just as we pass parameters to any URL:

```
curl -XGET -HContent-type:text/xml
http://localhost:8080/queryparams/resources/customer?id=1
```

Sending query parameters via the JAX-RS client API

The JAX-RS client API provides an easy and straightforward way of sending query parameters to RESTful web services. The following example illustrates how to do this:

```java
package com.ensode.javaee8book.queryparamsclient;

import com.ensode.javaee8book.queryparamsclient.entity.Customer;
import javax.ws.rs.client.Client;
import javax.ws.rs.client.ClientBuilder;

public class App {

    public static void main(String[] args) {
        App app = new App();
        app.getCustomer();
    }

    public void getCustomer() {
        Client client = ClientBuilder.newClient();
        Customer customer = client.target(
"http://localhost:8080/queryparams/resources/customer").
                queryParam("id", 1L).
                request().get(Customer.class);

        System.out.println("Received the following customer
        information:");
        System.out.println("Id: " + customer.getId());
        System.out.println("First Name: " +
        customer.getFirstName());
        System.out.println("Middle Name: " +
        customer.getMiddleName());
        System.out.println("Last Name: " + customer.getLastName());
    }
}
```

As we can see, all we need to do to pass a parameter is to invoke the `queryParam()` method on the instance of `javax.ws.rs.client.WebTarget` returned by the `target()` method invocation on our `Client` instance. The first argument to this method is the parameter name and must match the value of the `@QueryParam` annotation on the web service. The second parameter is the value that we need to pass to the web service. If our web service accepts multiple parameters, we can chain `queryParam()` method invocations, using one for each parameter our RESTful web service expects.

Path parameters

Another way we can pass parameters to our RESTful web services is via `path` parameters. The following example illustrates how to develop a JAX-RS RESTful web service that accepts `path` parameters:

```
package com.ensode.javaee8book.pathparams.service;

import com.ensode.pathparams.entity.Customer;
import javax.ws.rs.Consumes;
import javax.ws.rs.DELETE;
import javax.ws.rs.GET;
import javax.ws.rs.POST;
import javax.ws.rs.PUT;
import javax.ws.rs.Path;
import javax.ws.rs.PathParam;
import javax.ws.rs.Produces;

@Path("/customer/")
public class CustomerResource {

  private Customer customer;

  public CustomerResource() {
    customer = new Customer(1L, "William",
        "Daniel", "Graystone");
  }

  @GET
  @Produces("text/xml")
  @Path("{id}/")
  public Customer getCustomer(@PathParam("id") Long id) {
      //in a "real" RESTful service, we would retrieve data from a
database
      //using the supplied id.
```

```java
    System.out.println("--- " + this.getClass().getCanonicalName()
        + ".getCustomer() invoked, id = " + id);

    return customer;
  }

  @PUT
  @Consumes("text/xml")
  public void createCustomer(Customer customer) {
    //in a "real" RESTful service, we would parse the XML
    //received in the customer XML parameter, then insert
    //a new row into the database.

    System.out.println("--- " + this.getClass().getCanonicalName()
        + ".createCustomer() invoked");
    System.out.println("customer = " + customer);

  }

  @POST
  @Consumes("text/xml")
  public void updateCustomer(Customer customer) {
    //in a "real" RESTful service, we would parse the XML
    //received in the customer XML parameter, then update
    //a row in the database.

    System.out.println("--- " + this.getClass().getCanonicalName()
        + ".updateCustomer() invoked");

    System.out.println("customer = " + customer);
     System.out.println("customer= " + customer);
  }

  @DELETE
  @Consumes("text/xml")
  @Path("{id}/")
  public void deleteCustomer(@PathParam("id") Long id) {
    //in a "real" RESTful service, we would invoke
    //a DAO and delete the row in the database with the
    //primary key passed as the "id" parameter.

    System.out.println("--- " + this.getClass().getCanonicalName()
        + ".deleteCustomer() invoked, id = " + id);

    System.out.println("customer = " + customer);
  }
}
```

Any method that accepts a `path` parameter must be decorated with the `@Path` annotation. The value attribute of this annotation must be formatted as "`{paramName}/`", where `paramName` is the parameter the method expects to receive. Additionally, method parameters must be decorated with the `@PathParam` annotation. The value of this annotation must match the parameter name declared in the `@Path` annotation for the method.

We can pass `path` parameters from the command line by adjusting our web service's URI as appropriate. For example, to pass an "`id`" parameter of `1` to the `getCustomer()` method above (which handles HTTP `GET` requests), we could do so from the command line, as follows:

```
curl -XGET -HContent-type:text/xml
http://localhost:8080/pathparams/resources/customer/1
```

Which returns the expected output of an XML representation of the `Customer` object returned by the `getCustomer()` method:

```
<?xml version="1.0" encoding="UTF-8"
standalone="yes"?><customer><firstName>William</firstName><id>1</id><lastNa
me>Graystone</lastName><middleName>Daniel</middleName></customer>
```

Sending path parameters via the JAX-RS client API

Sending path parameters to a web service via the JAX-RS client API is easy and straightforward; all we need to do is add a couple of method invocations to specify the path parameter and its value. The following example illustrates how to do this:

```
package com.ensode.javaee8book..pathparamsclient;

import com.ensode.javaee8book.pathparamsclient.entity.Customer;
import javax.ws.rs.client.Client;
import javax.ws.rs.client.ClientBuilder;

public class App {

    public static void main(String[] args) {
        App app = new App();
        app.getCustomer();
    }

    public void getCustomer() {
        Client client = ClientBuilder.newClient();
        Customer customer = client.target(
```

```
"http://localhost:8080/pathparams/resources/customer").
                    path("{id}").
                    resolveTemplate("id", 1L).
                    request().get(Customer.class);

        System.out.println("Received the following customer
        information:");
        System.out.println("Id: " + customer.getId());
        System.out.println("First Name: " +
        customer.getFirstName());
        System.out.println("Middle Name: " +
        customer.getMiddleName());
        System.out.println("Last Name: " + customer.getLastName());
    }
}
```

In this example, we invoke the `path()` method on the instance of `WebTarget` returned by `client.target()`. This method appends the specified `path` to our `WebTarget` instance. The value of this method must match the value of the `@Path` annotation in our RESTful web service.

After invoking the `path()` method on our `WebTarget` instance, we then need to invoke `resolveTemplate()`. The first parameter for this method is the name of the parameter (without the curly braces), and the second parameter is the value we wish to pass as a parameter to our RESTful web service.

If we need to pass more than one parameter to one of our web services, we simply need to use the following format for the `@Path` parameter at the method level:

```
@Path("/{paramName1}/{paramName2}/")
```

Then, annotate the corresponding method arguments with the `@PathParam` annotation:

```
public String someMethod(@PathParam("paramName1") String param1,
@PathParam("paramName2") String param2)
```

The web service can then be invoked by modifying the web service's URI to pass the parameters in the order specified in the `@Path` annotation. For example, the following URI would pass the values 1 and 2 for `paramName1` and `paramName2`:

```
http://localhost:8080/contextroot/resources/customer/1/2
```

The above URI will work both from the command line or through a web service client we develop with the JAX-RS client API.

Server-sent events

Typically, every interaction between a web service and its client is initiated by the client; the client sends a request (GET, POST, PUT, or DELETE), then receives a response from the server. Server-sent events technology allows RESTful web services to "take the initiative" to send messages to a client, that is, to send data that is not a response to a client request. Server-sent events are useful for sending data continuously to a client, for applications such as stock tickers, news feeds, sports scores, and so on.

JAX-RS 2.1 introduces server-sent event support. The following example illustrates how to implement this functionality into our JAX-RS RESTful web services:

```java
package net.ensode.javaee8book.jaxrs21sse;

import java.util.List;
import java.util.concurrent.Executor;
import java.util.concurrent.Executors;
import java.util.concurrent.TimeUnit;
import java.util.stream.Collectors;
import java.util.stream.Stream;
import javax.ws.rs.GET;
import javax.ws.rs.Path;
import javax.ws.rs.Produces;
import javax.ws.rs.core.Context;
import javax.ws.rs.core.MediaType;
import javax.ws.rs.sse.OutboundSseEvent;
import javax.ws.rs.sse.Sse;
import javax.ws.rs.sse.SseEventSink;

@Path("serversentevents")
public class SseResource {

    List<Float> stockTickerValues = null;
    Executor executor = Executors.newSingleThreadExecutor();

    @GET
    @Produces(MediaType.SERVER_SENT_EVENTS)
    public void sendEvents(@Context SseEventSink sseEventSink,
      @Context Sse sse) {
        initializeStockTickerValues();
        executor.execute(() -> {
            stockTickerValues.forEach(value -> {
                try {
                    TimeUnit.SECONDS.sleep(5);
                    System.out.println(String.format(
                      "Sending the following value: %.2f", value));
```

```
                        final OutboundSseEvent outboundSseEvent =
                          sse.newEventBuilder()
                        .name("ENSD stock ticker value")
                        .data(String.class,
                          String.format("%.2f", value))
                        .build();
                          sseEventSink.send(outboundSseEvent);
                    } catch (InterruptedException ex) {
                        ex.printStackTrace();
                    }

                });

            });
        }

        private void initializeStockTickerValues() {
            stockTickerValues = Stream.of(50.3f, 55.5f, 62.3f,
                70.7f, 10.1f, 5.1f).collect(Collectors.toList());
        }
    }
```

The preceding example simulates sending stock prices for a fictitious company to the client. To send server-sent events to the client, we need to utilize instances of the `SseEventSink` and `Sse` classes, as illustrated in our example. Both of these classes are injected into our RESTful web service via the `@Context` annotation.

To send an event, we first need to build an instance of `OutboundSseEvent` via the `newEventBuilder()` method of our `Sse` instance. This method creates an instance of `OutboundSseEvent.Builder`, which is then used to create the necessary `OutboundSseEvent` instance.

We give our event a name by invoking the `name()` method on our `OutboundSseEvent.Builder` instance, then set the data to be sent to the client via its `data()` method. The `data()` method takes two arguments: the first one is the type of data we are sending to the client (`String`, in our case), and the second one is the actual data we send to the client.

Once we have set our event's name and data via the corresponding method, we build an instance of `OutboundSseEvent` by invoking the `build()` method on `OutboundSseEvent.Builder`.

Once we have built our instance of `OutboundSseEvent`, we send it to the client by passing it as a parameter to the `send()` method of `SseEventSink`. In our example, we loop through the simulated stock prices and send it to the client.

JavaScript Server-sent events client

So far, all of our client examples have either used the curl command-line utility or the JAX-RS RESTful web server client API. It is very common to use JavaScript code running on a browser as a RESTful web service client, therefore, in this section, we will take that approach. The following example illustrates an HTML/JavaScript client receiving server-sent events:

```html
<!DOCTYPE html>
<html>
    <head>
        <title>Stock Ticker Monitor</title>
        <meta http-equiv="Content-Type" content="text/html;
charset=UTF-8">
    </head>
    <body onload="getStockTickerValues()">
        <h2>Super fancy stock ticker monitor</h2>
        <table cellspacing="0" cellpadding="0">
            <tr>
                <td>ENSD Stock Ticker Value: </td>
                <td> <span id="stickerVal"></span></td>
            </tr>
            <tr>
                <td></td><td><button>Buy!</button></td>
            </tr>
        </table>
        <script>
            function getStockTickerValues() {
              var source = new
                EventSource("webresources/serversentevents/");
              source.addEventListener('ENSD stock ticker value',
              function (event) {
              document.getElementById("stickerVal").
                  innerHTML = event.data;
                }, false);
            }
        </script>
    </body>
</html>
```

The `getStockTickerValues()` JavaScript function creates an `EventSource` object. This constructor takes a `String` representing the URL of the server sending the events as a parameter. In our case, we used a relative URL, since the preceding HTML/JavaScript code is hosted on the same server as the server code. If this wasn't the case, we would have needed to use a full URL.

We implement the functionality to be executed when the client receives an event by adding an event listener to our `EventSource` instance via its `addEventListener()` function. This function takes the event name (notice that the value matches the name we sent in the Java code for our RESTful web service), and a function to be executed when an event is received. In our example, we simply update the contents of a `<span>` tag with the data of the received message.

Summary

In this chapter, we discussed how to easily develop RESTful web services using JAX-RS, a new addition to the Java EE specification.

We covered how to develop a RESTful web service by adding a few simple annotations to our code. We also explained how to automatically convert data between Java and XML by taking advantage of the **Java API for XML Binding (JAXB)**.

Additionally, we covered how to pass parameters to our RESTful web services via the `@PathParam` and `@QueryParam` annotations.

Finally, we discussed how to develop web services that are able to send server-sent events to all of their clients, utilizing the new JAX-RS 2.1 Server-Sent event support.

11
Microservices Development with Java EE

Microservices is an architectural style in which code is deployed in small, granular modules. A microservices architecture reduces coupling and increases cohesion. Typically, microservices are implemented as RESTful web services, usually using JSON to pass data to one another by invoking HTTP methods (GET, POST, PUT or DELETE) on each other. Since communication between microservices is done via HTTP methods, microservices written in different programming languages can interact with each other. In this chapter, we will cover how we can use Java EE to implement microservices.

In this chapter, we will cover the following topics:

- Introduction to microservices
- Advantages of a microservices architecture
- Disadvantages of a microservices architecture
- Developing microservices using Java EE

Introduction to microservices

Architecting applications as a series of microservices offer some advantages over traditionally designed applications, as well as some disadvantages. When considering a microservices architecture for our applications, we must carefully weigh the advantages and disadvantages before we make our decision.

Advantages of a microservices architecture

Developing an application as a series of microservices offers several advantages over traditionally designed applications:

- **Smaller code bases**: since each microservice is a small, standalone unit, code bases for microservices tend to be smaller and easier to manage than traditionally designed applications.
- **Microservices encourage good coding practices:** a microservices architecture encourages loose coupling and high cohesion.
- **Greater resilience:** traditionally designed applications act as a single point of failure; if any component of the application is down or unavailable, the whole application is unavailable. Since microservices are independent modules, one component (that is, one microservice) being down does not necessarily make the whole application unavailable.
- **Scalability:** since applications developed as a series of microservices are composed of a number of different modules, scalability becomes easier; we can focus only on those services that may need scaling, without having to waste effort on parts of the application that do not need to be scaled.

Disadvantages of a microservices architecture

Developing and deploying applications adhering to microservice architecture comes with its own set of challenges, regardless of which programming language or application framework is used to develop the application:

- **Additional operational and tooling overhead:** each microservice implementation would require its own (possibly automated) deployment, monitoring systems, and so on.
- **Debugging microservices may be more involved than debugging traditional enterprise applications:** if an end user reports a problem with their application and that application utilizes multiple microservices internally, it is not always clear which of the microservices may be the culprit. This may be especially difficult if the microservices involved are developed by different teams with different priorities.

- **Distributed transactions may be a challenge:** rolling back a transaction involving several microservices may be hard. A common approach to working around this is to isolate microservices as much as possible, treating them as single units, then have local transaction management for each microservice. For example, if microservice A invokes microservice B, if there is a problem with microservice B, a local transaction in microservice B would roll back, then it would return an HTTP status code 500 (server error) to microservice A. Microservice A could then use this HTTP status code as a signal to initiate a compensating transaction to bring the system back to its initial state.

- **Network latency:** since microservices rely on HTTP method calls for communication, performance can sometimes suffer due to network latency.

- **Potential for complex interdependencies:** while independent microservices tend to be simple, they are dependent on each other. A microservices architecture can potentially create a complex dependency graph. This situation can be worrisome if some of our services depend on microservices developed by other teams who may have conflicting priorities (for example, if we find a bug in their microservice, however, fixing the bug may not be a priority for the other team).

- **Susceptible to the fallacies of distributed computing:** applications developed following microservice architecture may make some incorrect assumptions, such as network reliability, zero latency, infinite bandwidth, and so on.

Microservices and Java EE

Some may think that Java EE is "too heavyweight" for microservices development, but this is simply not the case. Because of this misconception, some may think that Java EE may not be suitable for a microservices architecture, when, in reality, Java EE fits microservices development well. In the past, Java EE applications were deployed to a "heavyweight" application server. Nowadays, most Java EE application server vendors offer lightweight application servers that use very little memory or disk space. Some examples of these Java EE compliant lightweight application servers include IBM's Open Liberty, Red Hat's WildFly Swarm, Apache TomEE, and Payara Micro.

Developing microservices with Java EE involves writing standard Java EE applications while limiting yourself to a certain subset of Java EE APIs—typically, JAX-RS and JSON-P or JSON-B, and perhaps some others, such as CDI and, if interacting with a relational database, JPA. Java EE developers can leverage their existing expertise when developing microservices. The main requirement is the development of RESTful web services using JAX-RS. Then, these web services are packaged in a WAR file and deployed to a lightweight application server as usual.

When using modern, embeddable Java EE application servers, usually only one application is deployed to each instance of the application server, and, in some cases, the "tables are turned" so to speak, by having the application server be just a library that the application uses as a dependency. With these modern application servers, several instances of the application server are often deployed to a server, making modern Java EE particularly suitable for microservices development. Many modern, lightweight Java EE application servers are embeddable, allowing the creation of an "uber jar", which includes both the application code and the application server libraries. This "uber jar" is then transferred to the server and run as a standalone application. In addition to "uber jars", modern application servers can be added to a container image (such as Docker), then applications can be deployed as a thin war, typically only a few kilobytes in size; this approach has the advantage of very fast deployments, usually under 2 seconds.

By deploying to a contemporary Java EE Web Profile compliant application server (or, as explained in the previous paragraph, creating an "uber jar"), Java EE developers can certainly leverage their existing expertise to develop microservice compliant applications.

Developing microservices using Java EE

Now that we have given a brief introduction to microservices, we are ready to see an example microservices application written using Java EE. Our example application should be very familiar to most Java EE developers. It is a simple **CRUD (Create, Read, Update, Delete)** application. Developed as a series of microservices, the application will follow the familiar MVC design pattern, with the "View" and "Controller" developed as microservices. The application will also utilize the very common DAO pattern, with our DAO developed as a microservice as well.

 Actually, the example code is not a full CRUD application. For simplicity, we decided to only implement the "Create" part of our CRUD application.

We will be using Payara Micro to deploy our example code. Payara Micro is a lightweight Java EE application server derived from GlassFish, it is open source and freely available, and supports the Java EE web profile, which includes a subset of all Java EE specifications, namely, Security, Bean Validation, CDI, EJB Lite (provides a subset of full EJB functionality), the Unified Expression Language, JAX-RS, JDBC, JNDI, JPA, JSF, JSON-P, JSP, Servlets, and WebSockets.

Payara Micro can be downloaded at
https://www.payara.fish/downloads.

Our application will be developed as three modules: first, a microservices client, followed by a microservices implementation of a controller in the MVC design pattern, then an implementation of the DAO design pattern implemented as a microservice.

Developing microservices client code

Before delving into developing our services, we will first develop a microservices client, in the form of an HTML5 page, using the popular Twitter Bootstrap CSS library as well as the ubiquitous jQuery JavaScript library. The JavaScript code in the frontend service will invoke the controller microservice, passing a JSON representation of user entered data. The controller service will then invoke the persistence service and save data to a database. Each microservice will return an HTTP code indicating success or an error condition.

The most relevant parts of our client code are the HTML form and the jQuery code to submit the form to our controller microservice.

We will only show small snippets of code here. The complete code for the sample application can be found at:
https://github.com/dheffelfinger/Java-EE-8-Application-Development-Code-Samples.

Markup for the form in our HTML5 page looks as follows:

```html
<form id="customerForm">
    <div class="form-group">
        <label for="salutation">Salutation</label><br/>
        <select id="salutation" name="salutation"
            class="form-control" style="width: 100px !important;">
            <option value=""> </option>
            <option value="Mr">Mr</option>
            <option value="Mrs">Mrs</option>
            <option value="Miss">Miss</option>
            <option value="Ms">Ms</option>
            <option value="Dr">Dr</option>
        </select>
    </div>
    <div class="form-group">
        <label for="firstName">First Name</label>
```

```html
        <input type="text" maxlength="10" class="form-control"
         id="firstName" name="firstName"  placeholder="First Name">
    </div>
    <div class="form-group">
        <label for="middleName">Middle Name</label>
        <input type="text" maxlength="10" class="form-control"
         id="middleName" name="middleName" placeholder="Middle
         Name">
    </div>
    <div class="form-group">
        <label for="lastName">Last Name</label>
        <input type="text" maxlength="20" class="form-control"
         id="lastName" name="lastName" placeholder="Last Name">
    </div>
    <div class="form-group">
        <button type="button" id="submitBtn"
         class="btn btn-primary">Submit</button>
    </div>
</form>
```

As we can see, this is a standard HTML form using Twitter Bootstrap CSS classes. Our page also has a script to send form data to the controller microservice.

```html
<script>
  $(document).ready(function () {
      $("#submitBtn").on('click', function () {
          var customerData = $("#customerForm").serializeArray();
          $.ajax({
              headers: {
                  'Content-Type': 'application/json'
              },
              crossDomain: true,
              dataType: "json",
              type: "POST",
              url:
"http://localhost:8180/CrudController/webresources/customercontroll
er/",
              data: JSON.stringify(customerData)
          }).done(function (data, textStatus, jqXHR) {
              if (jqXHR.status === 200) {
                  $("#msg").removeClass();
                  $("#msg").toggleClass("alert alert-success");
                  $("#msg").html("Customer saved successfully.");
              } else {
                  $("#msg").removeClass();
                  $("#msg").toggleClass("alert alert-danger");
                  $("#msg").html("There was an error saving
                   customer data.");
              }
```

```
    }).fail(function (data, textStatus, jqXHR) {
        console.log("ajax call failed");
        console.log("data = " + JSON.stringify(data));
        console.log("textStatus = " + textStatus);
        console.log("jqXHR = " + jqXHR);
        console.log("jqXHR.status = " + jqXHR.status);
    });
    });
});
</script>
```

The script is invoked when the **Submit** button on the page is clicked. It uses jQuery's `serializeArray()` function to collect user-entered form data and create a JSON-formatted array with it. The `serializeArray()` function creates an array of JSON objects. Each element on the array has a name property matching the name attribute on the HTML markup, and a `value` property matching the user-entered value.

For example, if a user selected `"Mr"` in the salutation drop down, entered `"John"` in the first name field, left the middle name blank, and entered `"Doe"` as the last name, the generated JSON array would look as follows:

```
[{"name":"salutation","value":"Mr"},{"name":"firstName","value":"Jo
hn"},{"name":"middleName","value":""},{"name":"lastName","value":"D
oe"}]
```

Notice that the value of each `"name"` property in the JSON array above matches the `"name"` attributes in the HTML form; the corresponding `"value"` attributes match the user entered values.

Since the generated HTTP request will be sent to a different instance of Payara Micro, we need to set the `crossDomain` property of the `Ajax` settings object to `true`, even though we are deploying all of our microservices to the same server (or, in our case, to our local workstation).

Notice that the `url` property value of the `Ajax` setting objects has a port of `8180`, we need to make sure our controller microservice is listening to this port when we deploy it.

We can deploy our View microservice to Payara Micro from the command line as follows:

```
java -jar payara-micro-4.1.2.173.jar --noCluster --deploy
/path/to/CrudView.war
```

Payara micro is distributed as an executable JAR file, therefore, we can start it via the `java -jar` command. The exact name of the JAR file will depend on the version of Payara Micro you are using.

By default, Payara Micro instances running on the same server form a cluster automatically. For our simple example, we don't need this functionality, therefore, we used the `--noCluster` command-line argument.

The `--deploy` command-line argument is used to specify the artifact we want to deploy. In our case, it is a WAR file containing the HTML5 page serving as the user interface of our example application.

We can examine the Payara Micro output to make sure our application was deployed successfully:

```
[2017-10-21T12:00:35.196-0400] [] [INFO] [AS-WEB-GLUE-00172]
[javax.enterprise.web] [tid: _ThreadID=1 _ThreadName=main] [timeMillis:
1508601635196] [levelValue: 800] Loading application [CrudView] at
[/CrudView]
[2017-10-21T12:00:35.272-0400] [] [INFO] [] [javax.enterprise.system.core]
[tid: _ThreadID=1 _ThreadName=main] [timeMillis: 1508601635272]
[levelValue: 800] CrudView was successfully deployed in 1,332 milliseconds.
[2017-10-21T12:00:35.274-0400] [] [INFO] [] [PayaraMicro] [tid: _ThreadID=1
_ThreadName=main] [timeMillis: 1508601635274] [levelValue: 800] Deployed 1
archive(s)
```

We can now point our browser to our CrudView application URL (`http://localhost:8080/CrudView` in our example). After entering some data, the page will look as shown in the following screenshot:

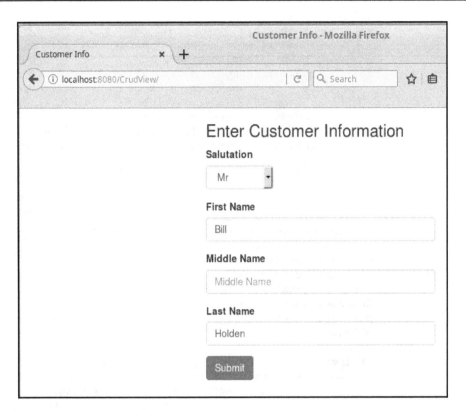

When the user clicks on the **Submit** button, the client passes a JSON representation of user-entered data to the controller service.

The controller service

The controller service is a standard RESTful web service implementation of a controller in the MVC design pattern, implemented using JAX-RS:

```
package
net.ensode.javaee8book.microservices.crudcontroller.service;
//imports omitted for brevity
@Path("/customercontroller")
public class CustomerControllerService {
    public CustomerControllerService() {
    }

    @OPTIONS
    public Response options() {
```

```
        return Response.ok("")
                .header("Access-Control-Allow-Origin",
                "http://localhost:8080")
                .header("Access-Control-Allow-Headers", "origin," +
                        "content-type, accept, authorization")
                .header("Access-Control-Allow-Credentials", "true")
                .header("Access-Control-Allow-Methods",
                        "GET, POST, PUT, DELETE, OPTIONS, HEAD")
                .header("Access-Control-Max-Age", "1209600")
                .build();
    }

    @POST
    @Consumes(MediaType.APPLICATION_JSON)
    public Response addCustomer(String customerJson) {
        Response response;
        Response persistenceServiceResponse;
        CustomerPersistenceClient client =
            new CustomerPersistenceClient();
        Customer customer = jsonToCustomer(customerJson);
        persistenceServiceResponse = client.create(customer);
        client.close();

        if (persistenceServiceResponse.getStatus() == 201) {
            response = Response.ok("{}").
                    header("Access-Control-Allow-Origin",
                            "http://localhost:8080").build();

        } else {
            response = Response.serverError().
                    header("Access-Control-Allow-Origin",
                            "http://localhost:8080").build();
        }
        return response;
    }

    private Customer jsonToCustomer(String customerJson) {
        Customer customer = new Customer();
        JsonArray jsonArray;
        try (JsonReader jsonReader = Json.createReader(
                new StringReader(customerJson))) {
            jsonArray = jsonReader.readArray();
        }

        for (JsonValue jsonValue : jsonArray) {
            JsonObject jsonObject = (JsonObject) jsonValue;
            String propertyName = jsonObject.getString("name");
            String propertyValue = jsonObject.getString("value");
```

```
            switch (propertyName) {
                case "salutation":
                    customer.setSalutation(propertyValue);
                    break;
                case "firstName":
                    customer.setFirstName(propertyValue);
                    break;
                case "middleName":
                    customer.setMiddleName(propertyValue);
                    break;
                case "lastName":
                    customer.setLastName(propertyValue);
                    break;
                default:
                    LOG.log(Level.WARNING, String.format(
                            "Unknown property name found: %s",
                            propertyName));
                    break;
            }
        }
        return customer;
    }
}
```

The `options()` method, annotated with the `javax.ws.rs.OPTIONS` annotation, is necessary since the browser automatically calls it before invoking the actual POST request containing the main logic of our server. In this method, we set some header values to allow **Cross-Origin Resource Sharing (CORS)**, which in simple terms means we allow our service to be invoked from a different server than the one our service is running on. In our case, the client is deployed to a different instance of Payara Micro, therefore, it is considered a different origin. These headers are necessary to allow our client code and controller service to communicate with each other. Notice that we explicitly allow requests from `http://localhost:8080`, which is the host and port where our client code is deployed.

The main logic of our controller service is in the `addCustomer()` method. This method receives the JSON string sent by the client as a parameter. In this method, we create an instance of `CustomerPersistenceClient()`, which is a client for the persistence service implemented using the JAX-RS client API.

We then create an instance of a `Customer` class by invoking the `jsonToCustomer()` method. This method takes the JSON string sent by the client and, using the standard Java EE JSON-P API, populates an instance of the `Customer` class with the corresponding values in the JSON string.

The Customer class is a simple **Data Transfer Object** (DTO) containing a few properties matching the input fields in the form in the client, plus corresponding getters and setters. The class is so simple we decided not to show it.

Our addCustomer() method then invokes the persistence service by invoking the create() method on CustomerPersistenceClient, checks the HTTP status code returned by the persistence service, then returns a corresponding status code to the client.

Let's now take a look at the implementation of our JAX-RS client code:

```
package
net.ensode.javaee8book.microservices.crudcontroller.restclient;
//imports omitted
public class CustomerPersistenceClient {

    private final WebTarget webTarget;
    private final Client client;
    private static final String BASE_URI =
    "http://localhost:8280/CrudPersistence/webresources";

    public CustomerPersistenceClient() {
        client = javax.ws.rs.client.ClientBuilder.newClient();
        webTarget =
        client.target(BASE_URI).path("customerpersistence");
    }

    public Response create(Customer customer) throws
      ClientErrorException {
        return webTarget.request(
        javax.ws.rs.core.MediaType.APPLICATION_JSON).
         post(javax.ws.rs.client.Entity.entity(customer,
          javax.ws.rs.core.MediaType.APPLICATION_JSON),
           Response.class);
    }

    public void close() {
        client.close();
    }
}
```

Our controller service only uses two standard Java EE APIs, namely JAX-RS and JSON-P. As we can see, our client code is a fairly simple class. Making use of the JAX-RS client API, we declare a constant containing the base URI of the service we are invoking (our persistence service). In its constructor, we create a new instance of `javax.ws.rs.client.ClientBuilder`, then set its base URI and path, matching the appropriate values for our persistence service. Our client class has a single method, which submits an HTTP POST request to the persistence service, then returns the response sent back from it.

We can deploy our controller service to Payara Micro from the command line as follows:

```
java -jar payara-micro-4.1.2.173.jar --noCluster --port 8180 --deploy
/path/to/CrudController.war
```

By examining Payara Micro's output, we can see that our code deployed successfully:

```
[2017-10-21T12:04:06.505-0400] [] [INFO] [AS-WEB-GLUE-00172]
[javax.enterprise.web] [tid: _ThreadID=1 _ThreadName=main] [timeMillis:
1508601846505] [levelValue: 800] Loading application [CrudController] at
[/CrudController]
[2017-10-21T12:04:06.574-0400] [] [INFO] [] [javax.enterprise.system.core]
[tid: _ThreadID=1 _ThreadName=main] [timeMillis: 1508601846574]
[levelValue: 800] CrudController was successfully deployed in 1,743
milliseconds.
[2017-10-21T12:04:06.576-0400] [] [INFO] [] [PayaraMicro] [tid: _ThreadID=1
_ThreadName=main] [timeMillis: 1508601846576] [levelValue: 800] Deployed 1
archive(s)
```

Now that we have successfully deployed our controller service, we are ready to go through the final component of our application, the persistence service:

```
package
net.ensode.javaee9book.microservices.crudpersistence.service;

//imports omitted for brevity
@ApplicationScoped
@Path("customerpersistence")
public class CustomerPersistenceService {
    @Context
    private UriInfo uriInfo;
    @Inject
    private CrudDao customerDao;

    @POST
    @Consumes(MediaType.APPLICATION_JSON)
    public Response create(Customer customer) {
```

```
        try {
            customerDao.create(customer);
        } catch (Exception e) {
            return Response.serverError().build();
        }
        return Response.created(uriInfo.getAbsolutePath()).build();
    }
}
```

In this case, since the client code invoking our service is developed in Java, there is no need to convert the JSON string we receive to Java code; this is done automatically under the covers. Our `create()` method is invoked when the controller service sends an HTTP POST request to the persistence service. This method simply invokes a `create()` method on a class implementing the DAO design pattern. Our persistence service returns an HTTP response 201 (created). If everything goes well, if the DAO's `create()` method throws an exception, then our service will return an HTTP error 500 (Internal Server Error).

Our DAO is implemented as a CDI-managed bean, using JPA to insert data into the database:

```
package net.ensode.microservices.crudpersistence.dao;
//imports omitted for brevity
@ApplicationScoped
@Transactional
public class CrudDao {
    @PersistenceContext(unitName = "CustomerPersistenceUnit")
    private EntityManager em;

    public void create(Customer customer) {
        em.persist(customer);
    }
}
```

Our DAO couldn't be much simpler; it implements a single method that invokes the `persist()` method on an injected instance of `EntityManager`.

 In our persistence service project, the `Customer` class is a trivial JPA entity.

We now deploy our persistence service to Payara Micro as usual:

```
java -jar payara-micro-4.1.2.173.jar --port 8280 --noCluster --deploy
/path/to//CrudPersistence.war
```

Examining Payara Micro's output, we can see that our persistence service was deployed successfully:

```
[2017-10-21T15:15:17.361-0400] [] [INFO] [AS-WEB-GLUE-00172]
[javax.enterprise.web] [tid: _ThreadID=1 _ThreadName=main] [timeMillis:
1508613317361] [levelValue: 800] Loading application [CrudPersistence] at
[/CrudPersistence]
[2017-10-21T15:15:17.452-0400] [] [INFO] [] [javax.enterprise.system.core]
[tid: _ThreadID=1 _ThreadName=main] [timeMillis: 1508613317452]
[levelValue: 800] CrudPersistence was successfully deployed in 4,201
milliseconds.
[2017-10-21T15:15:17.453-0400] [] [INFO] [] [PayaraMicro] [tid: _ThreadID=1
_ThreadName=main] [timeMillis: 1508613317453] [levelValue: 800] Deployed 1
archive(s)
```

Now that we have deployed all three components of our application, we are ready to see it in action.

Once the user enters some data and clicks the **Submit** button, we should see a *success* message at the top of our page:

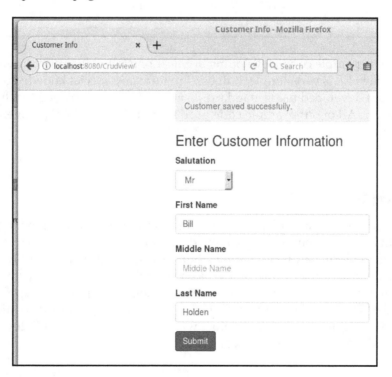

If we take a look at the database, we should see that the user-entered data was persisted successfully:

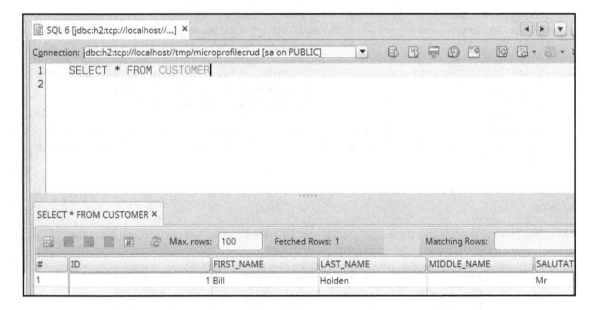

As shown by our example code, developing applications following microservices architecture in Java EE is very simple; it doesn't require any special knowledge. Microservices are developed using standard Java EE APIs and deployed to a lightweight application server. All of our example code used standard Java EE APIs, covered in previous chapters.

Summary

As we can see, Java EE is particularly suitable for microservices development. Java EE developers can leverage their existing knowledge to develop a microservice architecture and deploy it to modern, lightweight application servers. Traditional Java EE applications can interact with microservices well, as well as being refactored iteratively into a microservice architecture when it makes sense. Whether developing new applications following a microservice architecture, refactoring an existing application to microservices, or modifying existing applications to interact with microservices, Java EE developers can leverage their existing skills for the task at hand.

12

Web Services with JAX-WS

The Java EE specification includes the JAX-WS API as one of its technologies. JAX-WS is the standard way to develop **SOAP (Simple Object Access Protocol)** web services in the Java platform and stands for Java API for XML Web Services. JAX-WS is a high-level API; invoking web services via JAX-WS is done via remote procedure calls. JAX-WS is a very natural API for Java developers.

Web services are application programming interfaces that can be invoked remotely. Web services can be invoked from clients written in any language.

Some of the topics we will cover include:

- Developing web services with the JAX-WS API
- Developing web service clients with the JAX-WS API
- Adding attachments to web service calls
- Exposing EJBs as web services

Developing web services with JAX-WS

JAX-WS is a high-level API that simplifies the development of SOAP-based web services. JAX-WS stands for **Java API for XML Web Services**. Developing a web service via JAX-WS consists of writing a class with public methods to be exposed as web services. The class needs to be decorated with the @WebService annotation. All public methods in the class are automatically exposed as web services. They can optionally be decorated with the @WebService annotation. The following example illustrates this process:

```
package net.ensode.glassfishbook;

import javax.jws.WebMethod;
```

```
import javax.jws.WebService;

@WebService
public class Calculator {

    @WebMethod
    public int add(int first, int second) {
        return first + second;
    }

    @WebMethod
    public int subtract(int first, int second) {
        return first - second;
    }
}
```

The preceding class exposes its two methods as web services. The `add()` method simply adds the two `int` primitives it receives as parameters and returns the result; the `substract()` method subtracts its two parameters and returns the result.

We indicate that the class implements a web service by decorating it with the `@WebService` annotation. Any methods that we would like to expose as web services can be decorated with the `@WebMethod` annotation, but this isn't necessary; all public methods are automatically exposed as web services. We can still use the `@WebMethod` annotation for clarity, but it isn't strictly necessary to deploy our web service; we simply need to package it in a WAR file as usual.

Web service clients need a **WSDL** (**Web Services Definition Language**) file in order to generate executable code that they can use to invoke the web service. WSDL files are typically placed in a web server and accessed by the client via its URL.

When deploying web services developed using JAX-WS, a WSDL is automatically generated for us. The exact URL for the generated WSDL varies depending on the Java EE 8 application server we are using. When using GlassFish, URLs for JAX-WS WSDLs follow the following format:

```
[http|https]://[server]:[port]/[context root]/[service name]?wsdl
```

In our example, the URL for our web service's WSDL (when deployed to GlassFish) would be `http://localhost:8080/calculatorservice/CalculatorService?wsdl` (assuming GlassFish is running on our local workstation, and GlassFish is listening for HTTP connections on its default 8080 port).

Developing a web service client

As we mentioned earlier, executable code needs to be generated from a web service's WSDL. A web service client will then invoke this executable code to access the web service.

The **Java Development Kit** (**JDK**) includes a utility to generate Java code from a WSDL. The name of the utility is `wsimport`. It can be found under `$JAVA_HOME/bin`. The only required argument for `wsimport` is the URL of the WSDL corresponding to the web service, for example:

```
wsimport http://localhost:8080/calculatorservice/CalculatorService?wsdl
```

The preceding command will generate a number of compiled Java classes that allow client applications to access our web service:

- `Add.class`
- `AddResponse.class`
- `Calculator.class`
- `CalculatorService.class`
- `ObjectFactory.class`
- `package-info.class`
- `Subtract.class`
- `SubtractResponse.class`

Keeping generated source code: By default, the source code for the generated class files is automatically deleted; it can be kept by passing the `-keep` parameter to `wsimport`.

These classes need to be added to the client's `CLASSPATH` in order for them to be accessible to the client's code.

If we are using Apache Maven to build our code, we can take advantage of the JAX-WS Maven plugin to automatically invoke `wsimport` when building our client code. This approach is illustrated in the following `pom.xml` file:

```xml
<?xml version="1.0" encoding="UTF-8"?>
<project xmlns="http://maven.apache.org/POM/4.0.0"
xmlns:xsi="http://www.w3.org/2001/XMLSchema-instance"
xsi:schemaLocation="http://maven.apache.org/POM/4.0.0
http://maven.apache.org/xsd/maven-4.0.0.xsd">
    <modelVersion>4.0.0</modelVersion>
```

```
        <groupId>net.ensode.javaee8book</groupId>
        <artifactId>calculatorserviceclient</artifactId>
        <version>1.0</version>
        <packaging>war</packaging>

        <name>calculatorserviceclient</name>

        <properties>
<endorsed.dir>${project.build.directory}/endorsed</endorsed.dir>
<project.build.sourceEncoding>UTF-8</project.build.sourceEncoding>
        </properties>
        <dependencies>
            <dependency>
                <groupId>javax</groupId>
                <artifactId>javaee-api</artifactId>
                <version>7.0</version>
                <scope>provided</scope>
            </dependency>
        </dependencies>

        <build>
            <plugins>
                <plugin>
                    <groupId>org.codehaus.mojo</groupId>
                    <artifactId>jaxws-maven-plugin</artifactId>
                    <version>2.4.1</version>
                    <executions>
                        <execution>
                            <goals>
                                <goal>wsimport</goal>
                            </goals>
                            <configuration>
                                <vmArgs>
                                    <vmArg>-
Djavax.xml.accessExternalSchema=all</vmArg>
                                </vmArgs>
                                <wsdlUrls>
                                    <wsdlUrl>
http://localhost:8080/calculatorservice/CalculatorService?wsdl
                                    </wsdlUrl>
                                </wsdlUrls>
                                <keep>true</keep>
                            </configuration>
                        </execution>
                    </executions>
                </plugin>
                <!-- additional plugins removed for brevity -->
            </plugins>
```

```
        </build>
    </project>
```

The preceding `pom.xml` Maven build file will automatically invoke the `wsimport` utility whenever we build our code via the `mvn package` or `mvn install` commands.

At this point, we are ready to develop a simple client to access our web service. We will implement our client as a JSF application. The most relevant parts of our client application source code are shown as follows:

```java
package net.ensode.javaee8book.calculatorserviceclient;
import javax.enterprise.context.RequestScoped;
import javax.faces.event.ActionEvent;
import javax.inject.Inject;
import javax.inject.Named;
import javax.xml.ws.WebServiceRef;
import net.ensode.javaee8book.jaxws.Calculator;
import net.ensode.javaee8book.jaxws.CalculatorService;
@Named
@RequestScoped
public class CalculatorClientController {
    @WebServiceRef(wsdlLocation =
"http://localhost:8080/calculatorservice/CalculatorService?wsdl")
    private CalculatorService calculatorService;
    @Inject
    private CalculatorServiceClientModel
    calculatorServiceClientModel;
    private Integer sum;
    private Integer difference;
    public void add(ActionEvent actionEvent) {
        Calculator calculator =
         calculatorService.getCalculatorPort();
        sum =
calculator.add(calculatorServiceClientModel.getAddend1(),
        calculatorServiceClientModel.getAddend2());
    }
    public void subtract(ActionEvent actionEvent) {
        Calculator calculator =
         calculatorService.getCalculatorPort();
        difference =
calculator.subtract(calculatorServiceClientModel.getMinuend(),
         calculatorServiceClientModel.getSubtrahend());
    }
    public Integer getSum() {
        return sum;
    }
    public void setSum(Integer sum) {
```

```
        this.sum = sum;
    }
    public Integer getDifference() {
        return difference;
    }
    public void setDifference(Integer difference) {
        this.difference = difference;
    }
}
```

The `@WebServiceRef` annotation injects an instance of the web service into our client application. Its `wsdlLocation` attribute contains the URL of the WSDL corresponding to the web service we are invoking.

Notice that the web service class is an instance of a class called `CalculatorService`. This class was created when we invoked the `wsimport` utility, as `wsimport` always generates a class whose name is the name of the class we implemented plus the service suffix. We use this service class to obtain an instance of the web "Service" class we developed. In our example, we do this by invoking the `getCalculatorPort()` method on the `CalculatorService` instance. In general, the method to invoke to get an instance of our web service class follows the pattern `getNamePort()`, where `Name` is the name of the class we wrote to implement the web service. Once we get an instance of our web service class, we can simply invoke its methods as with any regular Java object.

Strictly speaking, the `getNamePort()` method of the service class returns an instance of a class implementing an interface generated by `wsimport`. This interface is given the name of our web service class and declares all of the methods we declared to be web services. For all practical purposes, the object returned is equivalent to our web service class.

The user interface for our simple client application is developed using Facelets, as customary when developing JSF applications:

```
<?xml version='1.0' encoding='UTF-8' ?>
<!DOCTYPE html PUBLIC "-//W3C//DTD XHTML 1.0 Transitional//EN"
"http://www.w3.org/TR/xhtml1/DTD/xhtml1-transitional.dtd">
<html xmlns="http://www.w3.org/1999/xhtml"
      xmlns:h="http://xmlns.jcp.org/jsf/html"
      xmlns:f="http://xmlns.jcp.org/jsf/core">
    <h:head>
        <title>Calculator Service Client</title>
    </h:head>
    <h:body>
        <h3>Simple JAX-WS Web Service Client</h3>
        <h:messages/>
```

```
<h:form>
    <h:panelGrid columns="4">
        <h:inputText id="addend1"
value="#{calculatorServiceClientModel.addend1}"/>
        <h:inputText id="addend2"
          value="#{calculatorServiceClientModel.addend2}"/>
        <h:commandButton value="Add"
          actionListener="#
            {calculatorClientController.add}">
            <f:ajax execute="addend1 addend2"
              render="sum"/>
        </h:commandButton>
        <h:panelGroup>
            Total: <h:outputText id="sum"
                value="#{calculatorClientController.sum}"/>
        </h:panelGroup>
    </h:panelGrid>
    <br/>
    <h:panelGrid columns="4">
        <h:inputText id="minuend"
value="#{calculatorServiceClientModel.minuend}"/>
        <h:inputText id="subtrahend"
          value="#
            {calculatorServiceClientModel.subtrahend}"/>
        <h:commandButton value="Subtract"
          actionListener="#
            {calculatorClientController.subtract}">
            <f:ajax execute="minuend subtrahend"
              render="difference"/>
        </h:commandButton>
        <h:panelGroup>
            Difference: <h:outputText id="difference"
                value="#
                    {calculatorClientController.difference}"/>
        </h:panelGroup>
    </h:panelGrid>
</h:form>
</h:body>
</html>
```

The user interface uses Ajax to invoke the relevant methods on the CalculatorClientController CDI named bean (refer to Chapter 2, *JavaServer Faces,* for details).

After deploying our code, our browser should render our page as follows (shown after entering some data and clicking the corresponding buttons):

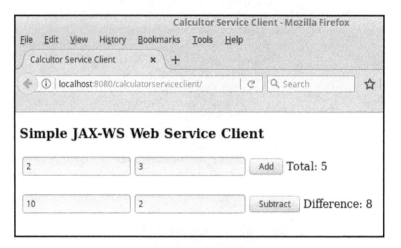

In this example, we passed `Integer` objects as parameters and return values. Of course, it is also possible to pass primitive types both as parameters and as return values. Unfortunately, not all standard Java classes or primitive types can be used as method parameters or return values when invoking SOAP-based web services implemented via JAX-WS. The reason for this is that, behind the scenes, method parameters and return types get mapped to XML definitions, and not all types can be properly mapped.

Valid types that can be used in JAX-WS web service calls are listed here:

- `java.awt.Image`
- `java.lang.Object`
- `Java.lang.String`
- `java.math.BigDecimal`
- `java.math.BigInteger`
- `java.net.URI`
- `java.util.Calendar`
- `java.util.Date`
- `java.util.UUID`
- `javax.activation.DataHandler`

- `javax.xml.datatype.Duration`
- `javax.xml.datatype.XMLGregorianCalendar`
- `javax.xml.namespace.QName`
- `javax.xml.transform.Source`

Additionally, the following primitive types can be used:

- `Boolean`
- `byte`
- `byte[]`
- `double`
- `float`
- `int`
- `long`
- `short`

We can also use our own custom classes as method parameters and/or return values for web service methods, but member variables of our classes must be one of the listed types.

Additionally, it is legal to use arrays both as method parameters and return values; however, when executing `wsimport`, these arrays get converted to lists, generating a mismatch between the method signature in the web service and the method call invoked in the client. For this reason, it is preferred to use lists as method parameters and/or return values, since this is also legal and does not create a mismatch between the client and the server.

> JAX-WS uses the Java Architecture for XML Binding (JAXB) internally to create SOAP messages from method calls. The types we are allowed to use for method calls and return values are the ones that JAXB supports. For more information on JAXB, see `https://github.com/javaee/jaxb-v2`.

Sending attachments to web services

In addition to sending and accepting the data types discussed in the previous sections, `web service` methods can send and accept file attachments. The following example illustrates how to do this:

```
package net.ensode.javaeebook.jaxws;

import java.io.FileOutputStream;
import java.io.IOException;

import javax.activation.DataHandler;
import javax.jws.WebMethod;
import javax.jws.WebService;

@WebService
public class FileAttachment {

    @WebMethod
    public void attachFile(DataHandler dataHandler) {
        FileOutputStream fileOutputStream;
        try {
            fileOutputStream =
              new FileOutputStream("/tmp/logo.png");
            dataHandler.writeTo(fileOutputStream);

            fileOutputStream.flush();
            fileOutputStream.close();
        } catch (IOException e) {
            e.printStackTrace();
        }

    }
}
```

In order to write a web service method that receives one or more attachments, all we need to do is add a parameter of type `javax.activation.DataHandler` for each attachment the method will receive. In the preceding example, the `attachFile()` method takes a single parameter of this type and simply writes it to the filesystem.

At this point, we need to package our code in a WAR file and deploy it as usual. Once deployed, a WSDL will automatically be generated. We then need to execute the `wsimport` utility to generate code that our web service client can use to access the web service. As previously discussed, the `wsimport` can be invoked directly from the command line or via an Apache Maven plugin.

Once we have executed `wsimport` to generate code to access the web service, we can write and compile our client code:

```
package net.ensode.javaee8book.fileattachmentserviceclient;

import java.io.ByteArrayOutputStream;
import java.io.IOException;
import java.io.InputStream;
import java.net.URL;
import javax.enterprise.context.RequestScoped;
import javax.inject.Named;
import javax.xml.ws.WebServiceRef;
import net.ensode.javaeebook.jaxws.FileAttachment;
import net.ensode.javaeebook.jaxws.FileAttachmentService;

@Named
@RequestScoped
public class FileAttachmentServiceClientController {

    @WebServiceRef(wsdlLocation =
"http://localhost:8080/fileattachmentservice/"
            + "FileAttachmentService?wsdl")
    private FileAttachmentService fileAttachmentService;

    public void invokeWebService() {
        try {
            URL attachmentUrl = new URL(
"http://localhost:8080/fileattachmentserviceclient/resources/img/lo
go.png");

            FileAttachment fileAttachment = fileAttachmentService.
                    getFileAttachmentPort();

            InputStream inputStream = attachmentUrl.openStream();

            byte[] fileBytes = inputStreamToByteArray(inputStream);
            fileAttachment.attachFile(fileBytes);
        } catch (IOException ioe) {
            ioe.printStackTrace();
        }
    }

    private byte[] inputStreamToByteArray(InputStream inputStream)
throws
        IOException {
        ByteArrayOutputStream byteArrayOutputStream =
            new ByteArrayOutputStream();
```

```
            byte[] buffer = new byte[1024];
            int bytesRead = 0;
            while ((bytesRead = inputStream.read(buffer, 0,
        buffer.length)) != -1) {
                byteArrayOutputStream.write(buffer, 0, bytesRead);
            }
            byteArrayOutputStream.flush();
            return byteArrayOutputStream.toByteArray();
        }
    }
```

Web service attachments need to be sent as a `byte` array to the web service, therefore, web service clients need to convert the file to attach to this type. In our example, we send an image as an attachment, we load the image into memory by creating an instance of `java.net.URL`, passing the URL of the image in question as a parameter to its constructor. We then obtain an `InputStream` instance corresponding to the image by invoking the `openStream()` method on our `URL` instance, convert our `InputStream` instance to a byte array, then pass this byte array to the `web service` method that expects an attachment.

Notice that, unlike when passing standard parameters, the parameter type used when the client invokes a method expecting an attachment is different from the parameter type of the method in the web server code. The method in the web server code expects an instance of `javax.activation.DataHandler` for each attachment; however, the code generated by `wsimport` expects an array of bytes for each attachment. These arrays of bytes are converted to the right type (`javax.activation.DataHandler`) behind the scenes by the `wsimport` generated code. As application developers, we don't need to concern ourselves with the details of why this happens; we just need to keep in mind that, when sending attachments to a web service method, parameter types will be different in the web service code and in the client invocation.

Exposing EJBs as web services

In addition to creating web services as described in the previous section, public methods of stateless session beans can easily be exposed as web services by simply adding an annotation to the EJB class. The following example illustrates how to do this:

```
package net.ensode.javaee8book.ejbws;

import javax.ejb.Stateless;
import javax.jws.WebService;

@Stateless
```

```
@WebService
public class DecToHexBean {

  public String convertDecToHex(int i) {
    return Integer.toHexString(i);
  }
}
```

As we can see, the only thing we need to do to expose a stateless session bean's public methods is to decorate its class declaration with the `@WebService` annotation. Needless to say, since the class is a session bean, it also needs to be decorated with the `@Stateless` annotation.

Just like regular stateless session beans, the ones whose methods are exposed as web services need to be deployed in a JAR file.

Just like standard web services, WSDL URLs for EJB web services depend on the application server being used. Consult your application server documentation for details.

EJB web service clients

The following class illustrates the procedure to be followed to access an EJB web service methods from a client application:

```
package net.ensode.javaee8book.ejbwsclient;

import javax.enterprise.context.RequestScoped;
import javax.inject.Inject;
import javax.inject.Named;
import javax.xml.ws.WebServiceRef;
import net.ensode.javaee8book.ejbws.DecToHexBeanService;

@Named
@RequestScoped
public class EjbClientController {

    @WebServiceRef(wsdlLocation =
    "http://localhost:8080/DecToHexBeanService/DecToHexBean?wsdl")
    private DecToHexBeanService decToHexBeanService;

    @Inject
    private EjbClientModel ejbClientModel;

    private String hexVal;
```

```
        public void convertIntToHex() {
            hexVal = decToHexBeanService.getDecToHexBeanPort().
                    convertDecToHex(ejbClientModel.getIntVal());
        }

        public String getHexVal() {
            return hexVal;
        }

        public void setHexVal(String hexVal) {
            this.hexVal = hexVal;
        }
    }
```

As we can see, nothing special needs to be done when accessing an EJB web service from a client. The procedure is the same as with standard web services.

The preceding class is a CDI named bean, and the following screenshot illustrates a simple JSF web-based user interface utilizing the preceding class to invoke our web service:

Summary

In this chapter, we covered how to develop web services and web service clients via the JAX-WS API. We explained how to incorporate web service code generation for web service clients when using ANT or Maven as a build tool. We also covered the valid types that can be used for remote method calls via JAX-WS. Additionally, we discussed how to send attachments to a web service. We also covered how to expose an EJB's methods as web services.

13

Servlet Development and Deployment

In this chapter, we will discuss how to develop and deploy Java servlets. Servlets allow us, as application developers, to implement server-side logic in Java web and enterprise applications.

Some of the topics covered include:

- An explanation of what servlets are
- Developing, configuring, packaging, and deploying our first servlet
- HTML form processing
- Forwarding HTTP requests
- Redirecting HTTP responses
- Persisting data across HTTP requests
- Initializing servlets via annotations
- Servlet filters
- Servlet listeners
- Servlet pluggability
- Configuring web applications programmatically
- Asynchronous processing
- HTTP/2 server push support

What is a servlet?

A servlet is a Java class used to extend the capabilities of servers that host server-side web applications. Servlets can respond to requests and generate responses. The base class for all servlets is `javax.servlet.GenericServlet`, defines a generic, protocol-independent servlet.

By far the most common type of servlet is an HTTP servlet. This type of servlet is used for handling HTTP requests and generating HTTP responses. An HTTP servlet is a class that extends the `javax.servlet.http.HttpServlet` class, which is a subclass of `javax.servlet.GenericServlet`.

A servlet must implement one or more methods to respond to specific HTTP requests. These methods are overridden from the parent `HttpServlet` class. As can be seen in the following table, these methods are named in such a way that knowing which one to use is intuitive:

HTTP request	HttpServlet method
GET	doGet(HttpServletRequest **request**, HttpServletResponse **response**)
POST	doPost(HttpServletRequest **request**, HttpServletResponse **response**)
PUT	doPut(HttpServletRequest **request**, HttpServletResponse **response**)
DELETE	doDelete(HttpServletRequest **request**, HttpServletResponse response)

Each of these methods takes the same two parameters, namely an instance of a class implementing the `javax.servlet.http.HttpServletRequest` interface and an instance of a class implementing `javax.servlet.http.HttpServletResponse`. These interfaces will be covered in detail later in this chapter.

Application developers never call the preceding methods directly, they are called automatically by the application server whenever it receives the corresponding HTTP request.

Of the four methods listed previously, `doGet()` and `doPost()` are, by far, the most commonly used.

An HTTP GET request is generated whenever a user types the servlet's URL in the browser, when a user clicks on a link pointing to the servlet's URL, or when a user submits an HTML form using the GET method where the form's action points to the servlet's URL. In any of these cases, the code inside the servlet's doGet() method gets executed.

An HTTP POST request is typically generated when a user submits an HTML form using the POST method and an action pointing to the servlet's URL. In this case, the servlet's code inside the doPost() method gets executed.

Writing our first servlet

In this section, we will develop a simple servlet to illustrate how to use the servlet API. The code for our servlet is as follows:

```java
package net.ensode.javaee8book.simpleapp;

import java.io.IOException;
import java.io.PrintWriter;

import javax.servlet.http.HttpServlet;
import javax.servlet.http.HttpServletRequest;
import javax.servlet.http.HttpServletResponse;

@WebServlet(urlPatterns = {"/simpleservlet"})
public class SimpleServlet extends HttpServlet {

    @Override
    protected void doGet(HttpServletRequest req,
     HttpServletResponse res) {
        try {
            res.setContentType("text/html");
            PrintWriter printWriter = res.getWriter();
            printWriter.println("<h2>");
            printWriter
                    .println("Hello servlet world!");
            printWriter.println("</h2>");
        } catch (IOException ioException) {
            ioException.printStackTrace();
        }
    }
}
```

The @WebServlet annotation specifies that our class is a servlet; its urlPatterns attribute specifies the relative URL of our servlet.

Servlets can also be configured via a web.xml deployment descriptor; however, since Java EE 6 annotation-based configuration is preferred.

Since this servlet is meant to execute when a user enters its URL in the browser window, we need to override the doGet() method from the parent HttpServlet class. Like we explained previously, this method takes two parameters, an instance of a class implementing the javax.servlet.http.HttpServletRequest interface, and an instance of a class implementing the javax.servlet.http.HttpServletResponse interface.

Even though HttpServletRequest and HttpServletResponse are interfaces, application developers don't typically write classes implementing them. When control goes to a servlet from an HTTP request, the application server provides objects implementing these interfaces.

The first thing our doGet() method does is to set the content type for the HttpServletResponse object to "text/html". If we forget to do this, the default content type used is "text/plain", which means HTML tags will be displayed on the page, as opposed to being interpreted by the browser.

Then we obtain an instance of java.io.PrintWriter by calling the HttpServletResponse.getWriter() method. We can then send text output to the browser by calling the PrintWriter.print() and PrintWriter.println() methods (the previous example uses println() exclusively). Since we set the content type to "text/html", any HTML tags are interpreted properly by the browser.

Testing the web application

To verify that the servlet has been properly deployed, we need to point our browser to our application's URL, for example, http://localhost:8080/simpleapp/simpleservlet. After doing so, we should see a page like the one shown in the following screenshot:

Processing HTML forms

Servlets are rarely accessed by typing their URL directly into the browser. The most common use for servlets is to process data entered by users in an HTML form. In this section, we illustrate this process.

The HTML file containing the form for our application looks like this:

```html
<!DOCTYPE html PUBLIC "-//W3C//DTD HTML 4.01 Transitional//EN"
"http://www.w3.org/TR/html4/loose.dtd">
<html>
    <head>
        <meta http-equiv="Content-Type" content="text/html;
charset=UTF-8">
        <title>Data Entry Page</title>
    </head>
    <body>
        <form method="post" action="formhandlerservlet">
            <table cellpadding="0" cellspacing="0" border="0">
                <tr>
                    <td>Please enter some text:</td>
                    <td>
                     <input type="text" name="enteredValue" />
                    </td>
                </tr>
                <tr>
                    <td></td>
```

```
                    <td><input type="submit" value="Submit"></td>
                </tr>
            </table>
        </form>
    </body>
</html>
```

The value for the form's `action` attribute must match the value of the servlet's `urlPatterns` attribute in its `@WebServlet` annotation. Since the value of the form's `method` attribute is `"post"`, our servlet's `doPost()` method will be executed when the form is submitted.

Now let's take a look at our servlet's code:

```java
package net.ensode.javaee8book.formhandling;

import java.io.IOException;
import java.io.PrintWriter;
import javax.servlet.annotation.WebServlet;

import javax.servlet.http.HttpServlet;
import javax.servlet.http.HttpServletRequest;
import javax.servlet.http.HttpServletResponse;

@WebServlet(urlPatterns = {"/formhandlerservlet"})
public class FormHandlerServlet extends HttpServlet {

    @Override
    protected void doPost(HttpServletRequest request,
     HttpServletResponse response) {
        String enteredValue;

        enteredValue = request.getParameter("enteredValue");

        response.setContentType("text/html");

        PrintWriter printWriter;
        try {
            printWriter = response.getWriter();

            printWriter.println("<p>");
            printWriter.print("You entered: ");
            printWriter.print(enteredValue);
            printWriter.print("</p>");
        } catch (IOException e) {
            e.printStackTrace();
        }
```

```
    }
  }
```

As can be seen in this example, we obtain a reference to the value the user typed by calling the `request.getParameter()` method. This method takes a single `String` object as its sole parameter, and the value of this string must match the name of the input field in the HTML file. In this case, the HTML file has a text field named `"enteredValue"`:

```
<input type="text" name="enteredValue" />
```

Therefore the servlet has a corresponding line:

```
enteredValue = request.getParameter("enteredValue");
```

This line is used to obtain the text entered by the user and store it in the `String` variable named `enteredValue` (the name of the variable does not need to match the input field name, but naming it that way is good practice; it makes it easy to remember what value the variable is holding).

After packaging the preceding three files in a WAR file called `formhandling.war`, then deploying the WAR file, we can see the rendered HTML file by entering a URL similar to the following in the browser (the exact URL will depend on the Java EE application server being used): `http://localhost:8080/formhandling`.

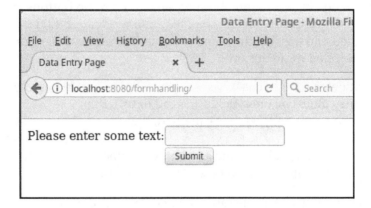

After the user enters **some text** in the text field and submits the form (either by hitting "Enter" or clicking on the **Submit** button), we should see the output of the servlet:

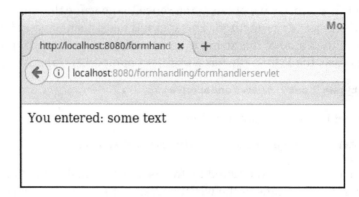

The `HttpServletRequest.getParameter()` method can be used to obtain the value of any HTML input field that can only return one value (text boxes, text areas, single selects, radio buttons, hidden fields, and so on). The procedure to obtain any of these fields' values is identical; in other words, the servlet doesn't care if the user typed in the value in a text field, selected it from a set of radio buttons, and so on. As long as the input field's name matches the value passed to the `getParameter()` method, the previous code will work.

 When dealing with radio buttons, all related radio buttons must have the same name. Calling the `HttpServletRequest.getParameter()` method and passing the name of the radio buttons will return the value of the selected radio button.

Some HTML input fields such as checkboxes and multiple select boxes allow the user to select more than one value. For these fields, instead of using the `HttpServletRequest.getParameter()` method, the `HttpServletRequest.getParameterValues()` method is used. This method also takes a `String` containing the input field's name as its only parameter, and returns an array of strings containing all the values that were selected by the user.

The following example illustrates this case. The relevant sections of our new HTML markup are shown as follows:

```
<form method="post" action="multiplevaluefieldhandlerservlet">
<p>Please enter one or more options.</p>
<table cellpadding="0" cellspacing="0" border="0">
  <tr>
    <td><input name="options" type="checkbox" value="option1" />
    Option 1</td>
```

```
  </tr>
  <tr>
    <td><input name="options" type="checkbox" value="option2" />
    Option 2</td>
  </tr>
  <tr>
    <td><input name="options" type="checkbox" value="option3" />
    Option 3</td>
  </tr>
  <tr>
    <td><input type="submit" value="Submit" /></td>
  </tr>
</table>
</form>
```

The new HTML file contains a simple form with three checkboxes and a submit button. Notice how every checkbox has the same value for its name attribute. Like we mentioned before, any checkboxes that are clicked by the user will be sent to the servlet.

Let's now take a look at the servlet that will handle the preceding HTML form:

```
package net.ensode.javaee8book.multiplevaluefields;

import java.io.IOException;
import java.io.PrintWriter;
import javax.servlet.annotation.WebServlet;

import javax.servlet.http.HttpServlet;
import javax.servlet.http.HttpServletRequest;
import javax.servlet.http.HttpServletResponse;

@WebServlet(urlPatterns = {"/multiplevaluefieldhandlerservlet"})
public class MultipleValueFieldHandlerServlet extends HttpServlet {

    @Override
    protected void doPost(HttpServletRequest request,
        HttpServletResponse response) {
        String[] selectedOptions =
        request.getParameterValues("options");

        response.setContentType("text/html");

        try {
            PrintWriter printWriter = response.getWriter();

            printWriter.println("<p>");
            printWriter.print("The following options were
```

```
            selected:");
            printWriter.println("<br/>");

            if (selectedOptions != null) {
              for (String option : selectedOptions) {
              printWriter.print(option);
              printWriter.println("<br/>");
              }
            } else {
                printWriter.println("None");
            }
            printWriter.println("</p>");
        } catch (IOException e) {
            e.printStackTrace();
        }
      }
    }
  }
```

The preceding code calls the `request.getParameterValues()` method and assigns its return value to the `selectedOptions` variable. Farther down the `doPost()` method, the code traverses the `selectedOptions` array and prints the selected values in the browser.

If no checkboxes are clicked, the `request.getParameterValues()` method will return `null`, therefore it is a good idea to check for null before attempting to traverse through this method's return values.

After packaging our new servlet in a WAR file and deploying it, we can see the changes in action by typing its URL in the browser window. For most application servers, the URL will be `http://localhost:8080/formhandling/`.

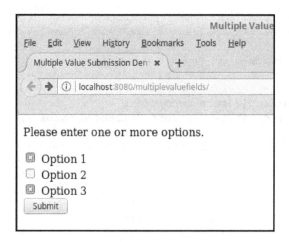

After submitting the form, control goes to our servlet, and the browser window should look something like this:

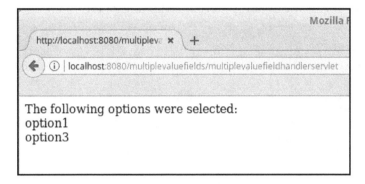

Of course, the actual message seen in the browser window will depend on what checkboxes the user clicked on.

Request forwarding and response redirection

In many cases, one servlet processes form data, then transfers control to another servlet or JSP to do some more processing or display a confirmation message on the screen. There are two ways of doing this, either the request can be forwarded or the response can be redirected to another servlet or page.

Request forwarding

Notice how text displayed in the previous section's example matches the value of the `value` attribute of the checkboxes that were clicked and not the labels displayed on the previous page. This might confuse the users. Let's modify the servlet to change these values so that they match the labels, then forward the request to another servlet that will display the confirmation message in the browser.

The new version of `MultipleValueFieldHandlerServlet` is shown as follows:

```
package net.ensode.javaee8book.formhandling;

import java.io.IOException;
import java.util.ArrayList;
```

```java
import javax.servlet.ServletException;
import javax.servlet.annotation.WebServlet;
import javax.servlet.http.HttpServlet;
import javax.servlet.http.HttpServletRequest;
import javax.servlet.http.HttpServletResponse;

@WebServlet(urlPatterns = {"/multiplevaluefieldhandlerservlet"})
public class MultipleValueFieldHandlerServlet extends HttpServlet {

    protected void doPost(HttpServletRequest request,
    HttpServletResponse response) {
        String[] selectedOptions =
        request.getParameterValues("options");
        ArrayList<String> selectedOptionLabels = null;

        if (selectedOptions != null) {
            selectedOptionLabels = new ArrayList<String>
            (selectedOptions.length);

            for (String selectedOption : selectedOptions) {
                if (selectedOption.equals("option1")) {
                    selectedOptionLabels.add("Option 1");
                } else if (selectedOption.equals("option2")) {
                    selectedOptionLabels.add("Option 2");
                } else if (selectedOption.equals("option3")) {
                    selectedOptionLabels.add("Option 3");
                }
            }
        }

        request.setAttribute("checkedLabels",
         selectedOptionLabels);

        try {
            request.getRequestDispatcher("confirmationservlet").
              forward(
              request, response);
        } catch (ServletException e) {
            e.printStackTrace();
        } catch (IOException e) {
            e.printStackTrace();
        }
    }
}
```

This version of the servlet iterates through the selected options and adds the corresponding label to an `ArrayList` of strings. This string is then attached to the `request` object by calling the `request.setAttribute()` method. This method is used to attach any object to the request so that any other code we forward the request to can have access to it later.

After attaching the `ArrayList` to the request, we then forward the request to the new servlet in the following line of code:

```
request.getRequestDispatcher("confirmationservlet").forward(
    request, response);
```

The `String` argument to this method must match the value of the `urlPatterns` tag of the servlet's `@WebServlet` annotation.

At this point, control goes to our new servlet. The code for this new servlet is shown as follows:

```
package net.ensode.javaee8book.requestforward;

import java.io.IOException;
import java.io.PrintWriter;
import java.util.List;
import javax.servlet.annotation.WebServlet;

import javax.servlet.http.HttpServlet;
import javax.servlet.http.HttpServletRequest;
import javax.servlet.http.HttpServletResponse;

@WebServlet(urlPatterns = {"/confirmationservlet"})
public class ConfirmationServlet extends HttpServlet {

    @Override
    protected void doPost(HttpServletRequest request,
    HttpServletResponse response) {
        try {
            PrintWriter printWriter;
            List<String> checkedLabels = (List<String>) request
                    .getAttribute("checkedLabels");

            response.setContentType("text/html");
            printWriter = response.getWriter();
            printWriter.println("<p>");
            printWriter.print("The following options were
            selected:");
            printWriter.println("<br/>");
```

```
            if (checkedLabels != null) {
                for (String optionLabel : checkedLabels) {
                    printWriter.print(optionLabel);
                    printWriter.println("<br/>");
                }
            } else {
                printWriter.println("None");
            }
            printWriter.println("</p>");
        } catch (IOException ioException) {
            ioException.printStackTrace();
        }
    }
}
```

This code obtains the ArrayList that was attached to the request by the previous servlet. This is accomplished by calling the request.getAttribute() method; the parameter for this method must match the value used to attach the object to the request.

Once the preceding servlet obtains the list of option labels, it traverses through it and displays them in the browser:

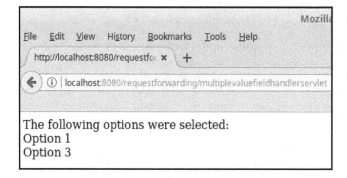

Forwarding a request as described previously only works for other resources (servlets and JSP pages) in the same context as the code doing the forwarding. In simple terms, the servlet or JSP we want to forward to must be packaged in the same WAR file as the code that is invoking the request.getRequestDispatcher().forward() method. If we need to direct the user to a page in another context (or even another server), we can do it by redirecting the response object.

Response redirection

One disadvantage of forwarding a request as described in the previous section is that requests can only be forwarded to other servlets or JSPs in the same context. If we need to direct the user to a page on a different context (deployed in another WAR file in the same server or deployed in a different server) we need to use the `HttpServletResponse.sendRedirect()` method.

To illustrate response redirection, let's develop a simple web application that asks the user to select their favorite search engine, then directs the user to his/her search engine of choice. The HTML page for this application would look like this:

```html
<!DOCTYPE html PUBLIC "-//W3C//DTD HTML 4.01 Transitional//EN"
"http://www.w3.org/TR/html4/loose.dtd">
<html>
    <head>
        <meta http-equiv="Content-Type" content="text/html;
charset=UTF-8">
        <title>Response Redirection Demo</title>
    </head>
    <body>
        <form method="post" action="responseredirectionservlet">
            <p>Please indicate your favorite search engine.</p>
            <table>
                <tr>
                  <td><input type="radio" name="searchEngine"
                      value="http://www.google.com">Google</td>
                </tr>
                <tr>
                    <td><input type="radio" name="searchEngine"
                        value="http://www.bing.com">Bing</td>
                </tr>
                <tr>
                    <td><input type="radio" name="searchEngine"
                        value="http://www.yahoo.com">Yahoo!</td>
                </tr>
                <tr>
                    <td><input type="submit" value="Submit" /></td>
                </tr>
            </table>
        </form>
    </body>
</html>
```

The HTML form in the previous markup code contains three radio buttons, the value for each of them is the URL for the search engine corresponding to the user's selection. Notice how the value for the name attribute of each radio button is the same, namely "searchEngine". The servlet will obtain the value of the selected radio button by calling the request.getParameter() method and passing the string "searchEngine" as a parameter, as is demonstrated in the following code:

```java
package net.ensode.javaee8book.responseredirection;

import java.io.IOException;
import java.io.PrintWriter;
import javax.servlet.annotation.WebServlet;

import javax.servlet.http.HttpServlet;
import javax.servlet.http.HttpServletRequest;
import javax.servlet.http.HttpServletResponse;

@WebServlet(urlPatterns = {"/responseredirectionservlet"})
public class ResponseRedirectionServlet extends HttpServlet {

    @Override
    protected void doPost(HttpServletRequest request,
    HttpServletResponse response)
            throws IOException {
        String url = request.getParameter("searchEngine");

        if (url != null) {
            response.sendRedirect(url);
        } else {
            PrintWriter printWriter = response.getWriter();

            printWriter.println("No search engine was selected.");
        }
    }
}
```

By calling request.getParameter("searchEngine"), the preceding code assigns the URL of the selected search engine to the url variable. Then (after checking for null, in case the user clicked on the submit button without selecting a search engine), it directs the user to the selected search engine by calling response.sendRedirect() and passing the url variable as a parameter.

The web.xml file for this application should be fairly straightforward and is not shown (it is part of this book's code download).

After packaging the code and deploying it, we can see it in action by typing a URL similar to the following in the browser: `http://localhost:8080/responseredirection/`.

After clicking the **Submit** button, the user is directed to their favorite search engine.

It should be noted that redirecting the response as illustrated previously creates a new HTTP request to the page we are redirecting to, therefore any request parameters and attributes are lost:

Persisting application data across requests

In the previous section, we saw how it is possible to store an object in the request by invoking the `HttpRequest.setAttribute()` method and how later this object can be retrieved by invoking the `HttpRequest.getAttribute()` method. This approach only works if the request was forwarded to the servlet invoking the `getAttribute()` method. If this is not the case, the `getAttribute()` method will return null.

It is possible to persist an object across requests. In addition to attaching an object to the request object, an object can also be attached to the session object or to the servlet context. The difference between these two is that objects attached to the session will not be visible to different users, whereas objects attached to the servlet context are.

Attaching objects to the session and servlet context is very similar to attaching objects to the request. To attach an object to the session, the `HttpServletRequest.getSession()` method must be invoked; this method returns an instance of `javax.servlet.http.HttpSession`. We then call the `HttpSession.setAttribute()` method to attach the object to the session. The following code fragment illustrates the process:

```
protected void doPost(HttpServletRequest request,
HttpServletResponse response)
{
  .
  .
  .
  Foo foo = new Foo(); //theoretical object
  HttpSession session = request.getSession();
  session.setAttribute("foo", foo);
  .
  .
  .
}
```

We can then retrieve the object from the session by calling the `HttpSession.getAttribute()` method:

```
protected void doPost(HttpServletRequest request,
HttpServletResponse response)
{
  HttpSession session = request.getSession();
  Foo foo =
  (Foo)session.getAttribute("foo");
}
```

Notice how the return value of `session.getAttribute()` needs to be cast to the appropriate type. This is necessary since the return value of this method is `java.lang.Object`.

The procedure to attach and retrieve objects to and from the servlet context is very similar. The servlet needs to call the `getServletContext()` method (defined in a class called `GenericServlet`, which is the parent class of `HttpServlet`, which in turn is the parent class of our servlets). This method returns an instance of `javax.servlet.ServletContext`, which defines a `setAttribute()` and a `getAttribute()` method. These methods work the same way as their `HttpServletRequest` and `HttpSessionResponse` counterparts.

The procedure to attach an object to the servlet context is illustrated in the following code snippet:

```
protected void doPost(HttpServletRequest request,
HttpServletResponse response)
{
    //The getServletContext() method is defined higher in
    //the inheritance hierarchy.
    ServletContext servletContext = getServletContext();

    Foo foo = new Foo();
    servletContext.setAttribute("foo", foo);
    .
    .
    .
}
```

The following code attaches the `foo` object to the servlet context; this object will be available to any servlet in our application and will be the same across sessions. It can be retrieved by calling the `ServletContext.getAttribute()` method, as is illustrated in the following code:

```
protected void doPost(HttpServletRequest request,
HttpServletResponse response)
{
    ServletContext servletContext = getServletContext();
    Foo foo = (Foo)servletContext.getAttribute("foo");
    .
    .
    .
}
```

This code obtains the `foo` object from the request context; again, a cast is needed since the `ServletContext.getAttribute()` method, like its counterparts, returns an instance of `java.lang.Object`.

 Objects attached to the servlet context are said to have a scope of *application*. Similarly, objects attached to the session are said to have a scope of *session*, and objects attached to the request are said to have a scope of *request*.

Passing initialization parameters to a servlet via annotations

Sometimes it is useful to pass some initialization parameters to a servlet; that way we can make sure the servlet behaves differently based on the parameters that are sent to it. For example, we may want to configure a servlet to behave differently in development and production environments.

In the old days, servlet initialization parameters were sent via the `<init-param>` parameter in `web.xml`. As of servlet 3.0, initialization parameters can be passed to the servlet as the value of the `initParams` attribute of the `@WebServlet` annotation. The following example illustrates how to do this:

```
package net.ensode.javaee8book.initparam;

import java.io.IOException;
import java.io.PrintWriter;
import javax.servlet.ServletConfig;
import javax.servlet.ServletException;
import javax.servlet.annotation.WebInitParam;
import javax.servlet.annotation.WebServlet;
import javax.servlet.http.HttpServlet;
import javax.servlet.http.HttpServletRequest;
import javax.servlet.http.HttpServletResponse;

@WebServlet(name = "InitParamsServlet", urlPatterns = {
  "/InitParamsServlet"}, initParams = {
  @WebInitParam(name = "param1", value = "value1"),
  @WebInitParam(name = "param2", value = "value2")})
public class InitParamsServlet extends HttpServlet {

  @Override
  protected void doGet(HttpServletRequest request,
```

```
                HttpServletResponse response)
                throws ServletException, IOException {
        ServletConfig servletConfig = getServletConfig();
        String param1Val = servletConfig.getInitParameter("param1");
        String param2Val = servletConfig.getInitParameter("param2");
        response.setContentType("text/html");
        PrintWriter printWriter = response.getWriter();

        printWriter.println("<p>");
        printWriter.println("Value of param1 is " + param1Val);
        printWriter.println("</p>");

        printWriter.println("<p>");
        printWriter.println("Value of param2 is " + param2Val);
        printWriter.println("</p>");
    }
}
```

As we can see, the value of the `initParams` attribute of the `@WebServlet` annotation is an array of `@WebInitParam` annotations. Each `@WebInitParam` annotation has two attributes—name, which corresponds to the parameter name, and `value`, which corresponds to the parameter value.

We can obtain the values of our parameters by invoking the `getInitParameter()` method on the `javax.servlet.ServletConfig` class. This method takes a single `String` argument as a parameter, corresponding to the parameter name, and returns a `String` corresponding to the parameter value.

Each servlet has a corresponding instance of `ServletConfig` assigned to it. As we can see in this example, we can obtain this instance by invoking `getServletConfig()`, which is a method inherited from `javax.servlet.GenericServlet`, the parent class of `HttpServlet`, which our servlets extend.

After packaging our servlet in a WAR file and deploying to our Java EE 8 application server of choice, we will see the following page rendered in the browser:

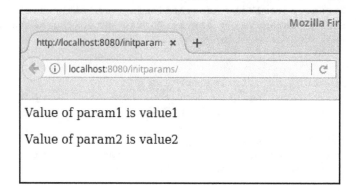

As we can see, the rendered values correspond to the values we set in each `@WebInitParam` annotation.

Servlet filters

Filters were introduced to the servlet specification in version 2.3. A filter is an object that can dynamically intercept a request and manipulate its data before the request is handled by the servlet. Filters can also manipulate a response after a servlet's `doGet()` or `doPost()` method finishes, but before the output is sent to the browser.

The only way to configure a filter in earlier servlet specifications was to use the `<filter-mapping>` tag in `web.xml`. Servlet 3.0 introduced the ability to configure servlets via the `@WebFilter` annotation.

The following example illustrates how to do this:

```
package net.ensode.javaee8book.simpleapp;

import java.io.IOException;
import java.util.Enumeration;
import javax.servlet.Filter;
import javax.servlet.FilterChain;
import javax.servlet.FilterConfig;
import javax.servlet.ServletContext;
import javax.servlet.ServletException;
import javax.servlet.ServletRequest;
import javax.servlet.ServletResponse;
```

```java
import javax.servlet.annotation.WebFilter;
import javax.servlet.annotation.WebInitParam;

@WebFilter(filterName = "SimpleFilter", initParams = {
 @WebInitParam(name = "filterparam1", value = "filtervalue1")},
  urlPatterns = {"/InitParamsServlet"})
public class SimpleFilter implements Filter {

  private FilterConfig filterConfig;

  @Override
  public void init(FilterConfig filterConfig) throws
          ServletException {
    this.filterConfig = filterConfig;
  }

  @Override
  public void doFilter(ServletRequest servletRequest,
          ServletResponse servletResponse, FilterChain filterChain)
          throws
          IOException, ServletException {
    ServletContext servletContext =
     filterConfig.getServletContext();
    servletContext.log("Entering doFilter()");
    servletContext.log("initialization parameters: ");
    Enumeration<String> initParameterNames =
            filterConfig.getInitParameterNames();
    String parameterName;
    String parameterValue;

    while (initParameterNames.hasMoreElements()) {
      parameterName = initParameterNames.nextElement();
      parameterValue =
       filterConfig.getInitParameter(parameterName);
      servletContext.log(parameterName + " = " + parameterValue);
    }

    servletContext.log("Invoking servlet...");
    filterChain.doFilter(servletRequest, servletResponse);
    servletContext.log("Back from servlet invocation");

  }

  @Override
  public void destroy() {
    filterConfig = null;
  }
}
```

As we can see in the example, the @WebFilter annotation has several attributes we can use to configure the filter. Of special importance is the urlPatterns attribute. This attribute takes an array of String objects as its value, and each element in the array corresponds to a URL that our filter will intercept. In our example, we are intercepting a single URL pattern, which corresponds to the servlet we wrote in the previous section.

Other attributes in the @WebFilter annotation include the optional filterName attribute, which we can use to give our filter a name. If we don't specify a name for our filter, then the filter name defaults to the filter's class name.

As we can see in the previous example, we can send initialization parameters to a filter. This is done the same way we send initialization parameters to a servlet. The @WebFilter annotation has an initParams attribute that takes an array of @WebInitParam annotations as its value. We can obtain the values of said parameters by invoking the getInitParameter() method on javax.servlet.FilterConfig, as illustrated in the example.

Our filter is fairly simple, it simply sends some output to the server log before and after the servlet is invoked. Inspecting the server log after deploying our application and pointing the browser to the servlet's URL should reveal our filter's output:

```
    [2017-05-31T20:02:46.044-0400] [glassfish 5.0] [INFO] []
[javax.enterprise.web] [tid: _ThreadID=112 _ThreadName=http-listener-1(5)]
[timeMillis: 1496275366044] [levelValue: 800] [[
    WebModule[/servletfilter] ServletContext.log():Entering doFilter()]]
    [2017-05-31T20:02:46.045-0400] [glassfish 5.0] [INFO] []
[javax.enterprise.web] [tid: _ThreadID=112 _ThreadName=http-listener-1(5)]
[timeMillis: 1496275366045] [levelValue: 800] [[
    WebModule[/servletfilter] ServletContext.log():initialization
parameters: ]]
    [2017-05-31T20:02:46.045-0400] [glassfish 5.0] [INFO] []
[javax.enterprise.web] [tid: _ThreadID=112 _ThreadName=http-listener-1(5)]
[timeMillis: 1496275366045] [levelValue: 800] [[
    WebModule[/servletfilter] ServletContext.log():filterparam1 =
filtervalue1]]
    [2017-05-31T20:02:46.045-0400] [glassfish 5.0] [INFO] []
[javax.enterprise.web] [tid: _ThreadID=112 _ThreadName=http-listener-1(5)]
[timeMillis: 1496275366045] [levelValue: 800] [[
    WebModule[/servletfilter] ServletContext.log():Invoking servlet...]]
    [2017-05-31T20:02:46.046-0400] [glassfish 5.0] [INFO] []
[javax.enterprise.web] [tid: _ThreadID=112 _ThreadName=http-listener-1(5)]
[timeMillis: 1496275366046] [levelValue: 800] [[
    WebModule[/servletfilter] ServletContext.log():Back from servlet
invocation]]
```

Servlet filters, of course, have many real uses. They can be used for profiling web applications, for applying security, and for compressing data, among many other uses.

Servlet listeners

During the lifetime of a typical web application, a number of events take place, such as HTTP requests getting created or destroyed, request or session attributes getting added, removed or modified, and so on and so forth.

The servlet API provides a number of listener interfaces we can implement in order to react to these events. All of these interfaces are in the `javax.servlet` package, and the following table summarizes them:

Listener interface	Description
ServletContextListener	Contains methods for handling context initialization and destruction events.
ServletContextAttributeListener	Contains methods for reacting to any attributes added, removed, or replaced in the servlet context (application scope).
ServletRequestListener	Contains methods for handling request initialization and destruction events.
ServletRequestAttributeListener	Contains methods for reacting to any attributes added, removed, or replaced in the request.
HttpSessionListener	Contains methods for handling HTTP session initialization and destruction events.
HttpSessionAttributeListener	Contains methods for reacting to any attributes added, removed, or replaced in the HTTP session.

All we need to do to handle any of the events handled by the interfaces described in the preceding table is to implement one of the previous interfaces and annotate it with the @WebListener interface, or declare it in the web.xml deployment descriptor via the <listener> tag. Unsurprisingly, the ability to use an annotation to register a listener was introduced in version 3.0 of the servlet specification.

The API for all of the preceding interfaces is fairly straightforward and intuitive. We will show an example for one of the preceding interfaces, and the others will be very similar.

 The JavaDoc for all of the preceding interfaces can be found at: https://javaee.github.io/javaee-spec/javadocs/.

The following example illustrates how to implement the ServletRequestListener interface, which can be used to perform an action whenever an HTTP request is created or destroyed:

```java
package net.ensode.javaee8book.listener;
import javax.servlet.ServletContext;
import javax.servlet.ServletRequestEvent;
import javax.servlet.ServletRequestListener;
import javax.servlet.annotation.WebListener;
  @WebListener()
public class HttpRequestListener implements ServletRequestListener
{
 @Override
   public void requestInitialized(ServletRequestEvent
   servletRequestEvent) {
ServletContext servletContext =
servletRequestEvent.getServletContext();
servletContext.log("New request initialized");
 }
 @Override
   public void requestDestroyed(ServletRequestEvent
   servletRequestEvent) {
ServletContext servletContext =
servletRequestEvent.getServletContext();
servletContext.log("Request destroyed");
 }
 }
```

As we can see, all we need to do to activate our listener class is to annotate it with the `@WebListener` annotation. Our listener must also implement one of the listener interfaces we listed previously. In our example, we chose to implement `javax.servlet.ServletRequestListener`; this interface has methods that are automatically invoked whenever an HTTP request is initialized or destroyed.

The `ServletRequestListener` interface has two methods, `requestInitialized()` and `requestDestroyed()`. In our previous, simple implementation we simply sent some output to the log, but of course we can do anything we need to do in our implementations.

Deploying our previous listener along with the simple servlet we developed earlier in the chapter, we can see the following output in the application server log:

```
[2017-05-31T20:15:57.900-0400] [glassfish 5.0] [INFO] []
[javax.enterprise.web] [tid: _ThreadID=109 _ThreadName=http-listener-1(2)]
[timeMillis: 1496276157900] [levelValue: 800] [[
WebModule[/servletlistener] ServletContext.log():New request initialized]]
[2017-05-31T20:15:58.013-0400] [glassfish 5.0] [INFO] []
[javax.enterprise.web] [tid: _ThreadID=109 _ThreadName=http-listener-1(2)]
[timeMillis: 1496276158013] [levelValue: 800] [[
WebModule[/servletlistener] ServletContext.log():Request destroyed]]
```

Implementing the other listener interfaces is just as simple and straightforward.

Pluggability

When the original servlet API was released back in the late 1990s, writing servlets was the only way of writing server-side web applications in Java. Since then, several standard Java EE and third-party frameworks have been built on top of the Servlet API. Examples of such standard frameworks include JSP and JSF, and third-party frameworks include Struts, Wicket, Spring Web MVC, and several others.

Nowadays, very few (if any) Java web applications are built using the Servlet API directly; instead, the vast majority of projects utilize one of the several available Java web application frameworks. All of these frameworks use the Servlet API "under the covers", therefore setting up an application to use one of these frameworks has always involved making some configuration in the application's `web.xml` deployment descriptor. In some cases, some applications use more than one framework, but this tends to make the `web.xml` deployment descriptor fairly large and hard to maintain.

Servlet 3.0 introduced the concept of pluggability. Web application framework developers now have not one, but two ways to avoid having application developers have to modify the web.xml deployment descriptor in order to use their framework. Framework developers can choose to use annotations instead of a web.xml to configure their servlets; after doing this, all that is needed to use the framework is to include the library JAR file(s) provided by the framework developers in the application's WAR file. Alternatively, framework developers may choose to include a web-fragment.xml as part of the JAR file to be included in web applications that use their framework.

web-fragment.xml is almost identical to web.xml, the main difference is that the root element of a web-fragment.xml is <web-fragment> as opposed to <web-app>. The following example illustrates a sample web-fragment.xml:

```xml
<?xml version="1.0" encoding="UTF-8"?>
<web-fragment version="3.0"
xmlns="http://java.sun.com/xml/ns/javaee"
  xmlns:xsi="http://www.w3.org/2001/XMLSchema-instance"
  xsi:schemaLocation="http://java.sun.com/xml/ns/javaee
  http://java.sun.com/xml/ns/javaee/web-fragment_3_0.xsd">
  <servlet>
    <servlet-name>WebFragment</servlet-name>
    <servlet-class>
      net.ensode.glassfishbook.webfragment.WebFragmentServlet
    </servlet-class>
  </servlet>
  <servlet-mapping>
    <servlet-name>WebFragment</servlet-name>
    <url-pattern>/WebFragment</url-pattern>
  </servlet-mapping>
</web-fragment>
```

As we can see, web-fragment.xml is almost identical to a typical web.xml. In this simple example, we only use the <servlet> and <servlet-mapping> elements, but all other usual web.xml elements, such as <filter>, <filter-mapping>, and <listener>, are available as well.

As specified in our web-fragment.xml, our servlet can be invoked via its URL pattern, /WebFragment, therefore the URL to execute our servlet once deployed as part of a web application would be http://localhost:8080/webfragmentapp/WebFragment. Of course, the host name, port, and context root must be adjusted as appropriate.

All we need to do for any Java EE-compliant application server to pick up the settings in web-fragment.xml is to place the file in the META-INF folder of the library where we pack our servlet, filter, and/or listener, then place our library's JAR file in the lib folder of the WAR file containing our application.

Configuring web applications programmatically

In addition to allowing us to configure web applications through annotations and through a web-fragment.xml, Servlet 3.0 also allows us to configure our web applications programmatically at runtime.

The ServletContext class has new methods to configure servlets, filters, and listeners programmatically. The following example illustrates how to configure a servlet programmatically at runtime, without resorting to the @WebServlet annotation or to XML:

```
package net.ensode.javaee8book.servlet;

import javax.servlet.ServletContext;
import javax.servlet.ServletContextEvent;
import javax.servlet.ServletContextListener;
import javax.servlet.ServletException;
import javax.servlet.ServletRegistration;
import javax.servlet.annotation.WebListener;

@WebListener()
public class ServletContextListenerImpl implements
        ServletContextListener {

  @Override
  public void contextInitialized(
          ServletContextEvent servletContextEvent) {
    ServletContext servletContext = servletContextEvent.
          getServletContext();
    try {
      ProgrammaticallyConfiguredServlet servlet = servletContext.
        createServlet(ProgrammaticallyConfiguredServlet.class);
      servletContext.addServlet(
        "ProgrammaticallyConfiguredServlet", servlet);
      ServletRegistration servletRegistration = servletContext.
        getServletRegistration(
        "ProgrammaticallyConfiguredServlet");
      servletRegistration.addMapping(
```

```
                    "/ProgrammaticallyConfiguredServlet");
          } catch (ServletException servletException) {
            servletContext.log(servletException.getMessage());
          }
        }

        @Override
        public void contextDestroyed(
                ServletContextEvent servletContextEvent) {
        }
      }
```

In this example, we invoke the `createServlet()` method of `ServletContext` to create the servlet that we are about to configure. This method takes an instance of `java.lang.Class` corresponding to our servlet's class. This method returns a class implementing `javax.servlet.Servlet` or any of its child interfaces.

Once we create our servlet, we need to invoke `addServlet()` on our `ServletContext` instance to register our servlet with the servlet container. This method takes two parameters, the first being a `String` corresponding to the servlet name, the second being the servlet instance returned by the call to `createServlet()`.

Once we have registered our servlet, we need to add a URL mapping to it. In order to do this, we need to invoke the `getServletRegistration()` method on our `ServletContext` instance, passing the servlet name as a parameter. This method returns the servlet container's implementation of `javax.servlet.ServletRegistration`. From this object, we need to invoke its `addMapping()` method, passing the URL mapping we wish our servlet to handle.

Our example servlet is very simple, it simply displays a text message in the browser:

```java
package net.ensode.javaee8book.servlet;

import java.io.IOException;
import javax.servlet.ServletException;
import javax.servlet.ServletOutputStream;
import javax.servlet.http.HttpServlet;
import javax.servlet.http.HttpServletRequest;
import javax.servlet.http.HttpServletResponse;

public class ProgrammaticallyConfiguredServlet extends HttpServlet
{

  @Override
  protected void doGet(HttpServletRequest request,
```

```
                    HttpServletResponse response)
                throws ServletException, IOException {
        ServletOutputStream outputStream = response.getOutputStream();

        outputStream.println(
                "This message was generated from a servlet that was "
                + "configured programmatically.");
    }
}
```

After packing our code in a WAR file, deploying to GlassFish, and pointing the browser to the appropriate URL (that is, `http://localhost:8080/programmaticservletwebapp/ProgrammaticallyConfigu redServlet`, assuming we packaged the application in a WAR file named `programmaticservletwebapp.war` and didn't override the default context root), we should see the following message in the browser:

This message was generated from a servlet that was configured programmatically.

The `ServletContext` interface has methods to create and add servlet filters and listeners, they work very similarly to the way the `addServlet()` and `createServlet()` methods work, therefore we won't be discussing them in detail. Refer to the Java EE API documentation at: `https://javaee.github.io/javaee-spec/javadocs/` for details.

Asynchronous processing

Traditionally, servlets have created a single thread per request in Java web applications. After a request is processed, the thread is made available for other requests to use. This model works fairly well for traditional web applications, for which HTTP requests are relatively few and far between. However, most modern web applications take advantage of Ajax (Asynchronous JavaScript and XML), a technique that makes web applications behave much more responsively than traditional web applications. Ajax has the side effect of generating a lot more HTTP requests than traditional web applications, if some of these threads block for a long time waiting for a resource to be ready, or do anything that takes a long time to process, it is possible our application may suffer from thread starvation.

To alleviate the situation described in the previous paragraph, the Servlet 3.0 specification introduced asynchronous processing. Using this new capability, we are no longer limited to a single thread per request. We can now spawn a separate thread and return the original thread back to the pool, to be reused by other clients.

The following example illustrates how to implement asynchronous processing using the new capabilities introduced in Servlet 3.0:

```java
package net.ensode.javaee8book.asynchronousservlet;

import java.io.IOException;
import java.util.logging.Level;
import java.util.logging.Logger;
import javax.servlet.AsyncContext;
import javax.servlet.ServletException;
import javax.servlet.annotation.WebServlet;
import javax.servlet.http.HttpServlet;
import javax.servlet.http.HttpServletRequest;
import javax.servlet.http.HttpServletResponse;

@WebServlet(name = "AsynchronousServlet", urlPatterns = {
 "/AsynchronousServlet"},
  asyncSupported = true)
public class AsynchronousServlet extends HttpServlet {

  @Override
  protected void doGet(HttpServletRequest request,
          HttpServletResponse response)
          throws ServletException, IOException {
    final Logger logger =
          Logger.getLogger(AsynchronousServlet.class.getName());
    logger.log(Level.INFO, "--- Entering doGet()");
    final AsyncContext ac = request.startAsync();
    logger.log(Level.INFO, "---- invoking ac.start()");
    ac.start(new Runnable() {

      @Override
      public void run() {
        logger.log(Level.INFO, "inside thread");
        try {
          //simulate a long running process.
          Thread.sleep(10000);
        } catch (InterruptedException ex) {
          Logger.getLogger(AsynchronousServlet.class.getName()).
                  log(Level.SEVERE, null, ex);
        }
        try {
          ac.getResponse().getWriter().
           println("You should see this after a brief wait");
          ac.complete();
        } catch (IOException ex) {
          Logger.getLogger(AsynchronousServlet.class.getName()).
```

```
                              log(Level.SEVERE, null, ex);
                }
            }
        });
        logger.log(Level.INFO, "Leaving doGet()");
    }
}
```

The first thing we need to do to make sure our asynchronous processing code works as expected is to set the `asyncSupported` attribute of the `@WebServlet` annotation to true.

To actually spawn an asynchronous process, we need to invoke the `startAsync()` method on the instance of `HttpServletRequest` that we receive as a parameter in the `doGet()` or `doPost()` method in our servlet. This method returns an instance of `javax.servlet.AsyncContext`. This class has a `start()` method that takes an instance of a class implementing `java.lang.Runnable` as its sole parameter. In our example, we used an anonymous inner class to implement `Runnable` in line; of course a standard Java class implementing `Runnable` can be used as well.

When we invoke the `start()` method of `AsyncContext`, a new thread is spawned and the `run()` method of the `Runnable` instance is executed. This thread runs in the background, the `doGet()` method returns immediately, and the request thread is immediately available to service other clients. It is important to notice that, even though the `doGet()` method returns immediately, the response is not committed until after the spawned thread finishes. It can signal it is done processing by invoking the `complete()` method on `AsyncContext`.

In the previous example, we sent some entries to the application server log file to better illustrate what is going on. By observing the application server log right after our servlet executes, we should notice that all log entries are written to the log within a fraction of a second of each other; the message **You should see this after a brief wait** doesn't show in the browser until after the log entry indicating that we are leaving the `doGet()` method gets written to the log.

HTTP/2 server push support

HTTP/2 is the newest version of the HTTP protocol. It offers several advantages over HTTP 1.1. For example, with HTTP/2 there is a single connection between the browser and the server and this connection remains open until the user navigates to another page. HTTP/2 also offers multiplexing, meaning that several concurrent requests from the browser to the server are allowed. Additionally, HTTP/2 features server push, meaning that the server can send resources to the browser without the browser specifically having to request them.

HTTP/2 server push support was added to the servlet specification in version 4.0, released as part of Java EE 8. In this section, we'll see how we can write code to take advantage of HTTP/2's server push functionality. The following example illustrates how this can be done:

```java
package net.ensode.javaee8book.servlet;

import java.io.IOException;
import java.io.PrintWriter;
import javax.servlet.ServletException;
import javax.servlet.annotation.WebServlet;
import javax.servlet.http.HttpServlet;
import javax.servlet.http.HttpServletRequest;
import javax.servlet.http.HttpServletResponse;
import javax.servlet.http.PushBuilder;

@WebServlet(name = "ServletPushDemoServlet", urlPatterns =
{"/ServletPushDemoServlet"})
public class ServletPushDemoServlet extends HttpServlet {
    @Override
    protected void doPost(HttpServletRequest request,
    HttpServletResponse response)
            throws ServletException, IOException {
        PushBuilder pushBuilder = request.newPushBuilder();

        if (pushBuilder != null) {
            //We know the browser is going to need the image
            //so we push it before it even requests it.
            //We could do the same for Javascript files, CSS, etc.
            pushBuilder.path("images/david_heffelfinger.png").
             addHeader("content-type", "image/png").
              push();
            response.sendRedirect("response.html");
        } else {
            //Gracefully handle the case when the browser does not
            //support HTTP/2.
        }
    }
}
```

We can push resources to the browser via the new PushBuilder interface, introduced in version 4 of the servlet specification. We can obtain an instance of a class implementing PushBuilder by invoking the new PushBuilder() method on the instance of HttpServletRequest we get as a parameter in our doPost() method.

As its name implies, the `PushBuilder` interface implements the Builder pattern, meaning that most of its methods return a new instance of `PushBuilder` we can use, allowing us to conveniently chain together method invocations.

We indicate the path of the resource we'd like to push to the browser by invoking the appropriately named `path()` method from `PushBuilder`. This method takes a single `String` argument indicating the path of the resource to push. Paths beginning with a forward slash (/) indicate an absolute path, all other paths indicate a path relative to our application's context root.

Once we have specified the path of our resource, we can optionally set some HTTP headers; in our case, we are pushing an image in PNG format, therefore we set the content type as appropriate.

Finally, we invoke the `push()` method on our `PushBuilder` instance to actually push our resource to the browser.

What we accomplished with our example was pushing a resource to the browser before the browser submitted a request for it; this task was impossible before the HTTP/2 protocol was released.

Summary

This chapter covered how to develop, configure, package, and deploy servlets. We also covered how to process HTML form information by accessing the HTTP request object. Additionally, forwarding HTTP requests from one servlet to another was covered, as well as redirecting the HTTP response to a different server.

We discussed how to persist objects in memory across requests by attaching them to the servlet context and the HTTP session. We also covered additional features of the servlet API, including configuring web applications via annotations, pluggability through `web-fragment.xml`, programmatic servlet configuration, and asynchronous processing. Finally, we covered the new Servlet 4.0 API that supports HTTP/2 server push.

Configuring and Deploying to GlassFish

At the time of writing, GlassFish 5 was the only released Java EE 8 compliant application server, as such, all the example code was tested against GlassFish, however, they should work on any Java EE 8 compliant application server.

Readers wanting to use GlassFish to run the example code can follow the instructions in this appendix to set it up.

Obtaining GlassFish

GlassFish can be downloaded from `https://javaee.github.io/glassfish/download`.

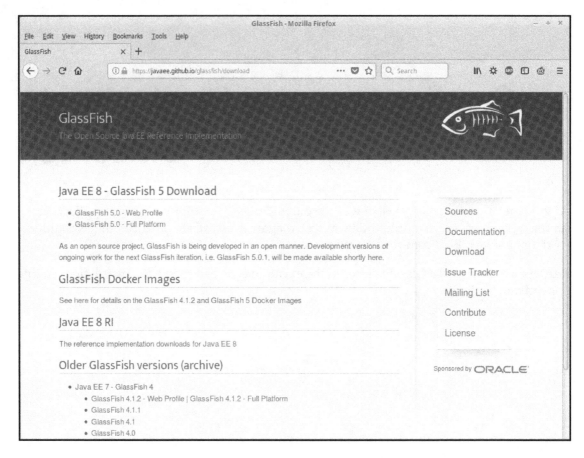

The Java EE specification has the concept of profiles, the Web Profile implements a subset of the full Java EE specification and is missing some features, such as JMS and some EJB features. To be able to successfully deploy all examples in the book, we should download the version of GlassFish implementing the full Java EE 8 specification by clicking the link labeled **GlassFish 5.0 - Full Platform**.

Installing GlassFish

GlassFish 5.0 is distributed as a zip file; installing GlassFish is as simple as extracting the zip file to a directory of our choosing.

GlassFish assumes some dependencies are present in your system.

GlassFish dependencies

In order to install GlassFish 5, a recent Java SE version must be installed on your workstation (Java SE 8 required), and the Java executable must be in your system PATH. Java SE 8 can be downloaded at
`http://www.oracle.com/technetwork/java/javase/downloads/jdk8-downloads-2133151.html`.

Performing the installation

Once the JDK has been installed, the GlassFish installation can begin by simply extracting the downloaded compressed file:

All modern operating systems, including Linux, Windows, and macOS, include out-of-the-box support for extracting compressed ZIP files, consult your operating system documentation for details.

After extracting the zip file, a new directory named glassfish5 will be created, this new directory contains our GlassFish installation.

Starting GlassFish

To start GlassFish from the command line, change the directory to [glassfish installation directory]/glassfish5/bin, and execute the following command:

```
./asadmin start-domain
```

The preceding command, and most commands shown in this chapter assume a Unix or Unix-like operating system, such as Linux or macOS. For Windows systems, the initial ./ is not necessary.

A few short seconds after executing the preceding command, we should see a message similar to the following at the bottom of the terminal:

```
Waiting for domain1 to start ..............
Successfully started the domain : domain1
domain  Location:
/home/heffel/glassfish-5/glassfish5/glassfish/domains/domain1
Log File: /home/heffel/glassfish-
  5/glassfish5/glassfish/domains/domain1/logs/server.log
Admin Port: 4848
Command start-domain executed successfully.
```

We can then open a browser window and type the following URL in the browser's location text field: http://localhost:8080.

If everything went well, we should see a page indicating that your GlassFish server is now running:

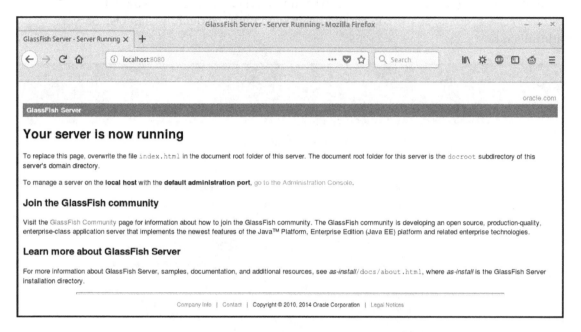

Deploying our first Java EE application

To further test that our GlassFish installation is running properly, we will deploy a WAR (Web ARchive) file and make sure it deploys and executes properly. Before moving on, please download the `simpleapp.war` file from this book's code bundle.

Deploying an application through the web console

To deploy `simpleapp.war`, open a browser and navigate to the following URL: `http://localhost:4848`. You should be greeted with the default GlassFish Server administration page:

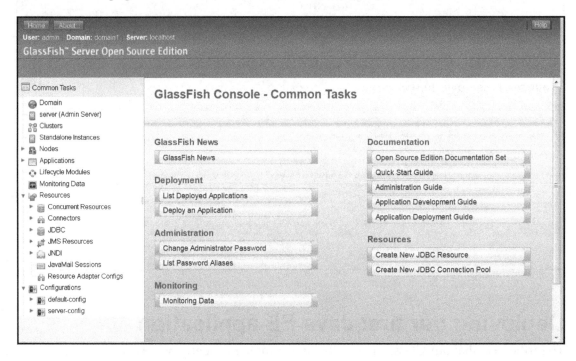

By default, GlassFish is installed in development mode, in this mode, it is not necessary to enter a username and password to access the GlassFish web console. In production environments, it is highly advisable to configure the web console so that it is password protected.

At this point, we should click the **Deploy an Application** item under the **Deployment** section in the main screen.

To deploy our application, we should select the **Local Packaged File or Directory That Is Accessible from GlassFish Server** radio button, and either type the path to our WAR file or select it by clicking the **Browse Files...** button:

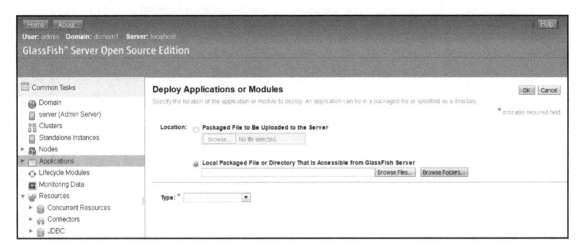

After we have selected our WAR file, a number of input fields allowing us to specify several options are shown. For our purposes, all defaults are fine, we can simply click the **OK** button at the top right of the page:

Once we deploy our application, the GlassFish web console displays the **Applications** window, with our application listed as one of the deployed applications:

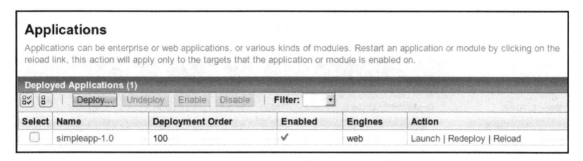

To execute the `simpleapp` application, type the following URL in the browser 's location text field: `http://localhost:8080/simpleapp-1.0/simpleServlet`. The resulting page should look like this:

That's it! We have successfully deployed our first Java EE application.

Undeploying an application through the GlassFish Admin Console

To undeploy the application we just deployed, log in to the GlassFish Admin Console by typing the following URL in the browser: `http://localhost:4848`.

Then, either click the **Applications** menu item in the navigation pane on the left or click the **List Deployed Applications** item on the administration console's home page.

Either way, should take us to the application management page:

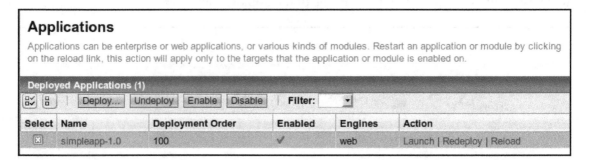

The application can be undeployed simply by selecting it from the list of deployed applications and clicking the **Undeploy** button above the list of deployed applications:

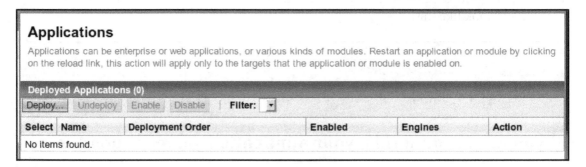

Deploying an application through the command line

There are two ways in which an application can be deployed through the command line: it can be done by copying the artifact we want to deploy to an `autodeploy` directory or by using GlassFish's `asadmin` command-line utility.

The Autodeploy directory

Now that we have undeployed the `simpleapp.war` file, we are ready to deploy it using the command line. To deploy the application in this manner, simply copy `simpleapp.war` to `[glassfish installation directory]/glassfish4/glassfish/domains/domain1/autodeploy`. The application will automatically be deployed just by copying it to this directory.

We can verify that the application has successfully been deployed by looking at the server log. The server log can be found at `[glassfish installation directory]/glassfish4/glassfish/domains/domain1/logs/server.log`. The last few lines of this file should look something like this:

```
    [2017-11-22T19:02:41.206-0500] [glassfish 5.0] [INFO] []
[javax.enterprise.system.tools.deployment.common] [tid: _ThreadID=91
_ThreadName=AutoDeployer] [timeMillis: 1511395361206] [levelValue: 800] [[
      visiting unvisited references]]
    [2017-11-22T19:02:41.237-0500] [glassfish 5.0] [INFO] [AS-WEB-
GLUE-00172] [javax.enterprise.web] [tid: _ThreadID=91
_ThreadName=AutoDeployer] [timeMillis: 1511395361237] [levelValue: 800] [[
      Loading application [simpleapp-1.0] at [/simpleapp-1.0]]]
    [2017-11-22T19:02:41.246-0500] [glassfish 5.0] [INFO] []
[javax.enterprise.system.core] [tid: _ThreadID=91 _ThreadName=AutoDeployer]
[timeMillis: 1511395361246] [levelValue: 800] [[
      simpleapp-1.0 was successfully deployed in 50 milliseconds.]]
    [2017-11-22T19:02:41.247-0500] [glassfish 5.0] [INFO] [NCLS-
DEPLOYMENT-02035] [javax.enterprise.system.tools.deployment.autodeploy]
[tid: _ThreadID=91 _ThreadName=AutoDeployer] [timeMillis: 1511395361247]
[levelValue: 800] [[
  [AutoDeploy] Successfully autodeployed :
/home/heffel/glassfish-5/glassfish5/glassfish/domains/domain1/autodeploy/si
mpleapp-1.0.war.]]
```

We can, of course, also verify the deployment by navigating to the URL for the application, which will be the same one we used when deploying through the web console, `http://localhost:8080/simpleapp/simpleservlet`, the application should execute properly.

An application deployed this way can be undeployed by simply deleting the artifact (the WAR file, in our case) from the `autodeploy` directory. After deleting the file, we should see a message similar to the following in the server log:

```
    [2017-11-22T19:04:23.198-0500] [glassfish 5.0] [INFO] [NCLS-
DEPLOYMENT-02026] [javax.enterprise.system.tools.deployment.autodeploy]
[tid: _ThreadID=91 _ThreadName=AutoDeployer] [timeMillis: 1511395463198]
[levelValue: 800] [[
      Autoundeploying application:  simpleapp-1.0]]
    [2017-11-22T19:04:23.218-0500] [glassfish 5.0] [INFO] [NCLS-
DEPLOYMENT-02035] [javax.enterprise.system.tools.deployment.autodeploy]
[tid: _ThreadID=91 _ThreadName=AutoDeployer] [timeMillis: 1511395463218]
[levelValue: 800] [[
      [AutoDeploy] Successfully autoundeployed :
/home/heffel/glassfish-5/glassfish5/glassfish/domains/domain1/autodeploy/si
mpleapp-1.0.war.]]
```

The asadmin command-line utility

An alternate way of deploying an application through the command line is to use the following command:

```
asadmin deploy [path to file]/simpleapp-1.0.war
```

 The preceding command must be run from the [glassfish installation directory]/glassfish4/bin.

We should see confirmation on the command-line terminal letting us know that the file was deployed successfully:

```
Application deployed with name simpleapp-1.0.
Command deploy executed successfully.
```

The server log file should show a message similar to the following:

```
    [2017-11-22T19:06:36.342-0500] [glassfish 5.0] [INFO] [AS-WEB-
GLUE-00172] [javax.enterprise.web] [tid: _ThreadID=128 _ThreadName=admin-
listener(6)] [timeMillis: 1511395596342] [levelValue: 800] [[
      Loading application [simpleapp-1.0] at [/simpleapp-1.0]]]
    [2017-11-22T19:06:36.349-0500] [glassfish 5.0] [INFO] []
[javax.enterprise.system.core] [tid: _ThreadID=128 _ThreadName=admin-
listener(6)] [timeMillis: 1511395596349] [levelValue: 800] [[
  simpleapp-1.0 was successfully deployed in 51 milliseconds.]]
```

The asadmin executable can be used to undeploy an application as well by issuing a command like the following:

```
asadmin undeploy simpleapp-1.0
```

The following message should be shown at the bottom of the terminal window:

```
[2017-11-22T19:06:36.349-0500] [glassfish 5.0] [INFO] []
[javax.enterprise.system.core] [tid: _ThreadID=128 _ThreadName=admin-
listener(6)] [timeMillis: 1511395596349] [levelValue: 800] [[
simpleapp-1.0 was successfully deployed in 51 milliseconds.]]
```

Please note that the file extension is not used to undeploy the application, the argument to asadmin undeploy should be the application name, which defaults to the WAR file name (minus the extension).

GlassFish domains

Alert readers might have noticed that the `autodeploy` directory is under a `domains/domain1` subdirectory. GlassFish has a concept of **domains**. Domains allow a collection of related applications to be deployed together. Several domains can be started concurrently. GlassFish domains behave like individual GlassFish instances, a default domain called `domain1` is created when installing GlassFish.

Creating domains

Additional domains can be created from the command line by issuing the following command:

```
asadmin create-domain domainname
```

The preceding command takes several parameters to specify ports where the domain will listen for several services (HTTP, Admin, JMS, IIOP, secure HTTP, and so on); type the following command in the command line to see its parameters:

```
asadmin create-domain --help
```

If we want several domains to execute concurrently on the same server, these ports must be chosen carefully since specifying the same ports for different services (or even the same service across domains) will prevent one of the domains from working properly.

The default ports for the default `domain1` domain are listed in the following table:

Service	Port
Admin	4848
HTTP	8080
Java Messaging System (JMS)	7676
Internet Inter-ORB Protocol (IIOP)	3700
Secure HTTP (HTTPS)	8181
Secure IIOP	3820
Mutual Authorization IIOP	3920
Java Management Extensions (JMX) Administration	8686

Please note that when creating a domain, the only port that needs to be specified is the admin port, if other ports are not specified, the default ports listed in the table will be used. Care must be taken when creating a domain, since, as explained above, two domains cannot run concurrently in the same server if any of their services listen for connections on the same port.

An alternate method of creating a domain without having to specify ports for every service is to issue the following command:

```
asadmin create-domain --portbase [port number] domainname
```

The value of the --portbase parameter dictates the base port for the domain; ports for the different services will be offsets of the given port number. The following table lists the ports assigned to all the different services:

Service	Port
Admin	portbase + 48
HTTP	portbase + 80
Java Messaging System (JMS)	portbase + 76
Internet Inter-ORB Protocol (IIOP)	portbase + 37
Secure HTTP (HTTPS)	portbase + 81
Secure IIOP	portbase + 38
Mutual Authorization IIOP	portbase + 39
Java Management Extensions (JMX) Administration	portbase + 86

Of course, care must be taken when choosing the value for portbase, making sure that none of the assigned ports collide with any other domain.

As a rule of thumb, creating domains using a portbase number greater than 8000 and divisible by 1000 should create domains that don't conflict with each other, for example, it should be safe to create a domain using a portbase of 9000, another one using a portbase of 10000, so on and so forth.

Deleting domains

Deleting a domain is very simple, it can be accomplished by issuing the following command in the command line:

```
asadmin delete-domain domainname
```

We should see a message like the following on the terminal window:

```
Command delete-domain executed successfully.
```

Please use the preceding command with care; once a domain is deleted, it cannot be easily recreated (all deployed applications will be gone, as well as any connection pools, datasources, and so on).

Stopping a domain

A domain that is running can be stopped by issuing the following command:

```
asadmin stop-domain domainname
```

This command will stop the domain named domainname.

If only one domain is running, the domainname argument is optional.

 This book assumes the reader is working with the default domain called domain1 and the default ports. If this is not the case, the instructions given need to be modified to match the appropriate domain and port.

Setting up database connectivity

Any non-trivial Java EE application will connect to a Relational Database Management Server (RDBMS). Supported RDBMS systems include JavaDB, Oracle, Derby, Sybase, DB2, Pointbase, MySQL, PostgreSQL, Informix, Cloudscape, and SQL Server. In this section, we will demonstrate how to set up GlassFish to communicate with a MySQL database, the procedure is similar for other RDBMS systems.

GlassFish comes bundled with an RDBMS called JavaDB. This RDBMS is based on Apache Derby. To limit the downloads and configuration needed to follow this book's code, most examples needing an RDBMS use the bundled JavaDB RDBMS. The instructions in this section are for illustrating how to connect GlassFish to a third party RDBMS.

Setting up connection pools

Opening and closing database connections is a relatively slow operation. For performance reasons, GlassFish and other Java EE application servers keep a pool of open database connections. When a deployed application requires a database connection, one is provided from the pool, when the application no longer needs the database connection, said connection is returned to the pool.

The first step to follow when setting up a connection pool is to copy the JAR file containing the JDBC driver for our RDBMS in the `lib` directory of the domain (consult your RDBMS documentation for information on where to obtain this JAR file). If the GlassFish domain where we want to add the connection pool is running when copying the JDBC driver, it must be restarted for the change to take effect. The domain can be restarted by executing `asadmin restart-domain`.

Once the JDBC driver has been copied to the appropriate location and the application server has been restarted, log in to the admin console by pointing the browser to `http://localhost:4848`.

Then click **Resources | JDBC | JDBC Connection Pools**, the browser should now look something like this:

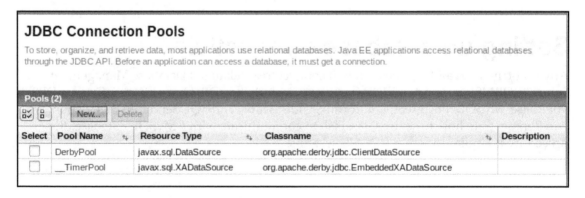

JDBC Connection Pools

To store, organize, and retrieve data, most applications use relational databases. Java EE applications access relational databases through the JDBC API. Before an application can access a database, it must get a connection.

Pools (2)

New... Delete

Select	Pool Name	Resource Type	Classname	Description
☐	DerbyPool	javax.sql.DataSource	org.apache.derby.jdbc.ClientDataSource	
☐	__TimerPool	javax.sql.XADataSource	org.apache.derby.jdbc.EmbeddedXADataSource	

Click the **New...** button; after entering the appropriate values for our RDBMS, the main area of the page should look something like this:

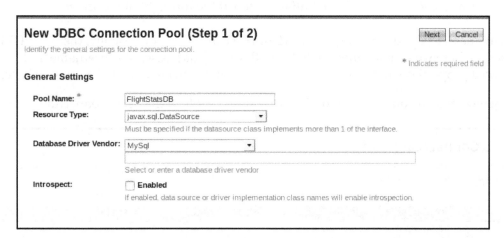

After clicking the **Next** button, we should see a page like the following:

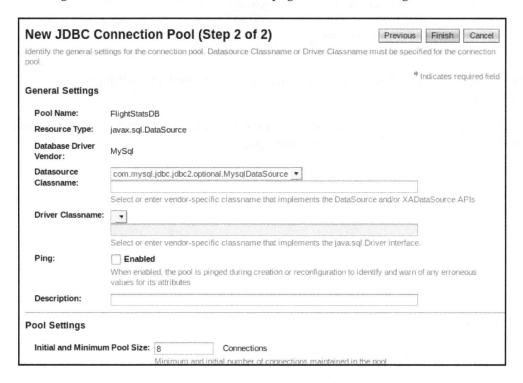

Most of the default values on the top portion of this page are sensible. Scroll all the way down and enter the appropriate property values for our RDBMS (at a minimum, username, password, and URL), then click the **Finish** button at the top right of the screen.

Property names vary depending on the RDBMS we are using, but usually, there is a URL property where we should enter the JDBC URL for our database, plus username and password properties where we should enter authentication credentials for our database.

Our newly-created connection pool should now be visible in the list of connection pools:

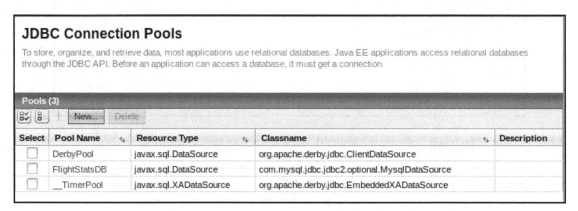

In some cases, the GlassFish domain may need to be restarted after setting up a new connection pool.

We can verify that our connection pool was successfully set up by clicking its **Pool Name**, then clicking the **Ping** button on the resulting page:

Our connection pool is now ready to be used by our applications.

Setting up data sources

Java EE applications don't access connection pools directly, instead, they access a data source that points to a connection pool. To set up a new data source, click the **JDBC Resources** menu item on the left-hand side of the web console, then click the **New...** button.

After filling out the appropriate information for our new data source, the main area of the web console should look something like this:

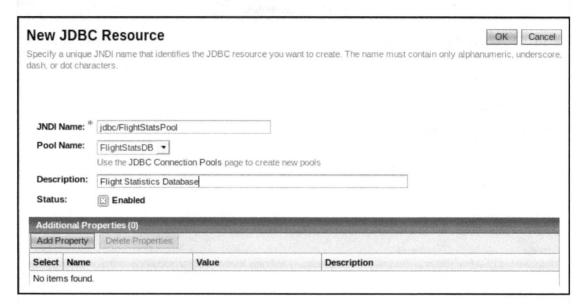

After clicking the **OK** button, we can see our newly created data source:

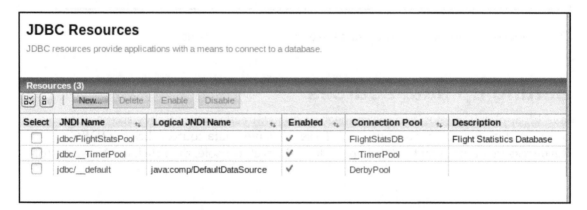

Setting JMS resources

Before we can start writing code to take advantage of the JMS API, we need to configure some GlassFish resources. Specifically, we need to set up a **JMS Connection Factory**, a **message queue**, and a **message topic**.

 Java EE 7 and Java EE 8 require all compliant application servers to provide a default JMS connection factory. GlassFish, being a fully compliant Java EE 8 application server (and the Java EE 8 reference implementation), complies with this requirement, so, strictly speaking, we don't really need to set up a connection factory. In many cases we may need to set one up, therefore in the following section, we illustrate how it can be done.

Setting up a JMS connection factory

The easiest way to set up a JMS connection factory is via GlassFish's web console. As previously mentioned from, `Chapter 1`, *Introduction to Java EE*, that the web console can be accessed by starting our domain by entering the following command on the command line:

```
asadmin start-domain domain1
```

We can then point the browser to `http://localhost:4848` and log in:

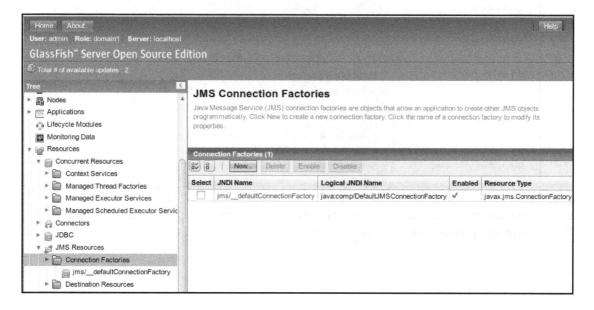

A connection factory can be added by expanding the **Resources** node in the tree at the left-hand side of the web console, expanding the **JMS Resources** node and clicking the **Connection Factories** node, then clicking the **New...** button in the main area of the web console:

New JMS Connection Factory

OK   Cancel

The creation of a new Java Message Service (JMS) connection factory also creates a connector connection pool for the factory and a connector resource.

General Settings

JNDI Name: *   jms/GlassFishBookConnectionFactory

Resource Type: javax.jms.ConnectionFactory

Description:

Status: ☒ Enabled

Pool Settings

Initial and Minimum Pool Size: 1   Connections
Minimum and initial number of connections maintained in the pool

Maximum Pool Size: 250   Connections
Maximum number of connections that can be created to satisfy client requests

Pool Resize Quantity: 2   Connections
Number of connections to be removed when pool idle timeout expires

Idle Timeout: 300   Seconds
Maximum time that connection can remain idle in the pool

Max Wait Time: 60000   Milliseconds
Amount of time caller waits before connection timeout is sent

On Any Failure: ☐ **Close All Connections**
Close all connections and reconnect on failure, otherwise reconnect only when used

Transaction Support:
Level of transaction support. Overwrite the transaction support attribute in the Resource Adapter in a downward compatible way.

Connection Validation: ☐ **Required**
Validate connections, allow server to reconnect in case of failure

For our purposes, we can take most of the defaults; the only thing we need to do is enter a **Pool Name** and pick a resource type for our connection factory.

It is always a good idea to use a pool name starting with `jms/` when picking a name for JMS resources. This way, JMS resources can be easily identified when browsing a JNDI tree.

In the text field labeled **JNDI Name**, enter `jms/GlassFishBookConnectionFactory`.

The **Resource Type** drop-down has three options:

- `javax.jms.TopicConnectionFactory`: Used to create a connection factory that creates JMS topics for JMS clients using the pub/sub messaging domain
- `javax.jms.QueueConnectionFactory`: Used to create a connection factory that creates JMS queues for JMS clients using the PTP messaging domain
- `javax.jms.ConnectionFactory`: Used to create a connection factory that creates either JMS topics or JMS queues

For our example, we will select `javax.jms.ConnectionFactory`; this way we can use the same connection factory for all of our examples, those using the PTP messaging domain, and those using the pub/sub messaging domain.

After entering the **Pool Name** for our connection factory, selecting a connection factory type and, optionally, entering a description for our connection factory, we must click the **OK** button for the changes to take effect:

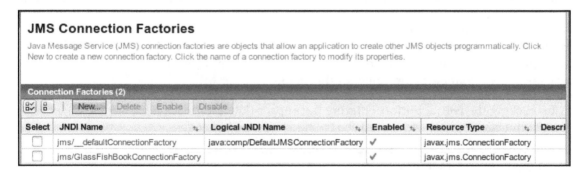

We should then see our newly-created connection factory listed in the main area of the GlassFish web console.

Setting up a JMS message queue

A JMS message queue can be added by expanding the **Resources** node in the tree at the left-hand side of the web console, expanding the **JMS Resources** node and clicking the **Destination Resources** node, then clicking the **New...** button in the main area of the web console:

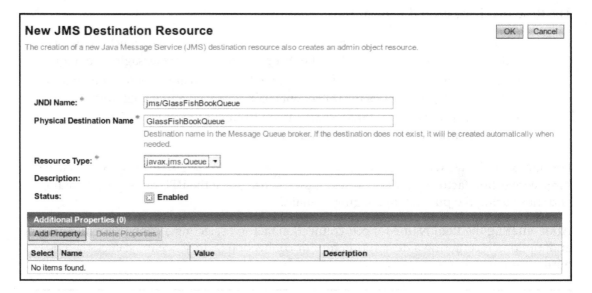

In our example, the JNDI name of the message queue is `jms/GlassFishBookQueue`. The resource type for message queues must be `javax.jms.Queue`. Additionally, a **Physical Destination Name** must be entered. In the preceding example, we use `GlassFishBookQueue` as the value for this field.

After clicking the **New...** button, entering the appropriate information for our message queue, and clicking **OK**, we should see the newly created queue:

Setting up a JMS message topic

Setting up a JMS message topic in GlassFish is very similar to setting up a message queue.

In the GlassFish web console, expand the **Resources** node in the tree at the left-hand side, then expand the **JMS Resouces** node, click the **Destination** node, then click the **New...** button in the main area of the web console:

Our examples will use a **JNDI Name** of jms/GlassFishBookTopic. Since this is a message topic, the **Resource Type** must be javax.jms.Topic. The **Description** field is optional. The **Physical Destination Name** property is required; for our example, we will use GlassFishBookTopic as the value for the **Name** property.

After clicking the **OK** button, we can see our newly created message topic:

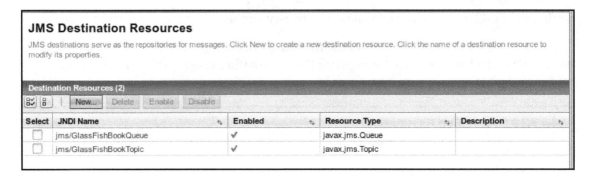

Now that we have set up a connection factory, a message queue, and a message topic, we are ready to start writing code using the JMS API.

Configuring durable subscribers

Like we mentioned before, the easiest way to add a connection factory is through the GlassFish web console. Recall that, to add a JMS connection factory through the GlassFish web console, we need to expand the **Resources** node on the left-hand side, then expand the **JMS Resources** node, click the **Connection Factories** node, then click the **New...** button in the main area of the page. Our next example will use the settings displayed in the following screenshot:

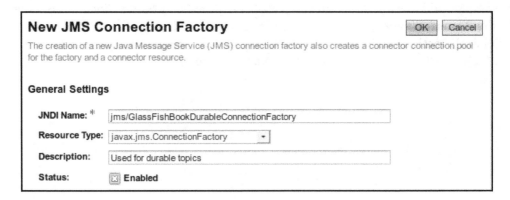

Before clicking the **OK** button, we need to scroll to the bottom of the page, click the **Add Property** button, and enter a new property named `ClientId`. Our example will use `ExampleId` as the value for this property:

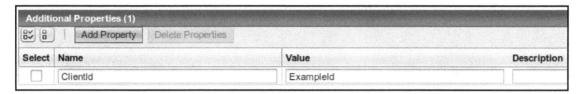

Summary

In this appendix, we discussed how to download and install GlassFish. We also discussed several methods of deploying the Java EE application through the GlassFish web console, through the `asadmin` command and by copying the file to the `autodeploy` directory. We also discussed basic GlassFish administration tasks, such as setting up domains and setting up database connectivity by adding connection pools and data sources.

Index

D

Data Access Objects (DAOs) 108
data
  deleting, with Criteria API 104
  updating, with Criteria API 102, 104
database connectivity setup
  about 339
  connection pools 340, 342
  data sources 343
dependency injection 152
domains
  creating 337, 338
  deleting 339
  stopping 339

E

EAR (Enterprise ARchive) 118
EJB client code
  implementing 114
EJB security
  about 143, 145, 146
  client authentication 146, 148
EJB timer service
  about 137, 139
  calendar-based EJB timer expressions 141, 142,
    143
EJB web service clients 287, 288
enterprise JavaBean life cycles
  about 131
  message-driven bean life cycle 137
  singleton session bean life cycle 135, 136
  stateful session bean life cycle 131, 132, 134
  stateless session bean life cycle 135, 136
enterprise JavaBeans
  exposing, as web services 286
  transactions 125
entity relationships
  about 72
  many-to-many relationships 84, 86, 88
  one-to-many entity relationships 78, 80, 82
  one-to-one relationships 73, 75, 76

F

Facelets 14, 16
form authentication mechanism 224, 225, 227

G

GlassFish Admin Console
  Java EE application, undeploying through 333
GlassFish domains 337
GlassFish
  dependencies 327
  download link 326
  durable subscribers, configuring 350
  installing 327, 328
  Java EE application, deploying 329
  obtaining 326
  starting 328, 329
Gson
  reference 186

H

HTTP methods
  DELETE 236
  GET 236
  POST 236
  PUT 236
HTTP/2
  about 321
  server push support 322, 323

I

ICEfaces
  reference 63
identity store
  about 217
  custom identity store 220
  setup, stored in LDAP database 219
  setup, stored in relational database 218, 219
initialization parameters
  passing, to servlet 308
Internet Engineering Task Force (IETF) 10, 182

CPSIA information can be obtained
at www.ICGtesting.com
Printed in the USA
LVHW100057010520
654814LV00013B/2284